T0305571

Cost Reduction Analysis

Cost Reduction Analysis

Tools and Strategies

STEVEN M. BRAGG

John Wiley & Sons, Inc.

Published by John Wiley & Sons, Inc., Hoboken, New Jersey.
Published simultaneously in Canada.

For general information on our other products and services or for technical support,
please contact our Customer Care Department within the United States at (800)
762-2974, outside the United States at (317) 572-3993 or fax (317) 572-4002.

Wiley also publishes its books in a variety of electronic formats. Some content that
appears in print may not be available in electronic books. For more information
about Wiley products, visit our web site at www.wiley.com.

Library of Congress Cataloging-in-Publication Data:
Bragg, Steven M.
   Cost reduction analysis : tools and strategies / Steven M. Bragg.
      p. cm.
   Includes index.
   ISBN 978-0-470-58726-3 (cloth)
1. Cost control. 2. Cost accounting. I. Title.
   HD47.3.B73 2010
   658.15'52—dc22   2009047255

Printed in the United States of America.

10 9 8 7 6 5 4 3 2 1

Contents

About the Author

Steven M. Bragg, CPA, has been the chief financial officer or controller of four companies, as well as a consulting manager at Ernst & Young and auditor at Deloitte & Touche. He received a master's degree in finance from Bentley College, an MBA from Babson College, and a bachelor's degree in economics from the University of Maine. He has been the two-time president of the Colorado Mountain Club and is an avid alpine skier, mountain biker, and certified master diver. Mr. Bragg resides in Centennial, Colorado. He has written the following books:

Accounting and Finance for Your Small Business
Accounting Best Practices
Accounting Control Best Practices
Accounting Policies and Procedures Manual
Advanced Accounting Systems
Billing and Collections Best Practices
Business Ratios and Formulas
The Controller's Function
Controller's Guide to Costing
Controller's Guide to Planning and Controlling Operations
Controller's Guide: Roles and Responsibilities for the New Controller
Controllership
Cost Accounting
Cost Reduction Analysis
Essentials of Payroll
Fast Close
Financial Analysis
GAAP Guide
GAAP Policies and Procedures Manual
GAAS Guide
Inventory Accounting
Inventory Best Practices

Investor Relations
Just-in-Time Accounting
Management Accounting Best Practices
Managing Explosive Corporate Growth
Mergers and Acquisitions
The New CFO Financial Leadership Manual
Outsourcing
Payroll Accounting
Payroll Best Practices
Revenue Recognition
Run the Rockies
Running a Public Company
Sales and Operations for Your Small Business
Throughput Accounting
Treasury Management
The Ultimate Accountants' Reference

Free Online Resources by Steven Bragg

The author issues a free accounting best practices podcast. You can sign up for it at www.accountingtools.com or access it through iTunes.

Preface

A central concern of any company is how to reduce its costs, since any cost reduction flows straight into profits. However, cost reduction must be accomplished without impacting customer loyalty or reducing the ability of the organization to achieve its long-term goals. Thus, the real issue is how to carefully pare away unnecessary costs while maintaining a robust organization. *Cost Reduction Analysis* shows how to do this. It describes a variety of cost reduction tools and the issues associated with using them, and then goes on to describe various forms of cost reduction in key expense areas, such as sales and marketing, production, payroll, and benefits.

The book is divided into four sections. In Part I, we address the primary areas of cost reduction. This begins with a discussion of the need for cost reduction, a multitude of cost reduction tools, and process analysis. It continues with specific cost reduction opportunities in the areas of sales and marketing, product design, production, payroll, and benefits.

In Part II, we cover the major cost reduction area of procurement. Coverage begins with a number of methods for improving the procurement process to reduce operational costs and then continues with discussions of spend management and the more specialized area of maintenance, repair, and operations spending.

Part III addresses asset reduction, which indirectly impacts cost reduction. The first chapter describes a broad array of techniques for reducing a company's investment in inventory while the next chapter delves into the best forms of analysis to follow when deciding whether to invest in a fixed asset.

Finally, Part IV describes two special topics that are extremely important in the realm of cost reduction. The first topic is throughput analysis, where a company centers its activities on its use of the bottleneck operation that drives its overall level of profitability. All cost reduction decisions should be based on how they impact the productivity of this bottleneck.

The second topic is how to reduce costs in an acquired company by maximizing and successfully implementing cost-related synergies.

These chapters are liberally sprinkled with examples to clarify concepts and also include a variety of metrics that are specifically designed to monitor cost reduction progress.

The book answers a multitude of questions involving cost reduction, such as:

- How do I calculate the productivity of a salesperson?
- How do I design a product to minimize its cost?
- When should I eliminate a product?
- Can cellular manufacturing reduce my production costs?
- How do I decide whom to lay off?
- How do I avoid institutionalized pay increases?
- What alternatives do I have for maximizing the cost effectiveness of my benefits package?
- How does an evaluated receipts system streamline my process flow?
- How do I use a spend database to reduce costs?
- How do I restructure my capital spending process so that I buy only the fixed assets that I really need?
- How can I manage my bottleneck operation to maximize my profitability?

In short, *Cost Reduction Analysis* is the ideal sourcebook for how to maximize profits using a successful system of cost reduction.

October 2009
Centennial, Colorado

Cost Reduction Analysis

PART I

Primary Areas of
Cost Reduction

CHAPTER 1

The Cost Reduction Process

Introduction

The reason for having an active cost reduction program is quite simple. A company can work extremely hard to obtain one extra incremental dollar of revenue, which will yield a net profit of perhaps 5 percent. Gaining that extra revenue dollar will be uncertain, and it may be difficult to attain the targeted profit. Alternatively, and using the same profit percentage, a cost reduction of one dollar would have required 20 dollars of revenue to generate. Further, a cost reduction is entirely within the control of a company, whereas a revenue increase is not.

The calculation for the equivalent amount of revenue needed rather than saving one dollar of cost is:

$$1/\text{profit margin} = \text{Equivalent amount of sales}$$

The next table shows the equivalent sales that would be needed at various profit margins in order to equal one dollar of cost savings:

Net Profit	Equivalent Revenue
1%	$100
2%	50
5%	20
10%	10
15%	7
20%	5
25%	4

Thus, even a spectacularly profitable company having 25 percent profitability would have the choice of either creating four dollars of revenue or reducing costs by one dollar.

Also, assume that a cost reduction is not a one-time event but rather is a continuing cost reduction that otherwise would have been incurred in every future year. By eliminating this type of cost on an ongoing basis, a company can achieve compounded gains that keep piling up in the future.

Given the obvious economics of cost reduction, why do companies not practice it more often? They typically ignore it until they get into financial difficulties and then impose a sudden across-the-board cost reduction. The better approach is a long-term, ongoing analysis of every part of a company, with an emphasis on maintaining full funding of the overall strategic direction and a careful paring of other costs with surgical precision. This chapter describes the advantages, disadvantages, tools, and process flow of a successful cost reduction program.

Need for Cost Reduction

An ongoing program of cost reduction is not really an option for a company that wants to remain competitive over the long term, since it is subject to many issues that can negatively impact its profits, as the next subsections reveal.

Revenue Declines

The need for cost reduction starts with revenue: If a company's products and services are subject to significant price declines, then costs have to also drop to keep pace. It is useful to stress test the sales forecast with a variety of worst-case scenarios to see what would happen to profitability in the event of a major price decline. Another option is to watch the results of other companies located in the same industry or tangential ones to determine the extent of price elasticity.

Rapid price declines are a particular problem when there are low barriers to entry, so that new competitors can easily enter the market and drive down prices. Price declines can also occur when fixed costs are a large part of the product cost structure, so companies have an incentive to fill their available capacity by driving down prices (see the next subsection). On a more short-term basis, prices also drop when there is a great deal of unsold inventory flooding the market.

In all of these cases, revenue declines can be so severe that a company that was initially awash in profits may very suddenly find itself in a significant loss position.

Fixed Cost Base

A company may have an exceptionally large fixed cost base, perhaps due to a fixation on high levels of automation, or simply because the market requires a great deal of equipment in order to compete. A high fixed cost base means that a company has to operate at a relatively high percentage of capacity in order to turn a profit. This is a major problem in industries where everyone has a large fixed cost base, since an industry slowdown means that prices will drop dramatically as everyone tries to keep their capacity levels high.

A determined and ongoing cost reduction campaign is an excellent way to avoid this trap. With a lower fixed cost base than competitors, a company is much more capable of riding out an industry downturn and may even be able to snap up any competitors that have not had the prescience to similarly engage in an active cost reduction campaign.

Creeping Costs

If there is no active campaign to reduce costs, then by default costs will increase; they will not hold steady. The next factors all work in parallel to increase costs:

- *Complexity.* Processes always become more complex over time, as they expand to encompass new products, services, and situations. Complexity increases a variety of expenses, but in particular requires more staffing. See the next subsection for an extended discussion of this topic.
- *Entitlements.* Benefits increase over time—they rarely decrease. Once a benefit is granted, it is very difficult to reduce it but quite easy to add to it.
- *Inflation.* Costs will naturally increase with the rate of inflation, but this is not acceptable if a company's revenue increases are not keeping pace with inflation.
- *Tradition and inertia.* In general, if an expense has always been incurred, then a company will continue it. There is rarely a discussion of reducing an expense, only of adding to it.

For these reasons, cost creep is an insidious and ongoing issue that slowly reduces a company's profitability at a pace that is barely recognizable over the short term. Since it is not a sudden event, management is not motivated to take action for a long time, at which point a great deal of effort will be needed to revert to the earlier level of profitability.

Complexity

One of the chief causes of excess costs is the presence of too many layers of management. Each manager requires a separate set of reports to monitor his or her area of responsibility (which takes time to create) and tends to acquire support staff. It is better to flatten the management structure of an organization, so that fewer managers supervise the activities of quite a large number of employees. Not only does this approach eliminate the complexity that comes with too many layers of management, but it also brings top management closer to a company's operational levels.

An excessive quantity of reports also contributes to complexity. Each one requires some data collection as well as aggregation into a report. Even if a report is automatically generated and distributed from a computer database, it may still waste the time of the reader, who no longer needs it. Further, an automated report may draw on information that was originally added to the database specifically to create the report, and which is now still being collected.

A report may originally have been created as a one-time report and morphed into an ongoing one. Or it may be associated with a process that is no longer used. Alternatively, it may have been created for someone who is no longer with the company, and it was inherited by her successor. All of these reasons can explain the presence of reports that are no longer needed but that continue to plague employees.

Quite a serious form of complexity is customized systems. A company will find that it can acquire commercial, off-the-shelf (COTS) software that is perfectly acceptable for most of its operations. However, these systems will not exactly match the company's underlying process flows, so there will be pressure from employees either to modify these packages or to create entirely new ones in-house. These customized systems are difficult to maintain and are much more expensive than COTS systems, so they introduce a significant amount of costs that are probably not necessary.

These examples show that complexity can arise in a variety of places in an organization—in its organizational structure, reports, systems, and so forth. Each type of complexity brings with it an increase in costs that can only be reduced through a considerable and ongoing change effort.

Acquisitions

The cost of complexity arises in particular when a company starts acquiring other businesses. An acquiree rarely serves precisely the same markets or has the same corporate structure or offers the same products. Consequently, an acquirer must somehow create an overall corporate structure that integrates two disparate businesses, which generally results in a combined entity that is less optimal than the original business. If these issues are expanded to a large number of acquisitions, then the cost of complexity becomes even more widespread.

However, there is one case where an acquisition strategy can *lower* costs. This is when an acquirer specifically searches for target companies that have lower costs than the acquirer and buys them specifically to spread that low-cost knowledge throughout the rest of the organization. This requires an excellent ability to force change throughout an organization.

Partnerships

A company may have a variety of partnerships, such as for research and development, or for production distribution, or for independent sales-people. Each of these partnerships requires some time by management to monitor and so increases costs to some extent. These partnerships may have been in existence for a long time and so may be continued more because of tradition than due to their profitability.

Because of their associated costs, all partnership agreements should be reviewed regularly to ensure that a company is earning a reasonable return. A major warning flag for these reviews should be any partnership that is characterized as "strategic," especially if it has not generated a return since its inception. Strategic partnerships typically have the support of a senior-level manager and so are not easily discarded, but their ongoing cost should be noted.

Advantages of Cost Reduction

Cost reduction is the easiest and most certain way to increase profits in the short term. It can also be a major driver of long-term growth, if handled properly. Why is it easy? Because cost reduction is entirely within the control of the company. Simply determine an area for cost reduction and implement it. It is completely unlike the uncertainty of trying to increase revenue, where one must be concerned about pricing, margins, the actions of competitors, and governmental regulation. Cost reduction is the simplest road to increased profitability and enhanced cash flow.

Cost reduction also works well for long-term profits, so long as the process becomes a core belief of the entire company and is constantly readdressed. The selection of cost reduction targets is key, since cost reduction over the long term cannot undercut a company's profit-making capabilities. Instead, the focus should be on constantly paring away unnecessary expenses, increasing efficiencies, and streamlining processes. In addition, it helps to continually reinvest some portion or all of the cost reduction savings back into the company's people, processes, and technology.

A company that publicizes its continual efforts to reduce costs is effectively signaling to potential market entrants that they will have a very difficult time competing on price, since the company can likely weather any such attacks with ease. Conversely, a low-cost company has a powerful tool available for undercutting companies in new markets and so can aggressively pursue its more bloated competitors.

Disadvantages of Cost Reduction

Cost reduction sometimes can earn a bad reputation if it is handled incorrectly. The worst form of cost reduction is the blanket percentage cost reduction that is imposed throughout a company. This arises when senior management suddenly realizes that the organization will not achieve its targeted numbers and decides that everyone will share equally in the pain of a cost reduction.

The blanket cost reduction has three bad effects.

1. Any department that has already voluntarily reduced its costs substantially must now find a way to cut expenses farther, probably to the point where it cannot complete its assigned tasks.
2. Managers who have experienced multiple rounds of these imposed cost reductions then realize that their best hope of survival is to pad their budgets with *extra* expenditures, so that they will have enough fat to cut from their budgets the next time a cost reduction mandate arrives.
3. A blanket cost reduction tends to result in the elimination of "soft" expenses that are needed for long-term growth, such as employee training or new investments in business development, additional salespeople, and fixed assets. If these expenses are trimmed, then a blanket reduction tends to harm a company's long-term growth prospects.

The effects noted here can be eliminated through the use of a more targeted cost reduction program, as noted later in the "Process Analysis" section. Even a well-run cost reduction program will face additional difficulties, as noted next in the "Cost Reduction Politics" section.

Cost Reduction Politics

There can be considerable dissension within a company if cost reductions have a particular impact on lower-paid employees; unless they see a comparable level of cost reductions on other employees in other pay grades, their morale will decline, and both employee turnover and work stoppages may not be too far behind. For this reason, it is best to apply cost reductions throughout an organization at the same time, so that everyone feels they are sharing the pain of the reductions.

In particular, the management team should share a greater proportion of the cost reductions than anyone else, so everyone can see that they are being equable. For example, if the management team takes a 20 percent pay reduction, they will meet with a much higher level of acceptance if they then ask everyone else to take a 10 percent pay reduction.

Another issue that can engender political maneuvering is the "sacred cow." From the perspective of cost reduction, this can be any expenditure that is clearly not needed for forwarding a company's strategy but that receives strong internal support. There may be a lengthy historical basis for continuing the expenditure, or perhaps it is supported by an especially powerful manager. In such cases, it may not be possible to eliminate the expense immediately. However, one should at least bring it to management's attention on a regular basis and be sure to charge the expense against the budget of the person who supports it.

Cost Reduction Priorities

When deciding on a course of action for cost reductions, the first step is to decide on the most strategically important part of the business that is needed for future growth and channel all cost reductions *around* it. If anything, some portion of the cost reductions from other areas should be shifted *into* this area.

The second cost reduction step occurs at the highest possible level and is the decision to retain or eliminate entire businesses or product lines. If there appears to be no hope of continuing profitability in such areas, and the company has no plans to invest aggressively in them, then management should make the decision to eliminate them. By doing so, the remaining parts of a company can focus clearly on cost reduction in other areas rather than having their efforts watered down in businesses that the company no longer wants. This is a particularly appealing approach if a company is essentially a conglomerate, with no discernible incremental profitability gains occurring because subsidiaries are part of a larger entity. In such an environment, all the costs related to aggregating financial information and "managing" subsidiaries introduces a level of complexity that merely increases costs with no offsetting benefit.

The third cost reduction step is to conduct a throughput analysis of the remaining parts of the business. Throughput is sales minus total variable expenses, and tells management where a business is (and is not) making money. Throughput analysis also involves finding out where a company's bottleneck operation (also called its constrained resource) is located and how to maximize throughput by focusing closely on the operations of that bottleneck. Throughput is an important concept for cost reduction, so Chapter 12, "Throughput Analysis," is devoted to it. For the purposes of this list, throughput tells management where they can safely reduce expenses and assets, and (more important) where they *cannot* do so (namely, in functions that support the bottleneck operation).

The fourth step is to see what costs can be reduced through outsourcing. This step is needed early in the cost reduction process, because management needs to decide if it should allocate significant cost reduction resources to an activity or simply hand it off in exchange for immediate cost savings. This step should follow the throughput analysis, since management needs to know how an outsourcing decision will impact a company's total throughput.

The fifth cost reduction priority is to clean up the company's financial reporting systems, so that management can clearly see where costs are being incurred and which functions are losing money. These items should be implemented:

- *Corporate overhead allocation.* No corporate overhead should be allocated anywhere. Corporate overhead is a discrete cost that is incurred by the corporate headquarters and should be examined for cost reduction purposes as part of that entity. Allocating overhead anywhere merely makes it less clear where costs truly are being incurred.
- *Service center allocations.* A company may elect to spread the cost of its service centers, such as the mail room, maintenance department, and power plant, to other departments. All of these allocations should be eliminated and shifted right back to the service centers, for two reasons.
  1. Allocations may not be on a usage basis—instead, they may depend on the negotiating ability of each department head, which makes them useless for cost analysis purposes.
  2. A cost reduction team can simply review the costs of each service center; it does not care about where costs are subsequently allocated, only where they originate.
- *Profit center reporting.* Whenever possible and reasonable, revenue should be assigned to a cost center, so that profitability can be determined. This information is useful for cost reduction triage—deciding which areas are in the most desperate need of cost reduction assistance.
- *Transfer pricing.* Transfer pricing should be at market rates only. When goods or services are transferred between company divisions, their cost should reflect what a subsidiary would have had to buy them for on the open market. Any other internally negotiated price merely reflects the ability of a company manager to negotiate a good rate and obscures costs.

At this point, a company has considered cost reduction issues at the business unit level and created enough throughput and financial reporting systems to know where there may be cost reduction opportunities. It is now time actually to reduce costs. There are a number of tools available for targeting possible areas of cost reduction, which are discussed in the next section, "Cost Reduction Tools." However, there are several issues to consider before using any specific cost reduction tool.

One such issue is to reduce costs in an area as remote as possible from customers. If a company scrimps on anything that a customer will experience, this can negatively impact customer purchases as well as increase customer turnover. For example, shifting customer service to a country where people speak with a strong accent is not going to improve the customer experience. Conversely, if a cost reduction program begins in the maintenance or accounting departments, management can make a number of mistakes and customers will never notice the difference. However, some prime cost reduction opportunities will certainly be in areas that are very noticeable to customers and cannot be ignored—in these cases, it is best to first test a cost reduction methodology elsewhere to gain experience with it and then roll it out in the areas noticeable to customers.

It is also necessary to select a cost reduction area where someone is clearly responsible for results. A cost reduction that is tied directly back to a specific manager is much more likely not only to be implemented but also to be maintained. Conversely, one should avoid a cost reduction project in an area where there is no clear responsibility for the expense, as is the case in a team or matrix environment. In such situations, it is best to recommend that management assign specific responsibility, and wait for this to happen before proceeding with a cost reduction project.

Finally, a company may find that the real underlying reason why its costs are increasing is that it is growing too fast for its internal systems to keep up with the growth. This could be due to exceptional organic growth, or perhaps a large number of acquisitions. Whatever the reason, it is entirely possible that there is no way to reduce costs at a pace fast enough to keep up with rampant growth. If this is the case, the solution may be to deliberately slow down or even halt the rate of growth. This gives a company time to install more robust systems, train its staff, and hire more people who are sufficiently qualified to handle high transactional volumes. In this case, slower growth may be the only way to quickly rein in expenses.

Cost Reduction Tools

There are a large number of cost reduction tools available, the most useful of which are described in this section. They are mostly based on various types of financial and operational analysis but also include such simple concepts as idea generation and a variation on the standard budgeting system. Companies have used all of them with considerable success.

5S Analysis

The 5S system is about organizing the workplace in order to eliminate waste. From a cost reduction perspective, it promotes workplace efficiency. As the name of this tool implies, there are five steps, and their names all begin with the letter S. They are:

1. *Sort.* Review all of the items within a work area, retain those needed for daily operations, and dispose of all other items (possibly involving a trip back to the supplies cabinet and/or the Dumpster).
2. *Straighten.* Reposition furniture and equipment to best serve the process flow, and move all other items out of the way.
3. *Scrub.* Clean the area completely.
4. *Systematize.* Establish schedules for repetitively cleaning the area.
5. *Standardize.* Incorporate the 5S system into standard company operations, so that it is performed on an ongoing basis. This should include a formal system for monitoring the results of the program.

A company should not embark on a 5S clean sweep of an entire company at the same time—that would create a great deal of disruption! Instead, this is a methodical process that is used to gradually address all locations, after which it starts over again in a continual cycle.

Benchmarking

Benchmarking is useful for deciding where to begin cost reduction activities. It provides information about the cost levels of other businesses, of other divisions of the same company, or simply of the company for earlier periods. Then match benchmark costs against current results and target unusually high variances for further analysis.

Internal benchmarking against other divisions is particularly useful. Every division is bound to have some best practice area for which clearly identifiable improvements can be copied to other divisions. Further, the corporate headquarters staff can order divisions to assist each other (which is not the case with external benchmarking, where the other company is providing information solely as a favor).

Differences in costs that are highlighted by a benchmarking review can result from a broad range of factors, such as plant layout, automation, employee training, management practices, and cultural issues. Even after a company identifies and copies every cost reduction technique that it can find at a benchmarking target, some portion of cost differences still may be tied to several residual issues that are not clearly identifiable. When a benchmarking review reaches this point of having no further identifiable practice improvements, then it is time to rebenchmark with some other entity and attempt to spot additional unique practices that the company can copy.

Breakeven Analysis

A product line may generate such minimal throughput (revenue minus total variable expenses) that it cannot pay for the cost of the overhead that is directly linked to it, unless it produces at near-maximum capacity levels. Run a simple breakeven analysis on company operations to see where this problem arises and target cost reductions in those areas where product lines are clearly at risk of not exceeding their breakeven levels.

The breakeven calculation is to divide the related overhead expenses by the throughput margin of the product line. For example, if a product line has an average throughput margin of 40 percent and the related overhead expense is $100,000, then it breaks even at a revenue level of $250,000. If there is only enough production capacity available to create $275,000 of product revenue, then there is very little room for the product line to earn any money.

Check Sheets

The check sheet is a structured form used for the collection and analysis of data. Its most common application is for the collection of data about the frequency or patterns of events. Data entry on the form is designed to be as simple as possible, with check marks or similar symbols. The check sheet is used most frequently in a production setting but can be easily applied anywhere in a company.

For example, what if the accounting manager is trying to increase the efficiency of the cash application process? Her first step is to determine the frequency of various issues impacting the process, so that she can focus her efforts on efficiency improvement. She discusses the project with the cash application staff and uses their input to construct the check sheet shown in Exhibit 1.1. The cash application staff fills it in during a one-week period, resulting in the determination that unauthorized payment deductions are the most frequent problem encountered during cash application, followed by missing remittance detail information. This information can then be used to prioritize efficiency improvement (and the resulting cost reduction) activities.

Reason	Day					
	Mon.	Tue.	Wed.	Thu.	Fri.	Total
Customer double pay		||		|		3
No remittance advice enclosed	|	||||	||	|	||||	13
Pays with multiple checks			|		|	2
Unauthorized deductions taken	||||	||||||	||||	||||||	||	25
Total	6	14	7	9	7	43

EXHIBIT 1.1 Cash Application Check Sheet

Employee Idea Systems

There are only a small number of really large cost reduction concepts, but there are a potentially infinite number of smaller cost reduction possibilities. The best way to obtain these smaller cost reductions is to create an employee idea collection system where a company actively solicits ideas from its employees. It is not unheard of for a company to solicit several dozen ideas per year from every employee and to implement most of the suggestions.

Installing hundreds or thousands of cost reduction ideas is also a significant way to build up a competitive position in an industry because small ideas are much less visible to competitors, so they are much less likely to be copied.

An employee idea system does not necessarily even require a reward system for suggestions. A reward system can require a considerable amount of time to calculate the savings from an idea, which in turn requires a small bureaucracy to hand out rewards. Further, employees will tend to focus on suggesting large-payback ideas only, so a reward system also tends to reduce the number of small-payoff ideas. A better approach is to include ideas generated in each employee's annual review, which can then focus on the quality of ideas generated.

There is a great deal of intrinsic value to an employee to see a suggestion implemented, so it is really more important to have a good implementation system in place than to have a reward system. Implementations should be handled as soon as possible by front-line staff, not routed up through the corporate chain of command for approval. If management requires multiple approvals for each idea, there is more chance that it will be rejected somewhere, which tends to discourage employees from making further suggestions. Also, a long approval process takes more time, money, and paperwork. Instead, the correct approach is to acknowledge receipt of an idea within one day and to make a go or no-go decision within just a few additional days.

A concern with employee idea systems is that they are very difficult to plan for; one cannot quantify precisely where or when cost reductions will be made, or the amount of savings. However, if ideas are generated and implemented in large numbers, a company can generally estimate the amount of savings that may be generated, based on historical results. In a company with fewer employees, planning for cost reductions will be more inaccurate.

Error Quantification

Any error that results in a scrapped or reworked product or documents piles up costs. A company can create an information tracking system to aggregate error information, which is then summarized into a report such as the one shown in Exhibit 1.2. The report notes the number of incidences of an error event during the measurement period. It also notes the lost throughput of each item. If an item is scrapped, then the associated throughput is lost forever. If an item is reworked, then the cost of the rework labor is offset against the lost throughput to yield a reduced level of throughput. Further, the report indicates the time and labor cost required for rework.

EXHIBIT 1.2 Error Quantification Report

Error Type	Number of Incidents	Lost Throughput per Incident	Total Lost Throughput	Total Rework Time	Total Rework Cost
Rework—Adjust paint gaps	14	$11.14	$155.96	3:30	$70.00
Rework—Cut off excess trim	29	8.23	238.67	5:00	100.00
Rework—Redrill unaligned hole	8	4.88	39.04	2:00	40.00
Rework—Smooth rough edges	11	7.35	80.85	1:00	20.00
Scrap—Broken base unit	10	19.20	192.00	—	—
Scrap—Crushed packaging	4	6.10	24.40	—	—
Scrap—Dented electronics	17	12.05	204.85	—	—

The error quantification report example reveals that the worst scrap issue to investigate is dented electronics, since the company loses the most throughput dollars from this problem. Among the rework issues, the cost of additional labor must be offset against the potential lost throughput to see if rework is worthwhile. The redrilling work costs more to fix than the throughput that would otherwise be lost, so these items can be scrapped instead. The other rework efforts all yield a higher throughput than would be the case if no rework were done.

Fixed Cost Analysis

A common decision point is whether to incur a large fixed cost (such as a high-capacity machine) in order to achieve higher margins through greater production efficiency. The answer, in many cases, is no. The reason is that a large fixed cost increases a company's breakeven point, so that it must make more sales before it can begin to earn a profit. This can be a risky scenario in a volatile market. The issue can even be reversed—should existing fixed costs be eliminated in exchange for variable costs that result in somewhat lower margins? In many cases, yes. It is worthwhile to be somewhat less profitable in exchange for having a more flexible company that can earn a profit over a broader range of revenues and margins. This issue can extend to a variety of nonproduction issues, such as leasing office space rather than buying a building.

Ishikawa Diagrams

Also known as a fishbone diagram or a cause-and-effect diagram, the Ishikawa diagram reveals the causes of a specified event. The diagram, as shown in Exhibit 1.3, has the general appearance of the bones of a fish. The problem to be solved lies at the head. Major bones represent groups of major causes, while minor bones represent subcauses. An Ishikawa diagram is an excellent starting point for a cost reduction analysis, since solving the issues listed along the various branches of the diagram will likely solve the initial problem, which may have been a source of considerable expense.

The exhibit shows the categories of issues causing late product deliveries to customers. The issues are clustered under general categories, such as Policy, Products, and Machine. For example, under the Machine category, incorrect machine setups are delaying the production of goods as well as inadequate preventive maintenance that increases machine downtime. Each of the items on the diagram can be addressed in order ultimately to reduce the incidence of late product deliveries to customers.

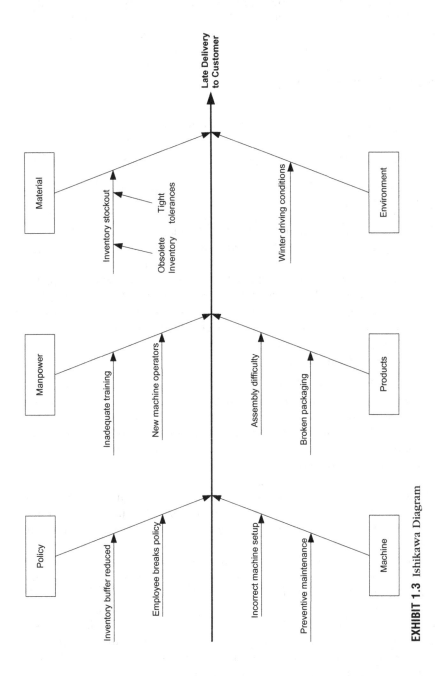

EXHIBIT 1.3 Ishikawa Diagram

17

There are a large number of major causes under which subcauses can be clustered. Possible headings include environment, equipment, inspection, manpower, materials, maintenance, management, policies, prices, procedures, processing, products, promotions, and suppliers.

Relevant Range Analysis

The management team should be aware of the activity range over which costs apply. In particular, they should know exactly when additional step costs must be incurred to support increased activity levels, the extent of those steps costs, and what alternatives are available to delay or mitigate them.

Total Cost Analysis

The removal of one cost may trigger the elimination of several other related costs. For example, laying off someone will also eliminate the cost of supplies, cell phones, and travel expense that the employee would also normally incur. There are also step costs that can be eliminated once certain volume points have been reached. For example, the layoff of one person will not also trigger the elimination of a human resources clerk, but laying off 100 employees might very well also eliminate this position.

Value Stream Mapping

Value stream mapping (VSM) focuses on the identification of waste across an entire process. A VSM chart identifies all of the actions required to complete a process while also identifying key information about each action item. Key information will vary by the process under review but can include total hours worked, overtime hours, cycle time to complete a transaction, error rates, and absenteeism.

The VSM chart shown in Exhibit 1.4 addresses the entire procurement cycle, from the initial placement of a requisition through processing of the resulting supplier invoice. Under each processing step, the VSM chart itemizes the amount of overtime, staffing, work shifts, process uptime, and transaction error rate. The chart then shows the total time required for each processing step as well as the time required between steps, and also identifies the types of time spent *between* steps (e.g., outbound batching, transit time, and inbound queue time).

The chart reveals that most of the procurement cycle time is used between processing steps, especially in the transit time of orders from suppliers to the company. If total cycle time is an issue, then a reasonable conclusion would be either to source locally or to spend more for faster delivery services. However, if the emphasis is on speedier in-house pro-

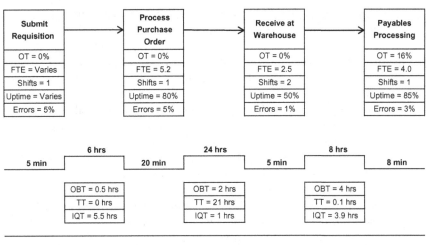

Submit Requisition		Process Purchase Order		Receive at Warehouse		Payables Processing
OT = 0%		OT = 0%		OT = 0%		OT = 16%
FTE = Varies		FTE = 5.2		FTE = 2.5		FTE = 4.0
Shifts = 1		Shifts = 1		Shifts = 2		Shifts = 1
Uptime = Varies		Uptime = 80%		Uptime = 50%		Uptime = 85%
Errors = 5%		Errors = 5%		Errors = 1%		Errors = 3%

	6 hrs		24 hrs		8 hrs	
5 min		20 min		5 min		8 min

OBT = 0.5 hrs	OBT = 2 hrs	OBT = 4 hrs
TT = 0 hrs	TT = 21 hrs	TT = 0.1 hrs
IQT = 5.5 hrs	IQT = 1 hrs	IQT = 3.9 hrs

Key:
FTE = Full-Time Equivalent   **OT** = Overtime
IQT = Inbound Queue Time   **TT** = Transit Time
OBT = Outbound Batch Time

EXHIBIT 1.4 Value Stream Map

cessing, then the chart shows that the purchase order processing stage is the most time consuming; it is also probably a bottleneck operation, given the amount of overtime incurred. Likely conclusions would be to reduce the error rate in the purchasing area by working on a reduction of errors in the upstream requisitioning area (note how the two error rates are identical, since the purchasing staff is likely copying errors from requisitions directly onto the purchase orders), offloading purchasing work with procurement cards, or bolstering capacity by adding purchasing staff.

Another option for shrinking the long cycle time is to have the receiving staff send receiving documents to the payables department more frequently than once every four hours; cutting the outbound batch time in half would eliminate two hours from the total cycle time.

VSM works best in highly focused, high-volume processes where it makes sense to spend time wringing a few seconds out of repetitive processes. Conversely, the analysis effort would be wasted in low-volume areas where the staff constantly switches between multiple tasks.

Waste Analysis

Cost reduction can be performed simply by identifying the various types of waste and then working to reduce them. Here are seven types of waste to be aware of:

1. *Additional processing.* This is any production process that does not directly add value to a product, such as a quality control review.
2. *Defects.* Any processing that destroys or harms production that has already passed through the bottleneck operation is a form of waste, because it eliminates valuable throughput and may require additional expenditures for rework.
3. *Inventory.* Inventory of all types requires a working capital investment, incurs storage costs, and is at risk of obsolescence. It also hides other cost issues, such as production imbalances and poor work practices.
4. *Motion.* Any motion by employees that does not add value is a waste. This includes any equipment setup time.
5. *Overproduction.* Any production exceeding specific customer orders is a waste, because it uses materials and other resources, which then incur storage costs and are subject to obsolescence.
6. *Transportation.* This is the movement of materials between any operations that transform the materials, such as between workstations in a production process. The more something moves, the more opportunity there is to damage materials. Spending on materials handling equipment or conveyor belts is also a form of waste.
7. *Waiting.* Any time when a machine or its operator is waiting is considered a waste of that resource. Waiting can be caused by unbalanced workloads, overstaffing, materials shortages, and so forth. However, analyze this type of waste with care; throughput analysis holds that only waiting at the bottleneck operation is truly a form of waste. (See Chapter 12.)

Some of the waste identified through this type of analysis does not add value but may be needed for legal or safety reasons, and so it cannot be eliminated.

Zero-Based Budgeting

Zero-based budgeting can be quite useful in cost reduction analysis. It requires that a company set up various levels of funding for different budgeted service levels. This typically means that there are budget levels *below* the current expenditure level. Then compare these lower levels of expenditure to actual expenditures to see how service levels will change if a lower level of expenditure is adopted. Creating a multitude of different expense levels within a zero-based budget can be quite time-consuming, so usually there are only a few levels to choose from.

Summary

The key point about cost reduction tools is that no single tool will be sufficient for every situation. Instead, the best results likely will be gained from a combination of tools, which may vary based on which functional area is under review. Also, there are a large number of acknowledged cost reduction tactics that are specific to each functional area of a company—those are listed in the following chapters.

Control charts are used primarily for the analysis of production problems, so they are discussed instead in Chapter 4, "Production Cost Reduction." Another tool is process analysis; it is a large enough topic to warrant two sections of its own, which follow.

Process Analysis

One of the best ways to reduce costs is to fundamentally restructure the processes that a company uses to complete transactions. Many processes are rife with an excessive number of controls, approvals, handoffs, and unnecessary tasks that have gradually built up. It is entirely natural for processes to become more complex over time, as any number of decisions impact what might originally have been a clean and simple process flow. Accordingly, a process analysis team should cycle through a company continually, reviewing every process for streamlining opportunities. Here are some of the issues that they should address:

- *Capture information once.* If a process runs through several people, it is possible that each one in turn collects and enters some of the same information. To avoid this issue, center processes around a central database, as would be available in an enterprise resources planning system, so that information is only entered once and is then available to all subsequent users.
- *Design around value-added steps.* In a typical process, there are only a few value-added steps, along with a number of reviews, controls, reports, approvals, tests, and inspections that do nothing to advance the process. In designing a better process, first focus on a process containing *only* value-added steps and then consider adding the *minimum* number of non-value-added steps.
- *Avoid formal quality review steps.* Any formal quality review activity is a waste of money, since it implies that a sufficient level of quality has not already been built into a process, and so requires extra labor to identify and fix. The solution may not be simple, since it involves error-proofing the entire process prior to a quality review step.

- *Reduce reviews and approvals.* Ideally, there should be no approvals at all, and certainly no more than one. Any additional approvals simply extend the length of a process and waste the time of the person doing the approving. A long string of approvals either indicates that the management team does not trust its employees to handle transactions with minimal oversight or that a number of processing errors in the past have triggered additional reviews. The solution to both problems is to locate the root cause of errors and improve the process flow to the point where errors no longer occur. Then management's confidence in the staff should improve to the point where no approvals are needed.

- *Center the process.* Ideally, a process should be performed by one person, which improves efficiency and also places responsibility squarely on that individual. In those cases where a process seemingly touches on everyone in a company, the solution will be a winnowing out of as many people as possible, shifting most of the work to the smallest number of people, and then reviewing the process again over multiple iterations to continually compress the number of involved employees.

  If there appear to be multiple people around whom a process can center, it is possible that the process should really be split into separate processes, with each one concentrated around a single individual.

- *Focus on the central process flow.* A process may include a variety of processing options, where some transactions must be shunted off to be dealt with differently from the majority of transactions. If so, the primary cost reduction gains will be from streamlining the tasks involved in the primary process flow. Secondary gains will be from entirely eliminating the decision points that shift some transactions off the central process flow. Thus, cost reductions are to be gained by increasing the efficiency of the core process and the volume of transactions running through it.

- *Simplify steps.* Task simplification is central to the reduction of processing errors. It can involve the elimination of processing options, or the elimination of various types of data, or the consolidation or elimination of forms, and so forth.

- *Select the simplest process path.* If a process improvement project yields several possible alternatives for a new process, it is generally best to select the simplest one, even if it is slightly more expensive than the other alternatives. The reason is that more complex solutions either require more oversight now or will in the future, as the process gradually becomes more complex again. If it is possible to adopt the simplest solution now, the odds are good that it will remain simple for a longer period of time.

- *Concentrate on high-cost items.* A process usually contains only a few steps that absorb costs. These few steps are where a cost reduction team should focus its efforts, since there is a greater payoff for eliminating or streamlining these steps.
- *Eliminate wasted time.* There is a great deal of wait time built into most processes, where a processing step sits in a person's work queue for an inordinate period of time, is then processed briefly, and then shifts forward to the work queue of the next person in line. It is not uncommon to experience 99 percent wait times during a process. It is extremely useful to measure wasted time in an existing process and use this information to alter the process flow, usually in the direction of more process centering and smaller batch sizes.
- *Identify and enhance bottleneck flows.* There is a bottleneck in every process, and it is where work tends to pile up. Once identified, either alter the process to reduce the work reaching the bottleneck or increase the capacity of the bottleneck operation.
- *Reduce batch sizes.* If processes flow among multiple people, then specify that document batches be reduced to the smallest possible number before shifting to the next downstream person. This reduces the opportunities for documents to be held up between people, thereby delaying process completion.
- *Introduce automation last.* Automation can be expensive, so automating a clunky process likely means that the existing process will be maintained for the foreseeable future, on the grounds that a large investment has been made in it. A better approach is *first* to streamline a process and *then* to introduce automation once the process appears to be working well, with no other significant cost reductions likely.
- *Install a feedback loop.* Even the best-designed process will generate errors occasionally, so include an error-reporting system in the process, along with a feedback loop that routes this information to the appropriate person for action.

Once a process has been fully redesigned, it is possible that the people performing it are no longer qualified to do so; their jobs may now require more skills than they have. If so, a special training regimen may be needed to bring the staff up to the minimum required skill level. Alternatively, it may be necessary to replace some employees.

Once a process has been improved and implemented, make sure that the same process is being used in all company locations. This may require that people using the new and improved process be sent to other locations to demonstrate the new system. Also, the internal audit staff should schedule a follow-up review to ensure that all locations are using the new system correctly. Otherwise, a company may find itself with an unwieldy group of disparate processes that all complete the same work with varying degrees of efficiency.

Top Processes to Review

Finally, there is the issue of which processes to select for an overhaul. There are dozens, if not hundreds, of processes to select from, so which ones go first? A process is in need of work if there is a great deal of turmoil around it. Indicators include finger-pointing about who caused an error, high error rates, lots of time researching and correcting errors, a multitude of manager approvals, and evidence that people are working around the process whenever possible. These are all symptoms of a process that touches too many departments and has too high a degree of complexity. It is not difficult to find these processes—just ask the employees.

Process Analysis Tools

There are a number of ways to analyze an existing process to see how it can be streamlined. A good overview of a process flow is the task chart, which shows the sequence of events in a process flow, what type of processing occurs, and the time required for each step. The task chart is very helpful for zeroing in on long-duration process steps that may be causing trouble for users. An example is shown in Exhibit 1.5.

The exhibit shows the steps used in a paper-based purchase requisition and purchase order flow. The steps are listed in their normal sequence, showing the duration and type of activity for each step. The chart makes it clear that there is a high annoyance factor and delay involved with any document approval or document transfer between employees. The other steps are so short that any improvements to them would not greatly reduce costs.

Another way of looking at a process is to see how many times it switches between different departments. The more handoffs there are in a process, the greater the chance for delays and errors. The format shown in Exhibit 1.6 for a simplified sales process reveals that a customer order is handled by no fewer than four departments, which explains why this process is a prime source of errors in many companies.

The process task chart is good for spotlighting specific areas for further investigation but does not provide a sufficient level of detail regarding exactly what activities are occurring. For that level of detail, we use a process cycle time analysis, such as the one shown in Exhibit 1.7. The matrix breaks down processing time into more clearly defined segments.

Task: Complete Purchase Requisition and Purchase Order

Sequence	Time	Symbol	Annoyance Factor	Task Description	Why Done
1	5 minutes	☑ ◇ ⇧ ◻ ▽	Low	Employee prepares purchase requisition	Relying on employees to inform the purchasing staff of stockout conditions
2	2 minutes	☑ ◇ ⇧ ◻ ▽	High	Supervisor reviews and approves purchase requisition	Managers want to know what items will be charged against their budgets
3	2 minutes	◻ ◇ ⇧ ◻ ▼	Low	Employee creates a copy of the requisition and retains it	Purchase requisitions are lost, either in transit to the purchasing department or by the purchasing staff, so employees want to retain a record
4	8 hours	◻ ◇ ⇧ ◻ ▽	High	Put requisition into interoffice mail, to the purchasing department	Resulting purchase order must be processed by a designated purchasing agent
5	30 minutes	☑ ◇ ⇧ ◻ ▽	Low	Locate supplier and prepare purchase order	Purchasing agent must source through a preferred supplier and create an authorization document
6	2 minutes	◻ ◆ ⇧ ◻ ▽	Low	Forward requisition and purchase order to purchasing manager if purchase order total exceeds $10,000	Purchasing manager wants to be assured that large purchases are authorized and placed with preferred suppliers; smaller orders are exempted
7	4 hours	◻ ◇ ⇧ ▼ ▽	High	Purchasing manager reviews and approves the purchase order, and returns it to the purchasing agent	Completion of review process
8	2 minutes	◻ ◇ ⇧ ◻ ▼	Low	Purchasing agent creates a copy of the purchase order, attaches the requisition to it, and retains it	Purchasing agent wants a copy of the transaction in case there are questions about it at a later date
9	4 minutes	◻ ◆ ⇧ ◻ ▽	Low	Purchasing agent creates a copy of the purchase order and sends it to the receiving department	Receiving department needs a copy of the purchase order to match against the delivery when it arrives
10	1 minute	◻ ◆ ⇧ ◻ ▽	Low	Purchasing agent sends two copies of the purchase order to the supplier	Purchase order triggers action by the supplier

◻ = Task   ◇ = Decision   ⇧ = Move   ◻ = Delay   ▽ = File

EXHIBIT 1.5 Process Task Chart

25

Sales Process Flow

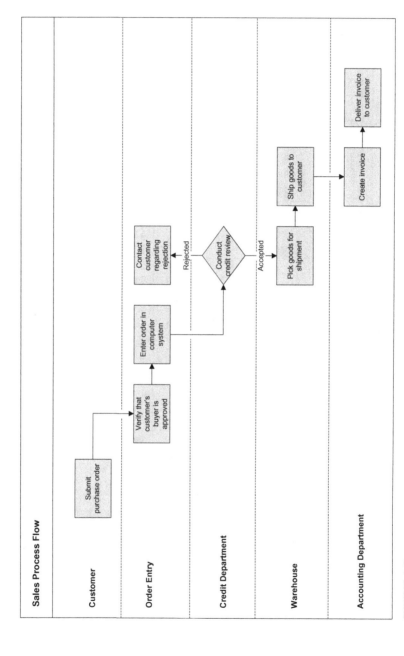

EXHIBIT 1.6 Process Flow across Departments

26

EXHIBIT 1.7 Process Cycle Time Analysis
Process: Plastic Part Injection Molding and Painting (minutes:seconds)

Sequence	Setup Time	Processing Time	Move Time	Wait Time	Inspection Time	Rework Time	Total Time
1	20:15	:05					20:20
2			:25	33:15			33:40
3					:01	:20	:21
4			:35	45:00			45:35
5	2:30	:05					2:35
6			:35	20:45			21:20
7					:01	:10	:11
8			:50				:50

EXHIBIT 1.8 Cycle Time Analysis

Sequence	Processing Time (hours)	Cycle Time (hours)	Processing Percentage
1	0.6	0.6	100%
2	0.2	0.3	67%
3	0.4	0.8	50%
4	1.0	4.9	20%
5	0.8	1.3	62%
Total	**3.0**	**7.9**	**38%**
Total Percentages	**38%**	**100%**	

The exhibit reveals that the wait times in processing steps 2, 4, and 6 are responsible for nearly all of the time in the process and so are worthy of further analysis.

As just noted, the wait time can be an extremely high proportion of the total process time. In Exhibit 1.8, the actual processing time for five steps is listed in the second column, with total cycle time (processing time plus wait time) in the third column. Processing time is then divided by cycle time in the fourth column. A very low percentage reveals the presence of an inordinate amount of wait time, which then becomes a target for more detailed analysis.

The cycle time analysis in Exhibit 1.8 reveals that the overall processing time during the process is 38 percent of the total, which means that 62 percent of the process is composed of wait time. The bulk of the wait time is centered on the fourth step in the sequence, which has a processing time percentage of only 20 percent. This would be an excellent spot to begin further investigation into compressing the cycle time.

Key Cost Reduction Questions

Before implementing a cost reduction, one should address a series of questions to see how the change will impact the organization. Just because there is a negative outcome to one or more of these questions does not mean that the change should be avoided; however, it does mean that management is now aware of the issue and can make any adjustments it feels necessary to counteract the problem. The questions are:

- *Will customer service levels decline?* This issue is listed first because it is important for revenues, customer satisfaction, and customer turnover. A negative response from management should not yield an automatic rejection of a proposed cost reduction, however. Instead, additional consideration should be given to the extent of the resulting service level decline and how much that decline will matter to customers.
- *Will it impact the lifetime value of customers?* In other words, will the cost reduction either increase customer turnover or reduce the profit from their purchases? If so, then the cost reduction needs to be so massive that it clearly offsets the projected customer losses. In most cases, a yes answer will provide sufficient grounds to cancel a proposed cost reduction.
- *Will it impact core functions?* This question is critical. A company should pare costs from a key company function only if the expenses are clearly extraneous. If anything, company resources should be flowing *into* these areas.
- *Will it impact product quality?* A yes answer does not automatically cancel the related cost reduction. One must determine if the current quality level matches customer expectations or if the design robustness is actually greater than needed.
- *Will employee skills be affected?* This question is targeted at reductions in training expenditures. The analysis should include a review of exactly which skills will be impacted and how critical they are to the company's long-term success.
- *Will there be a related exit cost?* There may be a variety of expenses that must be recognized as a result of a cost reduction, such as severance pay, writing off assets, or paying a termination fee to a business partner. These costs should have been included in the initial cost reduction analysis already, but the question is listed here to ensure that it is addressed.

Some variation on these questions can be included in a standard company checklist of items to be discussed before management approves a cost reduction.

Cost Reduction Reports

A well-organized cost reduction analysis project should start with a general overview of the target area that results in a graphical presentation of potential cost reductions. The format shown in Exhibit 1.9 is a good layout, showing the potential cost reduction impact of numerous projects across the bottom axis and implementation difficulty on the vertical axis. Cost reductions in the lower right corner are low-hanging fruit that generate significant returns in exchange for a modest effort. Conversely, items in the upper left corner require a great deal of effort and produce minimal returns. This format is a good guideline for deciding which projects to address first and which can safely be delayed.

In Exhibit 1.9, the commission restructuring in the upper left corner is projected to have such a low payback and high difficulty of implementation that it is not worth doing, whereas the procurement card program is highly worthwhile, since it has the reverse characteristics.

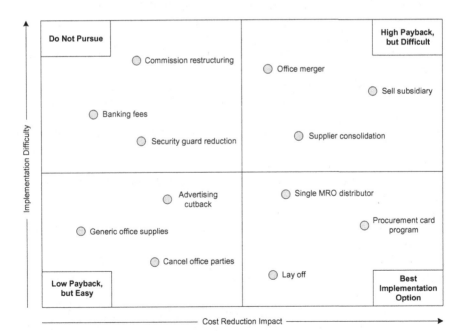

EXHIBIT 1.9 Cost Reduction Payoff Matrix

EXHIBIT 1.10 Cost Reduction Risk Matrix

	Cost Overrun	Customer Turnover	Extended Implementation	Management Support	Project Failure
Advertising cutback	1	4	3	2	1
Layoffs	2	1	2	4	1
Office merger	3	1	4	5	4
Single MRO distributor	1	1	4	1	2
Supplier consolidation	2	1	5	1	3
Scoring	1 = low risk 5 = high risk	1 < 1 month 5 > 1 year	1 < 1 month 5 > 1 year	1 = high 5 = low	1 = low risk 5 = high risk

A variation on the cost reduction payoff matrix is one that itemizes a number of additional factors, such as the risk of project failure, implementation duration, and level of support. If any prospective project has a high risk score in any category, then the project manager should either consider alternative projects or work on risk mitigation strategies. A sample risk matrix is shown in Exhibit 1.10. In the exhibit, the riskiest project appears to be the office merger, which contains three high-risk scores, while the single maintenance, repair, operations (MRO) distributor option is the safest, with four low-risk scores.

Exhibits 1.9 and 1.10 provide only an overview of potential cost reduction projects. The next step in an organized cost reduction system is to generate greater detail regarding potential reductions. The format is shown in Exhibit 1.11, which begins with the general topics already shown in the cost reduction payoff matrix, and then notes and quantifies specific opportunities. The matrix is split into two parts, with those projects estimated to have low levels of implementation difficulty listed at the top and those with more difficult implementation difficulty listed at the bottom.

Another way of stating Exhibit 1.11 is to create a before-and-after income statement showing the expected impact of the cost reduction program. An example, using all of the Exhibit 1.11 cost reductions, is shown in Exhibit 1.12. This can be an extremely effective way to convince senior management to support cost reductions, especially when they see the improvement in net profit, as shown in the example.

Once proposed cost reductions have been selected from the list in Exhibit 1.11, a tracking report is needed to show the progress of the reduc-

EXHIBIT 1.11 Cost Reduction Itemization Matrix

Topic Area	Opportunity	Action	Implementation Difficulty	Cost Reduction (000s)
Advertising cutback	All of advertising is spent on NASCAR sponsorship	Drop sponsorship and switch to mix of Internet and magazine advertising	Low	$380
Cancel office parties	Currently have Christmas and summer parties for 14 offices	Eliminate all summer office parties	Low	170
Generic office supplies	Using brand names for 140+ types of office supplies	Standardize on generic office supplies	Low	30
Layoff	10% of production staff is currently idle	Conduct a layoff of 5% of the production staff, leaving the remainder on staff to maintain capacity	Low	490
Procurement card program	Purchase orders used for virtually all purchases	Implement a procurement card program, and mandate its usage for purchases under $500	Low	640
Single MRO distributor	Currently use 15 MRO distributors	Centralize orders and shift to standard generic supplies	Low	520
		Total Cost Reduction		**$2,230**

(Continued)

EXHIBIT 1.11 *(Continued)*

Topic Area	Opportunity	Action	Implementation Difficulty	Cost Reduction (000s)
Banking fees	Currently paying account fees for a separate bank account for each office, and not aggregating cash for investing purposes	Switch all accounts to a single bank, and roll all cash into an investment account, using zero-balance accounts	High	40
Commission restructuring	Junior-level base pay is 25% higher than comparable rates in the market	Drop base pay to market rate for all new hires	High	75
Office merger	The Denver and Boulder offices service approximately the same group of customers	Eliminate the Boulder office, sublease the space, and shift staff to the Denver office	High	390
Security guard reduction	Currently have evening on-site security guards for all 14 offices	Switch to a private contractor that patrols the area periodically	High	85
Sell subsidiary	The Wynona Brewery is the only brewery still owned by the company	Sell the subsidiary	High	790
Supplier consolidation	Have over 1,000 suppliers for 5,400 stock keeping units	Consolidate the supply base to 300 suppliers, and realize a 3% overall cost reduction	High	500
		Total Cost Reduction		**$1,880**

EXHIBIT 1.12 Before and After Income Statement (000s)

	Prior to Reductions	Reductions	After Reductions
Sales	$79,400		$79,400
Cost of goods sold			
Sales compensation	3,850	$75	3,775
Materials	34,000	1,020	32,980
Labor	19,850	490	19,360
Total cost of goods	57,700		56,115
Gross margin	21,700		23,285
Administrative expenses			
Advertising	1,700	380	1,320
Events	410	170	240
Leases	5,460	390	5,070
Salaries	6,010	725	5,285
Supplies	830	30	800
Other	1,730	40	1,690
Total administrative	16,140		14,405
Gain on asset sale	0	790	790
Net profit	**$5,560**	**$4,110**	**$9,670**
Net profit percentage	**7%**		**12%**

EXHIBIT 1.13 Cost Reduction Status Report (000s)

Expense Category	Cost Reduction Goal	Identified Cost Reductions	Completed Cost Reductions	Achieved Reduction Run Rate
Direct labor	$490	$0	$0	$0
Direct materials	0	0	0	0
Administration labor	640	600	340	220
Production supplies	520	120	40	40
Supplies	200	180	180	140
Advertising	380	280	100	100
Totals	**$2,230**	**$1,180**	**$660**	**$500**

tion project. The report shown in Exhibit 1.13 itemizes the expense categories to be impacted as well as the progress of cost reductions. Of particular interest is the last column, which summarizes the achieved run rate of lowered costs that a company can expect to continue to experience in the future.

The cost reduction status report reveals that the layoff noted in Exhibit 1.11 has not yet taken place, since that would have appeared in the direct labor category. The remaining programs have all been initiated but not yet completed. In fact, the completed cost reductions currently comprise only 30 percent of the total cost reduction goal, so management clearly needs to monitor the situation closely for some time to come.

The reports shown here start at the very high-level cost reduction payoff matrix, add an analysis of project risk, and then drill down to individual cost reduction projects and the continuing progress of those projects. This level of reporting is needed to give management a complete top-to-bottom view of a cost reduction campaign.

Metrics

There is no single metric to monitor for a cost reduction program. Instead, a measurement system must be created for each type of cost reduction, showing historical costs and related activities, and then following the same metrics in the future, to warn of any backsliding in cost reductions. These metrics should be linked with a number of *failure metrics*. A failure metric reveals if a key type of performance is failing as a result of a cost reduction. For example, switching to lower-quality raw materials can be linked to a warranty claims failure metric; if warranty claims go up substantially as a result of the lower product quality, management should reevaluate the cost reduction program. Examples of other failure metrics are service delivery times and customer satisfaction ratings.

When setting up historical metrics for a cost reduction project, the costs incurred during the past 12 months are sufficient; they reflect the most recent activity as well as cost variations over a full-year cycle. Any metrics farther back in time likely reflect different activity levels and business conditions, and so are not relevant to the current cost structure.

Finally, the best measurement system is one that drills down to the lowest cost center or profit center level. Since costs generally are eliminated at the individual location and related general ledger subcode level, this type of highly localized metric will generate the best information about the success of a cost reduction effort.

Summary

This chapter has addressed the economics of cost reduction as well as other reasons for engaging in an ongoing program of cost reduction. We have also noted the general work flow to be used when engaging in a cost reduction project, and some of the tools that are available for this work. However, not all tools are applicable to all cost reduction areas. The next chapters reveal that different types of analysis are applicable to different expenses. For example, the use of a pull system is critical for minimizing an inventory investment, whereas throughput analysis is quite useful for evaluating fixed asset purchases, and a simple laundry list of options should be incorporated into an employee benefits review. Further, cost reductions in spend analysis are closely tied to supplier consolidation, while maintenance, repair, and operations spending calls for close cooperation with a preferred distributor. In short, there is no easy way to reduce expenses; doing so requires knowledge of a broad set of tools.

CHAPTER 2

Selling and Marketing Cost Reduction

Introduction

An old saying is that it takes money to make money. This is very true in the sales and marketing area, where a large cutback in costs can lead to a considerable reduction in sales volume. Accordingly, the emphasis in this is area is not necessarily on *reducing* costs but rather on *reapportioning* it to maximize throughput (revenue minus variable expenses), which results in the highest possible levels of profitability. In this chapter, we delve into analyzing the customer base as well as making alterations to the effectiveness and efficiency of its sales force. Additional topics include price optimization, the sales process flow, and marketing analysis.

Customer Mix Analysis

The sales team may be expending their efforts on customers who produce small overall sales volume or low margins. If so, the sales manager should periodically review this information for the entire list of active customers and reposition the sales staff to sell only to the best customers. A sample report that provides this information is shown in Exhibit 2.1.

The report divides all customers into a matrix, where the highest-volume and most profitable customers are listed in the upper right quadrant and lower-volume but still high-margin customers are listed in the upper left quadrant. These are a company's most important customers, since they provide the bulk of its margins. The lower two quadrants itemize the company's lower-margin customers. The low-volume, low-margin customers in the lower left quadrant typically require significant sales effort in exchange

Customer Margin Matrix

High Margin (30%)

		Margin %	Annual Dollars
No. Customers = 16	**No. Customers = 5**		
Percent of Sales = 5%	**Percent of Sales = 42%**		
Annual Sales = $531K	**Annual Sales = $3,922K**		
Annual Margin = 47%	**Annual Margin = 37%**		
AMG Industries	Acme	33%	$607,600
Audabon Park	Estes Door Frames	38%	$340,400
Boulder Technology	Hudson River Upholstery	35%	$1,586,200
Brindle Corporation	Killer Kitchen Products	39%	$964,400
Bucktooth Inc.	Monster Equipment	32%	$423,300
Bushmaster Weaponry			$3,921,900
Chemical Devices Corp.			
Huntington Brickworks			
Initial Response Units			
International Clearance Co.			
Mann's Cutlery			
Material Upgrade Company			
Newco Pottery			
Oliphaunt Fencing			
Peak Industries			
Quorum Software			

Low Margin

		Margin %	Annual Dollars
No. Customers = 10	**No. Customers = 4**		
Percent of Sales = 5%	**Percent of Sales = 48%**		
Annual Sales = $493K	**Annual Sales = $3,937K**		
Annual Margin = 11%	**Annual Margin = 22%**		
Poly Cracker Bird Supply	Early Research Corp.	24%	$925,000
Primary Rescue Services	Kanberra Koala	19%	$1,559,500
Rocky Mountain Oil	Optimum Energy	22%	$904,500
Scott Primary Services	Terrible Trouble Kid Stores	16%	$548,300
Sun Tanning Oil Co.			$3,937,300
Tofu Deluxe			
Aston Davidson Aerospace			
Backup Services			
Immediate Response Co.			
Jervis Book Binders			

Low Revenue — $100K — High Revenue

EXHIBIT 2.1 Customer Margin Matrix

for low margins and hence should be terminated. The company should make an effort to shift the higher-volume but still low-margin customers in the lower right quadrant into the higher-margin category in the upper right corner; this can be achieved by raising prices or by altering the mix of products sold to them.

The information required for this customer mix matrix can require considerable effort to assemble but provides an invaluable view of where a company really makes its money and therefore where it should target its selling efforts.

Customer Class Analysis

Another way to review selling costs is to create an income statement that is differentiated by class of customer. Marketing and distribution costs may differ for each class, resulting in substantially different profits for each one. A sample report is shown in Exhibit 2.2.

In the exhibit, there are substantially different results for each customer class. The company is earning essentially all of its profits from its sales through retailers and mail order houses and is earning almost nothing on its jobbers and direct sales, which may call for either the cancellation of sales through these last two classes or a substantial revision of how sales are conducted. Of particular interest are the direct sales noted in the last category, where the cost of goods sold is quite low (since there is no middleman) but operating and marketing costs are so high that the class is not substantially profitable. In this area, the sales manager should seriously consider dropping the entire customer class.

Sales Region Analysis

A key method for investigating the profitability of a sales department is an examination of how its resources are spread through its various sales territories. A company's products may sell better in some territories than others (such as blankets selling better in arctic regions than tropical ones), while the sales manager may be investing in a new territory, which requires some time to ramp up before it can aspire to the profitability of more established locations. Another key factor is the ability of the sales staff assigned to each territory to produce sales. A sample report that reveals this information is shown in Exhibit 2.3.

The report centers on three results for each sales territory: sales, throughput, and net profits. In this case, it shows that profits directly correlate with sales volume. Operating expenses are approximately the same

EXHIBIT 2.2 Income Statement by Class

Holmes Fencing Supply Company
Income Statement by Customer Class
For the Year-to-Date through June 30, 20xx

Description	Total Amount	% of Net Sales	Retailers Amount	% of Net Sales	Jobbers Amount	% of Net Sales	Mail Order Houses Amount	% of Net Sales	Direct Amount	% of Net Sales
Gross sales	1,495,000		690,000		220,000		310,000		275,000	
Less: sales deductions	(41,000)		(20,000)		(3,000)		(10,000)		(8,000)	
Net sales	1,454,000	100%	670,000	100%	217,000	100%	300,000	100%	267,000	100%
Variable expenses	1,096,600	75%	503,800	75%	187,700	86%	266,100	89%	139,000	52%
Throughput	357,400	25%	166,200	25%	29,300	14%	33,900	11%	128,000	48%
Marketing expenses	169,300	12%	82,400	12%	20,800	10%	5,100	2%	61,000	23%
Operating expenses	118,400	8%	40,900	6%	8,900	4%	3,600	1%	65,000	24%
Net profit before taxes	69,700	5%	42,900	6%	(400)	0%	25,200	8%	2,000	1%

EXHIBIT 2.3 Income Statement by Territory

Watson Wallpaper Company
Income Statement by Territory
For the Year-to-Date through June 30, 20xx

Description	Total Amount	% of Net Sales	West Amount	% of Net Sales	Midwest Amount	% of Net Sales	Mid-Atlantic Amount	% of Net Sales	New England Amount	% of Net Sales
Gross sales	840,000		50,000		390,000		240,000		160,000	
Less: sales deductions	(51,009)		(5,620)		(18,440)		(16,340)		(10,609)	
Net sales	788,991	100%	44,380	100%	371,560	100%	223,660	100%	149,391	100%
Variable expenses	559,127	71%	37,066	84%	251,514	68%	160,745	72%	109,802	73%
Throughput	229,864	29%	7,314	16%	120,046	32%	62,915	28%	39,589	27%
Operating expenses	120,510	15%	29,107	66%	31,951	9%	30,932	14%	28,520	19%
Net profit before taxes	109,354	14%	(21,793)	−49%	88,095	24%	31,983	14%	11,069	7%

41

in each territory, which reflects the base pay and travel costs of the sales-person assigned to each one. However, sales volumes vary considerably between the regions, from which we may infer that the high-volume Midwest region has been operational the longest, and so generates the most sales volume per dollar of sales activity invested. Conversely, the West region is presumably a new one, so it generates minimal sales while still incurring about the same expenses as the other regions.

A sales manager can use this type of report to obtain an overview of results by region and then work with the accounting department to drill down on any sales or expenses that look unusual.

A variation on the income statement by territory is a rolling 12-month income statement by territory, such as the one shown in Exhibit 2.4 for the Midwest region. This type of report offers more detail and makes it easier to spot sudden changes from month to month.

The exhibit includes a percentage analysis of each key line item as a percentage of sales, which makes it easier to spot trends in the data. In the exhibit, the proportion of sales deductions is steadily declining over time, which indicates either better customer service or an improving ability to avoid sales to marginal customers. The throughput percentage is also increasing over time, which highlights the salesperson's ability to continu-ally improve the mix of products sold to maximize profits. Finally, there is an obvious pay raise at year-end that appears in the operating expenses line, which is easily offset by increasing profitability within the territory. In short, the report reveals a territory whose salesperson's performance is steadily improving over time.

Dropped Customer Analysis

It is useful to have a report that identifies key customers who may be dropping the company. By identifying these customers as early as possible, the sales department can initiate contacts to determine why the customers apparently are switching their purchases elsewhere, and preferably before they are locked in to the products or services of a new supplier.

To create such a report, the first step is to determine which customers create sufficient sales volume to be worthy of detailed tracking; this can be accomplished by exporting a sales by customer report to Excel, sorting it by dollar volume, and retaining for further analysis the top 20 percent of all customers that typically comprise 80 percent of all sales volume.

Next, for this reduced set of customers, access the customer orders database and create a report that shows the exact dates on which the last three orders were placed by each customer. A quick examination of this information will reveal the average frequency with which each customer

EXHIBIT 2.4 Trailing 12-Month Income Statement by Territory

Watson Wallpaper Company
Trailing 12 Months Income Statement by Territory
For the 12 Months through June 30, 20xx
Midwest Region

Description	Jul 20x1	Aug 20x1	Sep 20x1	Oct 20x1	Nov 20x1	Dec 20x1	Jan 20x2	Feb 20x2	Mar 20x2	Apr 20x2	May 20x2	Jun 20x2	Totals
Gross sales	45,900	47,029	48,664	49,998	53,269	55,009	57,926	62,347	64,001	66,799	68,803	70,124	689,869
Less: sales deductions	(3,778)	(3,725)	(3,690)	(3,600)	(3,578)	(3,409)	(3,384)	(3,102)	(3,146)	(3,103)	(2,805)	(2,900)	(40,220)
Deduction %	*8%*	*8%*	*8%*	*7%*	*7%*	*6%*	*6%*	*5%*	*5%*	*5%*	*4%*	*4%*	*6%*
Net sales	42,122	43,304	44,974	46,398	49,691	51,600	54,542	59,245	60,855	63,696	65,998	67,224	649,649
Variable expenses	30,524	31,274	32,240	33,124	35,158	36,306	38,056	40,526	41,281	43,085	43,862	44,704	450,138
Throughput	11,599	12,030	12,734	13,274	14,533	15,294	16,486	18,719	19,574	20,611	22,136	22,520	199,511
Throughput %	*25%*	*26%*	*26%*	*27%*	*27%*	*28%*	*28%*	*30%*	*31%*	*31%*	*32%*	*32%*	*29%*
Operating expenses	4,793	4,793	4,793	4,793	4,793	4,793	5,325	5,325	5,325	5,325	5,325	5,326	60,709
Operating expenses %	*10%*	*10%*	*10%*	*10%*	*9%*	*9%*	*9%*	*9%*	*8%*	*8%*	*8%*	*8%*	*9%*
Net profit before taxes	6,806	7,237	7,941	8,481	9,740	10,501	11,161	13,394	14,249	15,286	16,811	17,194	138,802
Net profit %	*15%*	*15%*	*16%*	*17%*	*18%*	*19%*	*19%*	*21%*	*22%*	*23%*	*24%*	*25%*	*20%*

43

places orders. Then load the average ordering frequency (in days) into an unused field in the customer master file.

The final step is to create a custom report that adds the average ordering frequency in days to the last date on which an order was placed and determines which customers have not ordered within their standard ordering interval. The report should be sorted so that those customers with the longest ordering delays beyond their normal ordering intervals appear at the top of the report.

Also, consider enhancing the report by showing annual purchasing volume for each customer in the report. If a report shows a customer with a combination of large sales volume and a significant ordering delay, then the sales manager should contact that customer immediately to see if there is a problem.

Finally, conduct an annual update of the average ordering frequency calculation and load any changes into the customer master file. This procedure maintains the accuracy of the report.

In short, a report that reveals any customers who may be in the process of switching their business elsewhere is an excellent addition to the standard sales department reporting package.

Price Setting with Throughput Analysis

Traditional cost accounting methodology holds that pricing should include fully absorbed costs plus an acceptable profit margin. The reason for this thinking is that all costs must be covered by an adequate level of pricing, or else there will be no profit once all product and operating costs are subtracted from the total of all prices paid by customers. The sales staff chafes under this approach, since it is sometimes confronted with offers from customers to sell large quantities of product at reduced prices—but the accountants will not approve the lower prices, even if the proposed price points exceed the variable cost of the products.

However, throughput theory holds that *any* price point that exceeds the totally variable cost of a product should be considered. Proposed price points and unit volumes for incremental sales can then be included in a mix of current production activity to determine what the change will do to the company's total throughput and its production bottleneck operation. If the result improves throughput and there is a way to handle the increased production volume, then the price point should be approved. Consequently, throughput analysis gives the sales staff a much greater degree of flexibility in setting prices. The sales staff does not need to wade through a complex absorption costing formula for each product that it needs to price. Instead, all it needs is the proposed price, the totally variable cost of the product under consideration, and a discussion with the production scheduling staff to see if the proposed job can be scheduled into the bottleneck operation without hurting other scheduled production.

Example

The Tasmanian Chutney Company (TCC) has received a request for a special garlic-flavored chutney, at a price of $1.50 per jar. TCC applies a standard overhead charge of $0.40 to each jar of chutney produced. When this overhead cost is added to the $1.25 variable cost of producing a jar of garlic-flavored chutney, TCC's cost accountant calculates that there will be a loss of $0.15 per jar and so rejects the proposed order. However, a throughput analysis of the pricing proposal is included in the next table of TCC's various products, which shows a positive throughput of $0.25 per jar, because the overhead allocation is ignored for pricing purposes. Thus, TCC should accept the offer if there is sufficient production capacity to handle the order.

Chutney Flavor	Price/Jar	Variable Cost	Overhead	Net Profit	Throughput
Apple	$2.80	$1.80	$0.40	$0.60	$1.00
Peach	2.55	1.65	0.40	0.50	0.90
Banana	2.40	1.60	0.40	0.40	0.80
Garlic	1.50	1.25	0.40	(0.15)	0.25

There are several objections to the exclusion of overhead costs from the pricing formula. First, it may result in extremely low price points that will not allow a company to cover all of its expenses, which results in a loss. Over the long term, this is an accurate assessment. However, in the short term, if a company has excess production capacity available and can use it to sell additional product that generates throughput, then it should do so in order to increase profits. If its production capacity is already maximized, then proposed sales having lower throughput levels than items already being manufactured should be rejected.

Second, traditional accounting holds that a small proposed order that requires a lengthy machine setup should have the cost of that setup assigned to the product; if the additional cost results in a loss on the proposed transaction, then the sale should be rejected. However, throughput analysis does not include the cost of setups in the totally variable cost of the product, since it assumes that the company's existing production capacity can absorb the cost of the incremental setup without incurring any additional cost. Under this logic, if there is excess production capacity, then setups are free. This approach tends to result in a company offering a much richer mix of order sizes and products to its customers, which can yield a greater market share. However, this concept must be used with caution, for at some point the ability of the company to continually set up small production jobs will maximize its capacity, at which point there will be an incremental cost to adding more production jobs.

In short, throughput analysis results in more pricing flexibility for the sales staff, since a product's totally variable cost represents the lowest possible price point rather than a fully burdened cost.

Sales Productivity Analysis

A salesperson may sell low-margin products if doing so results in high sales volume. However, this may yield so little margin that the company would be better off without any of this type of sale. Consequently, sales productivity analysis should focus on the throughput achieved by a salesman, less his direct costs (which can include wages, commissions, travel and entertainment, cell phone, etc.). Sales productivity can also be expressed as a ratio, with throughput in the numerator and all salesperson expenses in the denominator. If used in ratio form, a salesperson's performance can be tracked on a trend line or in comparison to the same ratio for other sales staff.

Example

The manager of the Pondicherry Corp. sales department has been informed that one of his three sales staff must be laid off. To determine performance, the manager decides to measure their sales productivity. The manager collects the next information that covers the sales performance of the staff for the past year:

	Salesperson A	Salesperson B	Salesperson C
Gross revenue	$1,000,000	$800,000	$750,000
Variable cost of sales	$750,000	$400,000	$375,000
Throughput	$250,000	$400,000	$375,000
Sales expense	$150,000	$82,000	$74,000
Sales productivity	1.7:1	4.9:1	5.1:1

The table reveals that, although Salesperson A sells the most volume, the products have a lower throughput than the sales made by the other two employees. In addition, Salesperson A is spending far more money to secure sales than are the other two sales employees. This results in the worst sales productivity ratio (of 1.7:1) for Salesperson A while Salesperson C, who has the lowest sales volume, has achieved the highest sales productivity score. Based on this information, Salesperson A is the least productive and therefore should be targeted for the layoff. However, the sales manager should also point out to management that this layoff will result in a net decline in overall throughput, since Salesperson A was creating more throughput than he cost the company in sales expense.

Inclusions in Sales Expense

Part of the sales productivity analysis is the compilation of the sales expense. This commonly is considered to be the salesperson's compensation and directly traceable costs, such as travel. However, another major consideration is the cost of sales support personnel. Some salespeople surround themselves with additional staff who work on proposals and sales lead generation but who do not directly bring in new sales themselves. In these cases, the sales expense should include the fully burdened cost of both the salesperson and all support staff who assist him.

Example

Pedestal Corporation sells office furniture to large corporations, and Scott Riley is its newest salesperson. He sells primarily to Fortune 500 firms and has brought in three staff people to assist him in finding leads and respond to requests for proposals. His results after his second year on the job are:

Sales	$4,257,000
Less: discounts granted	(852,000)
Net sales	3,405,000
Variable expenses	3,138,000
Throughput	267,000
Scott Riley compensation	185,000
Riley other expenses	49,000
Additional support staff compensation	162,000
Net loss	$(129,000)

Continued

Clearly, Pedestal is losing money on Mr. Riley's sales efforts. A key part of the loss is the sales discounts he is granting in order to land large deals, while the cost of his large support staff is eliminating any residual profitability. Pedestal might be better off with a low-key salesperson who offers fewer discounts.

Sales Effectiveness Analysis

The sales staff should sell a mix of products that maximizes the use of a company's primary production bottleneck. If too many products are sold that require a large proportion of bottleneck time, then a company will soon find itself unable to increase sales without a large investment to increase the capacity of the bottleneck operation. The next example illustrates the concept.

Example

The Hard Rock Candy Company has maximized the output from its bottleneck operation, which is a candy cooker, and cannot produce a higher level of output without purchasing an additional cooker. The president instructs the salespeople to shift their efforts into product sales that require less cooker time. The president compiles the before-and-after information in the next table about the salespeople's performance to see if they are following her instructions.

	Before	After
Gross revenue	$1,000,000	$950,000
Variable cost of goods sold	$750,000	$700,000
Bottleneck time used	168 hours	153 hours
Sales effectiveness	$1,488/hr	$1,634/hr

The table reveals that the salespeople have achieved a slightly lower level of sales but have altered the gross margin mix, so the same gross margin (of $250,000) has been achieved both before and after the change in sales instructions. The primary change is that the number of hours of cooker time required by the sales has dropped from 168 hours to 153, which means that the gross margin earned per hour of bottleneck time has increased from $1,488 per hour to $1,634 per hour. In short, the sales staff is following the president's instructions.

Sales effectiveness analysis is all about reviewing *what* is being sold. However, this is a useful analysis only if the sales staff is made aware of which products they should be selling. If the company simply gives them a product list and tells them to go out and sell, then the analysis merely becomes a passive review of what they sold rather than a comparison of what they should have sold to what they did sell.

It can be difficult to accumulate and dispense the information needed for a sales effectiveness tracking system. A company must trace product throughput back to individual product sales while also keeping the sales staff informed of bottleneck usage times for each product.

Salesperson Analysis

The sales manager should have a standard report that shows the performance of each salesperson. The report shown in Exhibit 2.5 provides a great deal of key information. It compares revenue and throughput to budget standards for each salesperson, but only for those sales staff who are under budget by more than 5 percent; all others are aggregated into a "satisfactory performance" line.

Of particular interest in this report is throughput variance, since this is the prime indicator of profitability by salesperson. For example, salespersons Gordon and Owens appear to have obtained higher revenue figures by selling products with a lower throughput, whereas Dunwiddy has obtained reasonable sales while also improving upon his throughput budget. Thus, the report makes it easy to see both gross and net performance for underperforming salespeople.

Incentive Plans

It is a rare salesperson who is not compensated at least in part based on sales activity, usually in the form of a commission plan. Many companies conduct an annual review of these commission plans to determine the likely total compensation that the sales staff will receive if they meet various predetermined targets. However, less attention is paid to the compensation mix, commission payment delays, and the type of sales behavior that is being incentivized. These other factors are of considerable importance.

The compensation mix is important, because a purely variable commission structure makes the sales staff more desperate to sell *anything* in order to obtain their commission, and they will be more likely to pursue virtually any sales prospect, irrespective of the customer's credit rating. As the compensation mix shifts more in the direction of a pure salary, the sales staff has more leisure to pursue a long-term sales strategy, which

EXHIBIT 2.5 Sales Analysis by Salesperson

Moriarty Manufacturing Company
Sales Analysis by Salesperson
Under Budget 5% or More
For the Year-to-Date through June 30, 20xx

| Description | Revenues | | | Throughput | | |
| | Actual Sales | Over (Under) Budget | | Throughput | Over (Under) Budget | |
		Amount	%		Amount	%
Satisfactory performance:	827,432	112,610	14%	330,973	42,094	13%
Under budget performance:						
Abernathy	17,433	(1,390)	−8%	5,579	(1,394)	−25%
Bristol	19,811	(1,320)	−7%	6,934	(990)	−14%
Caldwell	24,033	(1,470)	−6%	9,133	(480)	−5%
Dunwiddy	32,016	(1,760)	−5%	13,446	640	5%
Fischer	8,995	(480)	−5%	4,048	450	11%
Gordon	27,666	(1,820)	−7%	8,023	(3,043)	−38%
Highsmith	4,277	(600)	−14%	1,754	43	2%
Mather	39,474	(3,800)	−10%	14,211	(1,579)	−11%
Owens	43,189	(4,400)	−10%	12,070	(5,206)	−43%
Subtotal	216,894	(17,040)	−8%	75,198	(11,560)	−15%
Grand total	1,044,326	95,570	9%	406,171	30,534	8%

encompasses a higher level of customer support, avoidance of bad-credit prospects, and following the direction of the sales manager regarding which products to sell. This paean to fixed compensation is not intended to be a recommendation for a pure salary structure, however. A significant proportion of compensation should be a commission, in order to create an ongoing incentive to pursue more sales.

Commission payment delay is another factor to consider. If commissions are based on cash received from customers, there is a greater incentive for the sales staff to sell only to prospects having high credit quality. However, this may involve the sales staff too much in postsale activities to ensure that customers are satisfied enough to pay and so could reduce the sales effectiveness of the salespeople.

Another issue is the type of sales behavior that is being incentivized. A compensation plan can encompass a range of possible incentives, such as a higher commission if sales are made prior to the end of the fiscal year-end, or a higher commission on sales made in a new territory, or lower commissions for recurring sales. If a company is pushing for higher year-end sales, this can cause an undue burden on the company's bottleneck operation, which may not be able to supply the requested products; or, if the goods come from a third party, then there is no bottleneck impact, but there will likely be a decline in sales during the next quarter, since the sales pipeline is now so full. Or, if lower commissions are paid on recurring sales, then the salesperson has less incentive to give a proper level of maintenance to existing customers, which may result in greater turnover among those customers. Based on these examples, it is evident that careful thought must be given to any change in compensation plan, to ensure that the correct type of sales behavior is being incentivized.

Strategic Sales

A common event is for a salesperson to request a "special" low price for a customer who is "strategic." This apparently means that if only the company will accept a loss or insignificant profit now on a new order, it will have the prospect of landing a really large (and presumably more profitable) deal in the future from that customer.

The overwhelming temptation is to accept the deal on the grounds that revenues will assuredly rise. However, the real test is whether this special sale is bumping out higher-throughput products that the company otherwise could have produced. The key factor is not the top-line revenue but the bottom-line margin, since that is what keeps the company in business. In such cases, it is better to take a hard-headed approach and maintain margins while letting a competitor take on the burden of a minimal-margin sale.

The only case where a strategic sale is warranted is when the customer is already actively inquiring about a follow-on order, and there is some assurance of obtaining it.

If a salesperson repeatedly brings up the prospect of strategic sales, it is time to consider why he is doing this—it may be because the salesperson is not capable of landing sales at normal margins and so is using large, low-margin sales prospects to cover this inadequacy.

Finding Throughput Problems in Sales

The basic concept of throughput management is to locate the bottleneck in an operation and implement a variety of techniques to eliminate or at least reduce its impact. Let us take a typical sales process as a example: The sales staff locates prospects, meets with them, issues a quote, conducts a product demonstration, negotiates the contract, and then passes the order to the rest of the company for delivery. If a company wants to increase sales, the usual response is to add more sales staff to drum up business—but what if they are drumming up plenty of initial leads and yet sales are still not increasing? If so, compare the capacity of each step in the sales process just noted to the amount of actual sales activity for the same step. For example, there may be only a small group assigned the task of creating quotes, and they cannot keep up with the inquiries brought to them by the sales staff. This leads to prospects becoming frustrated and taking their business elsewhere.

The key task in discovering these problems is to measure the capacity of each activity in the sales process and match it to the amount of actual activity. Every time the capacity and actual activity measures match, there is a bottleneck. It is also easy to spot bottlenecks by measuring the backlog in front of each process step—large backlogs indicate the presence of a bottleneck. Locating these problems is the crucial first step to increasing a company's sales.

Example

Fells Dunaway Corporation sells network analysis software to major corporations. Despite having a large and well-trained sales force, it is having difficulty increasing sales. To identify the problem, an analyst creates the next table of each step in the sales process, which shows the hours spent by the sales staff on each activity in comparison to the hours theoretically available during the past month.

Steps in Sales Funnel	Actual Time Used (hours)	Theoretical Capacity (hours)
Initial customer identification	450	700
Customer qualification	120	240
Needs assessment	300	300
Letter of understanding	50	80
Product demonstration	620	800
Solution proposal	2,400	3,100
Negotiation	280	400
Closing	100	200

The table reveals that there is a bottleneck in the needs assessment step, for which the actual time used matches the theoretical maximum available. To correct the problem, Fells's sales manager hires additional staff to work on the needs assessment step.

Sales Process Flow

Sometimes the sales staff may be excellent but not productive because of an inefficient sales process flow. The basic sales task is to sell high-margin products to creditworthy customers and then hand off the order to other departments. The reality can be quite a bit different. A salesperson may become involved in *every* step of the sales process and even continue in production monitoring, collections, and warranty claims issues. This multitude of activities takes up so much time that there is little room left in which to generate new sales.

In such a situation, create a flowchart of all current activities that a salesperson is involved in to complete a sale, then create a more segmented flow, such as the one shown in Exhibit 2.6, where the salesperson hands off the bulk of all sales-related activities to specialists who are more efficient at handling specific functional areas. In the exhibit, the salesperson makes the initial contact, creates a needs assessment, and is a marginal participant in proposal writing; all other tasks are handled by specialists. This task segmentation approach works well in high-volume situations where the sales staff can be fully utilized in just a few key roles.

These additional process flow improvements can reduce the workload of the sales staff:

- *Reduce customer iterations.* If the sales process includes a number of mandatory customer meetings or document approvals by the customer, then try to compress them into a single meeting. Otherwise, the customer has too many opportunities to stop the sale.
- *Push down decision making.* Avoid sales approvals by high-level staff, since they may not be available to render a decision for some time. Instead, push decision-making authority as far down in the company as possible, so that approvals take place closer to the actual events. Also, avoid approvals by multiple people—one should be enough.
- *Focus on work stoppages.* The sales process flow is largely about converting a customer need into a firm order—and there are a multitude of places where that flow can be inadvertently halted for long periods of time. Hunt down these work stoppage points and find ways to avoid them.

In general, consider each step in the sales process flow to be non–value added, and figure out ways to eliminate it, merge it into another step, or reduce the amount of time required to complete it.

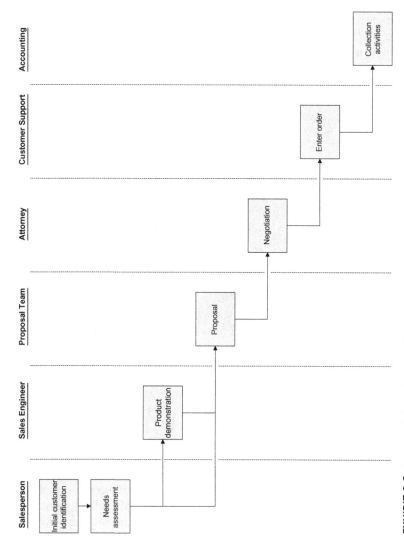

EXHIBIT 2.6 Improved Sales Process Flow

Sales Deduction Systems

The sales department may become involved in customer billing deductions, on the grounds that the sales staff has the best contacts with the customer. Reviewing deductions and negotiating settlements may take up a considerable amount of the sales staff's time. Here are some alternative arrangements to improve the efficiency of deduction handling:

- *Centralize deduction management.* One person should be assigned responsibility for the deductions of a small group of customers, and should monitor the status of each open deduction on a daily basis.
- *Create a standardized deduction procedure.* Create a tiered procedure for collecting information, developing a course of action, obtaining approvals, and processing the deduction. By doing so, no one wastes time with deductions that otherwise bounce around among the staff and remain unresolved for months.
- *Resolve underlying issues.* Enter all deductions in a database and summarize them by reason code. Management uses this information to prioritize and fix the product and delivery problems causing the deductions.
- *Push down deduction resolution authority.* Most deductions are quite small and are not worth management time to review and approve proposed resolutions. Instead, push decision-making authority for smaller deductions down to the customer service staff.
- *Request that customers bill the company for trade promotions.* If a company offers to pay customers for trade promotions, they will likely deduct these amounts from invoices payable to the company. Rather than having these items clutter up the deductions backlog, have customers bill them directly to the company, so that they are handled through the accounts payable system.
- *Cut off customers for ongoing deduction abuse.* If a customer continually takes large numbers of deductions, the cost of processing the deductions may fully offset any profit that would otherwise be earned by the company. If so, consider dropping the customer entirely, or switching to cash in advance payments.

Of the systemic improvements noted here, the key ones are to centralize and standardize the process. The next most important is to eliminate the reasons why deductions are taken in the first place, so that the total volume of deductions decline and cannot interfere with the work of the sales department.

Collections by the Sales Staff

The sales staff is generally not involved in the collection of overdue receivables from customers, and for a good reason—this is a coordination of payment documentation between the accounting staffs of the two companies, who are quite capable of handling most issues themselves.

However, the sales staff should be aware of customers who are having continuing late payment issues, so that they can focus their sales efforts elsewhere. This can be accomplished either through a periodic conference call with the collections manager, or by sending an aged accounts receivable report to each salesperson, highlighting overdue accounts. If a salesperson continually sells to a high-credit-risk customer, then it is acceptable to require that salesperson's collection assistance in advance, or to even collect payment on behalf of the company.

The primary role of the salesperson in the collection function is to act as a last resort who can step in and beseech the customer for payment after a variety of other collection methods have been attempted by the collection department.

Marketing Cost Reductions

Marketing expenditures do not always have a discernible cause-and-effect impact on corporate sales, which makes it difficult to apply a rigorous level of analysis to this area. Nonetheless, the next points can be useful in directing funds into those activities where they can have the greatest positive impact.

Incremental Advertising Analysis

When determining the correct amount of advertising to invest in, a common approach is simply to roll forward the expenditure from the previous year or to use a fixed percentage of estimated sales. This approach is hardly scientific and can be improved on with incremental advertising analysis. Under the incremental approach, the marketing staff estimates the number of unit sales it expects that will be triggered by a specific incremental amount of advertising activity. This should yield a narrow range of advertising expenditures within which the expense results in an offsetting (and larger) profit. If advertising expenditures increase above that range, then there is a reduced incremental benefit that results in a loss. The concept is shown in Exhibit 2.7, where throughput is maximized if the company spends a total of $100,000 on advertising, which yields a cumulative margin of $131,900. If the company makes additional advertising expenditures

EXHIBIT 2.7 Incremental Advertising Analysis

Incremental Block	Incremental Advertising Expense	Additional Units Estimated to Be Sold	Estimated Marginal Unit Throughput	Incremental Unit Advertising Cost	Unit Increment or (Decrement) Margin	Total Margin	Cumulative Margin
1	$ —	20,000	$ 1.00	$ —	$ (1.00)	$ 20,000	$ 20,000
2	$ 25,000	30,000	$ 1.20	0.83	0.37	$ 11,100	$ 31,100
3	$ 25,000	70,000	$ 1.30	0.36	0.94	$ 65,800	$ 96,900
4	$ 25,000	50,000	$ 0.90	0.50	0.40	$ 20,000	$ 116,900
5	$ 25,000	50,000	$ 0.80	0.50	0.30	$ 15,000	$ 131,900
6	$ 25,000	30,000	$ 0.70	0.83	(0.13)	$ (3,900)	$ 128,000
7	$ 25,000	30,000	$ 0.60	0.83	(0.23)	$ (6,900)	$ 121,100
8	$ 25,000	20,000	$ 0.50	1.25	(0.75)	$ (15,000)	$ 106,100
9	$ 25,000	10,000	$ 0.40	2.50	(2.10)	$ (21,000)	$ 85,100

above this level, then the resulting margins on additional incremental sales will not offset the additional advertising expenditure.

The analysis in the exhibit admittedly is based on a considerable amount of guessing and, it is hoped, some historical experience with how advertising correlates to product sales. Nonetheless, this approach can be valuable for those advertising campaigns that are targeted specifically at increasing product sales. It is not as useful when dealing with marketing that is only aimed at increasing brand awareness.

Marketing Efficiency

Marketing efforts can be associated with an entire company, a product line, or individual products. If a company has a large number of subsidiaries, product lines, or separately identifiable products, then it must spread its marketing activities quite thinly across all of them. A more cost-effective alternative is to reduce the number of each of these categories. By doing so, either the total marketing expenditure can be reduced or the same amount of marketing dollars can be concentrated on fewer subsidiaries, product lines, or products. If the latter approach is used, then consider also using the incremental advertising analysis noted above, which is a good tool for keeping from spending too much.

Marketing Effectiveness

It is extremely difficult to discern which types of marketing are impacting customers and which have minimal impact. One way to obtain this information is to ask customers where they heard about the company. If no paying customer claims to have heard about the company through a specific type of marketing, this is reasonable grounds for eliminating that expenditure.

However, use this approach with some care. If there are few respondents to a company's inquiries, it may simply mean that other customers do not like to fill out surveys. Thus, in low-response situations, the level of customer response regarding a specific marketing approach is not necessarily an indicator of its effectiveness.

New Markets and Products

An extreme misuse of cost cutting is in the establishment of new markets and products. This requires a significant outpouring of funds to create general awareness, and niggardly marketing expenditures will effectively strangle any prospects that a company might otherwise have. Admittedly, there are low-cost possibilities for viral marketing through the Internet, the recruiting of opinion leaders, videos, and podcasts; while these options can provide low-cost marketing alternatives, they do not usually provide a comprehensive solution to all of a company's marketing needs. Consequently, it is better to continue to channel significant funding into new market and product endeavors while also searching for low-cost alternatives that can provide additional support.

Special Promotions

The marketing department sometimes feels compelled to run special promotions because they have traditionally always been done. This approach is not a good one, because it may bullwhip demand; sales will peak for the promotion and then decline by a similar amount immediately thereafter. As a result, the production facility incurs overtime expenses during the busy period, machine maintenance may be delayed, *and* the company is offering the products at a discount—which is a recipe for lower profitability. Consequently, if a promotion is being offered simply because it has always been done this way, then consider a new way—which is no special promotions without a really good reason.

Sales and Marketing Metrics

The first three metrics noted next were described earlier in the chapter as being key determinants of the success of the sales department. The final two metrics are useful in specialized situations where a company operates an Internet store or where there is a quoting process that requires follow-up by the sales staff.

1. *Sales productivity.* The sales department's efficiency can best be addressed by matching the total throughput dollars it has booked in each period to the department's expenses. This metric is especially useful for judging the efficiency of sales that require a considerable amount of sales effort, such as those requiring product or service customization, multiple quote iterations, or extensive salesperson travel. The calculation is to divide throughput dollars booked during the period by the total sales department expense for the same period.
2. *Sales effectiveness.* The sales staff can be encouraged to sell products that use the least amount of production bottleneck time, which can lead to significant sales and profit increases. The calculation is to subtract the variable cost of goods sold from gross revenue and then divide the result by the amount of bottleneck time used to produce the item sold.

3. *Customer turnover.* This is useful for determining the impact of customer service on a company's customers. A very low turnover rate is important in situations where the cost of acquiring new customers is high. The calculation is to subtract from the total customer list those that have been invoiced (or sold to on a cash basis) within a standard sales cycle and then divide the remainder by the total number of customers on the customer list.

4. *Browse-to-buy conversion ratio.* If a company maintains a Web store, use this ratio to determine how many customers who initially browse the store then complete a purchase. The calculation is to divide the number of buying customers by the number of browsing customers, based on the Web site's analysis package.

5. *Quote-to-close ratio.* This metric reveals which sales personnel have the best ability to close a deal once it has been quoted. Though this measures the effectiveness of only one step in the sales funnel, it is nonetheless an important one. The calculation is to divide the dollar value of orders received by the dollar value of quoted orders.

Summary

The emphasis in this chapter has been on repositioning funding within the sales and marketing functions in order to maximize throughput, rather than outright cost cutting. This strategy is based on the assumption that this is the one area in a company where expenditures must be made in order to maintain or increase sales levels. If one *must* engage in cost cutting, then at least do so in areas of the department that are remote from the customer or that do not impact the order taking process flow.

A much better alternative to cost cutting is to shift non–value-added work away from the sales staff, tightly focus them on the sales mission, and measure them constantly to see who is not succeeding. If a salesperson is not generating enough sales and throughput, then the sales manager should replace that person as soon as possible and do everything possible to make the replacement succeed.

CHAPTER 3

Product Analysis

Introduction

There are a large number of cost reduction issues related to a company's products. Chief among them is the use of several target costing techniques to ensure that a product is initially designed to have a sufficient profit. In addition, the decisions to add, cancel, outsource, and customize a product require considerable deliberation. All of these topics are addressed within this chapter, as well as a number of product-related metrics.

Target Costing

Most costing methodologies are concerned primarily with the interpretation of costing data after it has already been incurred. Target costing differs from them in that it describes the costs that are *expected* to be incurred and how this will impact product profitability levels. By describing costs in a proactive and future-oriented manner, managers can determine how they should alter product designs before they enter the manufacturing process in order to ensure that the company earns a reasonable profit on all new products.

To use this methodology, a product design team continually compiles the projected cost of a product as it moves through the design process. Managers use this information not only to make product alterations, but also to drop a product design if it cannot meet its cost targets.

The target costing method addresses the costs designed into a product with this four-step process:

1. *Conduct market research.* The design team conducts market research to determine the price points that a company is most likely to achieve

if it creates a product with a certain set of features. The research should include information about the perceived value of certain features on a product, so that the design team can add or subtract features from the design with full knowledge of what these changes probably will do to the final price at which the product will be sold.

2. *Determine margin and cost feasibility.* Subtract from the prospective product price a gross margin that must be earned on the product; this can be a standard company-wide margin that must be earned on all new products or perhaps a more specific one that management has imposed based on the perceived risk of the project. By subtracting the required margin from the expected price, we arrive at the maximum amount that the product can cost. This total cost figure drives the next step.

3. *Meet margin targets through design improvements.* The design team then uses value engineering to drive down the cost of the product until it meets its overall cost target. Value engineering requires considerable attention to the elimination of production functions, a product design that is cheaper to manufacture, a planned reduction of product durability in order to cut costs, a reduced number of product features, less expensive component parts, and so on—in short, any activity that will lead to a reduced product cost. This process also requires the team to confirm costs with the suppliers of raw materials and outsourced parts as well as the processing costs that will be incurred internally. A standard procedure at this point is to force the team to come within a set percentage of its cost target at various milestones (such as being within 12 percent of the target after three months of design work, 6 percent after four months, and on target after five months); if the team cannot meet increasingly tighter costing targets, then the project will be canceled.

4. *Implement continuous improvement.* The target costing effort shifts into follow-on activities that will reduce costs even further after the product has entered its production phase. This final step is used to create additional gross margin over time, which allows the company to reduce the price of the product to respond to presumed increases in the level of competition. The sources of these cost reductions can be through either planned supplier cost reductions or through waste reductions in the production process (known as kaizen costing). The concepts of value engineering and kaizen costing can be used repeatedly to gradually reduce the cost of a product over time; typically, the market price of a product follows a steady downward trend, which is caused by ongoing competitive pressure as the market for the product matures. To meet this pricing pressure with corresponding reductions in costs, the company initially creates Product A and uses value engineering to

design a preset cost into the product. Once the design is released for production, kaizen costing is used to reduce costs further in multiple stages until there are few additional reductions left to squeeze out of the original design. At this point, the design team uses value engineering to create a replacement Product B that incorporates additional cost savings (likely including the cost reduction experience gleaned from the kaizen costing stages used for Product A) that result in an even lower initial cost. Kaizen costing is then used once again to further reduce the cost of Product B, thereby keeping the cost reduction process moving in an ever-downward direction. These target costing steps are shown graphically in Exhibit 3.1.

Value Engineering

Value engineering was mentioned in phase 2 of the preceding process. The term is a collective one for several activities used to lower the cost of a product. Here are some of the issues that are dealt with during a value engineering review:

- *Can we eliminate functions from the production process?* This involves a detailed review of the entire manufacturing process to see if there are any steps, such as interim quality reviews, that add no value to the product. By eliminating them, one can take their associated direct or overhead costs out of the product cost. However, these functions were originally included for a reason, so the engineering team must ensure that it can develop work-around steps that eliminate the need for the original functions.
- *Can we eliminate some durability or reliability?* It is possible to design an excessive degree of sturdiness into a product. For example, a vacuum cleaner can be designed to withstand a one-ton impact, although there is only the slightest chance that such an impact will ever occur; designing it to withstand an impact of 100 pounds may account for 99.999 percent of all probable impacts while also eliminating a great deal of structural material from the design. However, this concept can be taken too far, resulting in a visible reduction in durability or reliability that may reduce customers' perception of product quality.
- *Can we eliminate unnecessary features?* If a company has an active feedback loop with its customers (such as with continual polling), it can ask them which product features really are needed and which are superfluous. If there is a consistent opinion among customers that a specific feature is not part of the purchasing decision, then remove that feature in the next iteration of the product design.

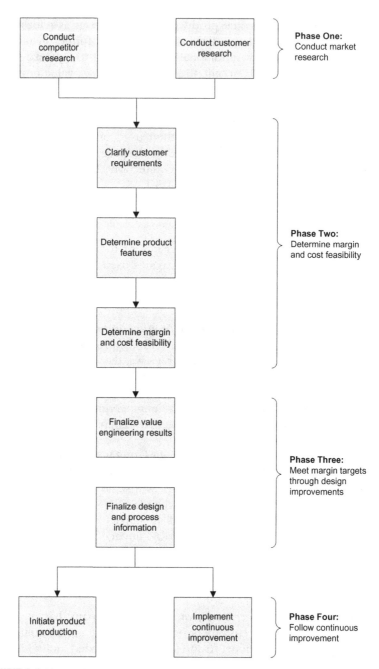

EXHIBIT 3.1 Target Costing Process

- *Are specifications too tight?* The component parts of a product may be designed to have extremely tight tolerances. Such parts are more expensive to produce than those having lower tolerances. If customers cannot tell the difference, and if the product functions in an acceptable manner with lower tolerances, then it may be possible to allow a broader range of variability in part sizes, resulting in lower costs.

- *Can we share parts with other products?* It is always better to use a smaller number of parts across a larger number of products. By doing so, the company can gain discounts by buying in larger volumes from its suppliers and has to track fewer inventory items. This approach calls for a great deal of design consistency across the engineering department and typically takes years to implement.

- *Can we minimize the design?* This involves the creation of a design that uses fewer parts or has fewer features. This approach is based on the assumption that a minimal design is easier to manufacture and assemble. Also, with fewer parts to purchase, less procurement overhead is associated with the product. However, reducing a product to extremes, perhaps from dozens of components to just a few, can result in excessively high costs for the few remaining parts, since they may be so complex or custom-made in nature that it would be less expensive to settle for a few extra standard parts that are more easily and cheaply obtained.

- *Can we shorten the design cycle time?* If the design cycle is quite short, a company can quickly launch new products to see what new features are popular with customers (or not), and then follow up with a string of incremental changes to match the product further to the market's requirements. A short cycle time is also beneficial for product testing, since any problems uncovered can be quickly fixed and incorporated into the next product iteration. It is also useful to examine the length of the testing period used before new products are released; by testing to see how long it usually takes to spot the bulk of all key issues, it may be possible to significantly shorten the testing period.

- *Can we design the product better for the manufacturing process?* Also known as design for manufacture and assembly (DFMA), this involves the creation of a product design that can be created in only a specific manner. For example, a toner cartridge for a laser printer is designed so that it can be inserted successfully into a printer only when the sides of the cartridge are correctly aligned with the printer opening; all other attempts to insert the cartridge will fail. When used for the assembly of an entire product, this approach ensures that a product is not incorrectly manufactured or assembled, which would call for a costly disassemble or product recall.

- *Can we reduce the amount of scrap?* Some manufacturing methods produce an inordinate amount of scrap. New production techniques may increase the yield for a given amount of material used, thereby reducing the overall cost of the product.
- *Can we substitute parts?* This approach encourages the search for less expensive components or materials that can replace more expensive parts currently used in a product design. However, sometimes the use of a different material impacts the types of materials that can be used elsewhere in the product, which may result in cost increases in these other areas, for a net cost increase. Thus, any parts substitution must be accompanied by a review of related changes elsewhere in the design.
- *Can we tear down competing products?* Competitors may have invented a unique design or used alternative parts that significantly reduce costs. If so, create a tear down room in which the engineering staff dismantles and examines competing products. Evaluate the cost and function of each component as well as its function in the context of the entire product.
- *Can we combine steps?* A detailed review of all the processes associated with a product sometimes reveals that some steps can be consolidated, which may mean that one can be eliminated or that several can be accomplished by one person rather than having people in widely disparate parts of the production process perform them. This is also known as process centering. By combining steps in this manner, one can eliminate some of the transfer and queue time from the production process, which in turn reduces the chance that parts will be damaged during those transfers.
- *Is there a better way?* Though this step sounds vague, it really strikes at the core of the cost reduction issue—the other value engineering steps previously mentioned focus on incremental improvements to the existing design or production process, whereas this one is a more general attempt to start from scratch and build a new product or process that is not based in any way on preexisting ideas. Improvements resulting from this step tend to have the largest favorable impact on cost reductions but can also be the most difficult for an organization to adopt.

The company's suppliers can be of great assistance in many of the preceding steps, since their particular knowledge of the components in which they specialize may lead to recommendations to use substitute parts, design changes, and even modifications to the production process.

A mix of all the value engineering steps just discussed must be applied to each product design to ensure that the maximum permissible cost is reached. Also, even if a minimal amount of value engineering is needed to reach a cost goal, conduct the full range of value engineering analysis anyway, since this can result in further cost reductions that improve the product margin to such an extent that management can either choose to reap exceptional profits or reduce the product price in order to gain market share.

If a product is highly regulated due to safety issues, then applying many of the preceding value engineering concepts may be subject to external review, which can be time-consuming. If so, consider downplaying product design changes, and focus instead on manufacturing process improvements as well as cost reductions in the supply chain. This approach should yield some cost reductions while avoiding regulatory issues.

Learning Curve

In addition to the cost savings that can be achieved through value engineering, it is also possible to reduce costs through sheer volume. It has been shown that costs decline by as much as 30 percent for every doubling of cumulative output, with the percentage declining as volumes increase. Thus, if a product initially costs $100 at an output level of 10,000 units, then its cost may decline to as much as $70 at an output level of 20,000 units. Again, the effect tends to decline as volumes continue to increase.

The learning curve has a number of causes, such as labor efficiency, standardization, task specialization, and better utilization of equipment—all of which presuppose active improvements on the part of the workforce. Thus, cost reductions are not automatically guaranteed to happen as volume rises, but it is easier to achieve reductions in such an environment.

The massive volume increases needed for the learning curve to take effect are most likely early in a product's life cycle, when it is easiest to obtain additional market share. Once the market consolidates, additional volume increases are most unlikely, so the learning curve is no longer a significant factor.

The learning curve effect can be accelerated if a company standardizes its use of components. By expanding the use of these components across multiple products, volume levels will increase to such an extent that measurable cost reductions can be achieved.

Kaizen Costing

Kaizen costing is a Japanese term for a number of cost reduction steps that can be used subsequent to issuing a new product design to the shop floor. Some of the activities in the kaizen costing methodology include the

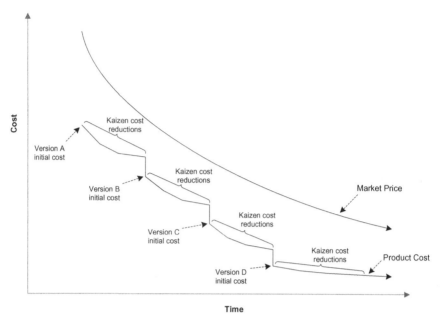

EXHIBIT 3.2 Stages of Cost Reduction

elimination of waste in the production, assembly, and distribution processes as well as the elimination of work steps in any of these areas. Kaizen costing repeats many of the value engineering steps used in the initial development of a product but does so for as long as a product is produced, constantly refining the process and thereby stripping out extra costs. The cost reductions resulting from kaizen costing are much smaller than those achieved with value engineering but are well worth the effort since competitive pressures are likely to force down product prices over time; any additional cost savings allow a company to still attain its targeted profit margins. This concept is illustrated in Exhibit 3.2.

Of particular interest in the exhibit is the use of multiple generations of products to meet the challenge of gradually reducing costs. In the example, the market price continues to drop over time, which forces the company to use both target and kaizen costing to reduce costs and retain its profit margin. However, prices eventually drop to the point where margins are reduced, which forces the company to develop a new product version with lower initial costs (Versions B, C, and D in the exhibit), and for which kaizen costing can again be used to further reduce costs. This pattern may be repeated many times as a company forces its costs down through successive generations of products. The exact timing of a switch to a new product is easy to determine well in advance, since the returns from kaizen costing follow the trend line of gradually shrinking savings, while prices also follow a predictable downward track; plotting these trend lines into the future reveals when a new product generation must be ready for market.

The type of cost reduction program used has an impact on the extent of cost reduction as well as on the nature of the components used in a product. When a design team sets cost reduction goals, it tends to focus on making incremental reductions, which is used most commonly during the redesign of products already on the market. An alternative is to create entirely new product configurations that may radically alter the product's design and yield greater cost savings. However, the latter approach is also a riskier one, since the resulting product concepts may not work and also may require so much extra design effort that new designs may miss their budgeted release dates. Therefore, the second method is generally reserved for situations where a company has a strong need to lower costs substantially.

The type of cost reduction path shown in Exhibit 3.2 is not worthwhile if a company is nearing the end of its life cycle. In such a case, a company will still use kaizen costing to extract some modicum of additional costs from the product but will no longer plan additional new versions. Further, as kaizen results gradually decline over time, managers must watch the resulting margins and decide when it is no longer profitable to continue the product. In low-competition markets, a product in this state may still be produced for years.

Profit Impact

Target costing improves profitability in two ways:

1. It places such a detailed and continuing emphasis on product costs throughout the product life cycle that it is unlikely that a company will experience runaway costs.
2. It improves profitability through precise targeting of the correct prices at which the company feels it can field a profitable product in the marketplace that will sell in a robust manner.

This is opposed to the more common cost-plus approach whereby a company builds a product, then determines its cost, tacks on a profit, and then does not understand why its resoundingly high price does not attract buyers. Thus, target costing results not only in better cost control but also in better price control.

Milestone Control

A target costing program eventually results in major cost reductions if design teams are given an unlimited amount of time to carry out a multitude of design iterations. However, there comes a point where the cost of maintaining the design team exceeds the savings to be garnered from additional iterations. Also, most products must be released within a reasonably short time frame or they will miss the appropriate market window when they can beat the delivery of competing products to the market. To avoid both these cost and time delays, use milestones as the principal method of control.

Several milestone reviews should be incorporated into a target costing program. Each one includes a thorough analysis of the progress of the design team since the last review, such as a comparison of the current cost of a design with its target cost. The main issue here is that the amount of cost yet to be worked out of a product must shrink, on a dollar or percentage basis, after each successive milestone review, or else management has the right to cancel the design project. For example, there may be a standard allowable cost variance of 12 percent for the first milestone meeting, 10 percent at the next meeting, and so on until the target cost must be reached as of a specific future milestone date. If a design team cannot quite reach its target cost but comes close, the management team should make a "go/no go" decision at that time that (1) sends the design into production, (2) allows more design time, or (3) terminates the project.

A milestone can be based on a time budget (e.g., one per month) or on the points in the design process at which specific activities are completed. For example, a milestone review can occur as soon as each successive design iteration is completed, when the conceptual drawings are finished, when the working model has been created, or when the production pilot has been run. There are many more steps that the management team can build into the milestone review process so that cost analyses become a nearly continual part of the target costing regimen.

Example

The GetLost Company is a manufacturer of global positioning systems (GPS) used in a variety of applications to determine a user's precise position on the surface of the planet. The founder of the company, Mr. Larry Ost, is concerned that the price point for handheld recreational GPS units has plummeted from more than $500 to about $100 in the past five years in response to severe pricing pressure from competitors. He decides to attack the problem by creating a target costing team.

The team conducts a number of marketing surveys to determine what features a prospective GPS unit should include. It finds that a key complaint of potential users is that all GPS units currently on the market are too bulky, which is a major concern for hikers, hunters, and trail runners who want to reduce the size of anything they carry with them into the outdoors. The marketing personnel on the team decide to combine the GPS unit with a standard walkie-talkie and weather instrument package, which many outdoorsmen also carry. The resulting device can then be marketed as a major space and weight saver compared to the alternative, which is to carry all three devices.

On initial review, the target costing team compiles a set of costs for a device that will cost $200, well above the $125 that surveys reveal is the most realistic price point for this type of device. Also, since the company wants to attain a 25 percent margin on this product, the team arrives at a cost reduction goal of $106 in this manner:

Target market price	$125
Target margin %	25%
Target margin $	$31
Target cost	$94
Current cost	$200
Target cost	−$94
Cost reduction goal	$106

To meet the cost reduction goal, the team begins its value engineering effort by reviewing combined functions in the radio, GPS, and weather instrument parts of the product. It finds that the radio and GPS share an antenna and a receiver; by merging these two components, the company can save $45 per unit. Also, by working with a supplier, the team finds that a new liquid crystal display (LCD) can be purchased for $2 less than the cost of the existing LCD. Finally, a design review of the circuitry reveals that combining multiple functions in a single chip will result in an additional $40 cost reduction while also creating a circuit board that is half the size of its predecessor. This allows the design team to create a much smaller plastic case for the device, reducing both the molding cost for the case and the cost of creating the injection mold used to create the case. The cost reduction resulting from these two innovations is $19. All these changes yield a new product cost of $94, which allows the GetLost Company to produce an innovative new product in a highly competitive market.

Continued

As a final measure, the target costing team assigns several staff members to review the production process with the objective of eliminating enough production waste to further reduce costs by 3 percent per year on a continual basis. Achieving this goal will allow the company to continue to reduce prices in the future, in the face of a heightened level of expected competition, while retaining a reasonable profit.

Targeted Price Increases

Product analysis would be somewhat limited if one only addresses cost reductions, when profit can also be achieved with price increases. In most markets, price competition does not allow for significant price increases. However, there are a few exceptions where highly targeted price increases can reap rich rewards.

First, consider product accessories. Unless there are third parties creating accessories for the company's products (only common for products having major market penetration), the company probably has this market to itself. Consequently, it is free to charge much higher prices for accessories than would be the case in a competitive market. One issue to consider is the cost of designing accessories, since probably only a few accessories will be bought frequently, beyond which additional accessories will experience minimal sales. Also, unusually high accessory pricing might drive customers away from buying the primary product. Within these constraints, accessory pricing is a rich opportunity and is available for however long the company chooses to market the primary product.

Second, anyone first to market has no competition, and so has the option of setting unusually high pricing. However, such a high-margin environment will inevitably attract competitors who are willing to accept lower margins, so this can be considered only a short-term pricing situation.

Third, the company can charge a premium for a lengthy time period if it can lock out the competition with a patent. If the market is sufficiently rich, competitors will strive to create work-arounds to the patent or simply invade the market with lower prices once the patent expires. Thus, this is a long-term pricing solution but with a definite termination date as represented by the patent expiration date.

All three of the preceding scenarios comprise a small minority of the areas in which a company competes, but they can make up a substantial proportion of its profitability. Thus, the management team should be aware of and exploit them to the greatest extent possible.

Eliminate Unprofitable Products

Pareto analysis holds that 80 percent of the activity in a given situation is caused by 20 percent of the population. This rule is strongly applicable to the profitability of a company's products, where 80 percent of the total profit is generated by 20 percent of the products. Of the remaining 80 percent of the product population, it is reasonable to assume that some make no profit at all. Consequently, financial analysis should encompass the regularly scheduled review of all company product offerings to determine which products should be withdrawn from the marketplace. This analysis is valuable for these reasons:

- *Complexity.* In general, too many products lead to an excessive degree of system complexity within a company in order to support those products.
- *Excessive inventory.* Each product usually contains some unique parts, which require additional storage space in the warehouse, as well as a working capital investment in those parts and the risk of eventual obsolescence.
- *Engineering time.* If there are changes to products, the engineering staff must update the bill of material and labor routing records, all of which takes time.
- *Marketing literature.* The marketing department usually maintains a unique set of literature for each product, which requires periodic updating and reprinting. The department may also run a separate advertising campaign for each product or group of products, which may not be cost effective.
- *Servicing cost.* The customer support staff must be trained in the unique features of each product, so they can adequately answer customer questions.
- *Warranty cost.* Some products have a considerable warranty cost, possibly due to design flaws or inadequate materials that require sizable warranty reserves.

Cancellation Decision

Only direct costs should be used in calculating the profitability of a product for purposes of the cancellation decision. This results in the next formula:

Standard list price (1)
- Commission (2)
- Buyer discounts (3)
- Material cost (4)
- Scrap cost (5)
- Outsourced processing (6)
- Inventory carrying cost (7)
- Packaging cost (8)
- Unreimbursed shipping cost (9)
- Warranty cost (10)

= Profit (loss)

Comments regarding the formula are presented next, and match the numbers next to each line item in the formula:

1. *Standard list price.* If a product has a number of prices based on volume discounts or other criteria, then create a model to determine the break-even price below which no profit is earned. The result may be a decision not necessarily to cancel the product but rather to not sell it at less than a certain discounted price, below which it makes no profit.
2. *Commission.* If a salesperson's commission is clearly identifiable with a specific product and will not be earned if the product is not sold, then include the commission in the product cost.
3. *Buyer discount.* The inclusion of buyer discounts in the calculation calls for some judgment. It should not be included if discounts are a rare event and comprise only a small dollar amount. If discounts are common, then calculate an average discount amount and deduct it from the standard list price.
4. *Material cost.* This is the cost of any materials included in the manufacture of a product.
5. *Scrap cost.* If a standard amount of scrap can be expected as part of the production process that is specifically identifiable with a product, then include this cost in the profitability calculation.
6. *Outsourced processing.* If any production work related to the product is completed by an outside entity, then the cost of this work should be included in the calculation on the grounds that the entire cost of the outsourced processing will be eliminated along with the product.
7. *Inventory carrying cost.* This should be only the incremental inventory carrying cost, which is usually just the interest cost of the company's investment in inventory specifically related to the product. It should not include the cost of warehouse storage space or insurance, since both of these costs are fixed in the short term and are very unlikely

to change as a result of the elimination of a single product. For example, a company may lease a warehouse and be obligated to make monthly lease payments irrespective of the amount of storage space being taken by inventory used for a specific product.

8. *Packaging cost.* Include the cost of any packaging materials used to contain and ship the product, but only if those materials cannot be used for other products.
9. *Unreimbursed shipping cost.* If the company is absorbing the cost of shipments to customers, then include this cost, net of volume discounts from the shipper.
10. *Warranty cost.* Though normally a small expense on a per-unit basis, an improperly designed product or one that includes low-quality parts may have an extremely high average warranty cost. If significant, this cost should be included in the profitability analysis.

In addition, please note that production labor costs are *not* included in the preceding calculation. The reason is that production labor rarely varies directly with the level of production; instead, a fixed number of workers will be in the production area every day, irrespective of the volume of work performed. Thus, the cancellation of a product will not impact the number of workers employed. If a product cancellation will result in the verifiable and immediate elimination of labor positions, however, then the incremental cost of the eliminated labor should be included in the calculation.

Exit Costs

An additional consideration when reviewing a potential product cancellation is the existence of any exit costs. These costs can include:

- *Contractual obligations.* Customers may have entered into contracts with the company for it to provide them with the product for a certain period of time. There may be an early termination fee contained within these contracts.
- *Fixed assets.* A variety of manufacturing equipment may no longer be needed if a product is canceled. In a cellular manufacturing environment, where smaller and more configurable equipment is used, such machines are more likely to be switched over to the manufacture of other products. If not, then the company should sell the equipment, which may involve the recognition of a gain or loss. It is generally best to sell off such equipment immediately, since it otherwise takes up valuable space, and the company will have immediate use of any sale proceeds.

- *Inventory.* There may be raw materials or finished goods on hand that must be dispositioned, probably at a loss. This is less of an issue for raw materials if there is extensive cross-usage of components among multiple products, since the raw materials can be used elsewhere. As for finished goods, they can be drawn down to zero before officially canceling a product, or they can be sold off to a third party in bulk at a lower price.
- *Severance costs.* If an entire product line is being shut down, then the company may lay off all of the people who worked on that line. This will likely involve a variety of severance costs.
- *Warranties.* The company may have an obligation to maintain product warranties for some period of time, during which it should retain trained customer service personnel and sufficient stocks of repair parts and replacement products.

Of the exit costs just noted, the inventory cost can be reduced by gradually draining inventory levels and then timing the product cancellation date to coincide with minimal remaining inventory. The fixed asset expense can be similarly managed by avoiding new equipment investments as the cancellation date approaches. The other expenses are not so easily managed but are still nonrecurring in nature—they are incurred only once. Thus, exit costs should be considered only for the *timing* of a product cancellation, not in regard to whether the cancellation should occur at all.

Application of Overhead to Product Costs

When conducting a product cancellation analysis, care must be taken not to assume that some expenses will be eliminated along with a product. Instead, an expense may have been allocated to a product but will still remain once the product has been canceled. The same pool of overhead costs must now be spread over a smaller number of remaining products, which increases the allocated cost per product and makes the remaining products appear to be even less profitable. This can lead to a continuous series of product eliminations that leaves a company in a much less profitable situation than when it started eliminating products.

Thus, a product should be eliminated *only* when its price is lower than its totally variable costs, which were described earlier. This should greatly reduce the number of cases where the product price will be low enough to warrant product elimination. By using this approach, a company will tend to have a broader diversity in its product offerings, but only under the assumption that it can continue to afford the extra labor required to keep track of these more diverse products, which can include a larger number of component parts, product designs, advertising campaigns, and so on.

Example

Acorn Company has three products, whose margins and other information are shown in the table. The company has $100,000 of overhead
costs, which it allocates based on the number of units sold. Acorn sells
a combined total of 15,000 units of all three of its products, so each
one receives an overhead charge of $6.66 ($100,000 overhead
expense/15,000 units).

	Product Alpha	Product Beta	Product Charlie	Totals
Units sold	1,500	3,500	10,000	15,000
Price each	$8.00	$12.00	$15.00	—
Variable cost each	3.00	5.00	6.00	—
Overhead allocation	6.66	6.66	6.66	—
Gross margin each	$(1.66)	$0.34	$2.34	—
Gross margin total	$(2,490)	$1,190	$23,400	$22,100

Based on this analysis, Acorn elects to stop selling Product Alpha,
which has a fully burdened loss of $2,490. The company does not lose
any overhead expenses as a result of this product elimination, so the
same $100,000 must now be allocated among products Beta and
Charlie; this results in an increased overhead charge per unit of $7.41
($100,000 overhead expense/13,500 units). The results appear in the
next table.

	Product Beta	Product Charlie	Totals
Units sold	3,500	10,000	13,500
Price each	$12.00	$15.00	—
Variable cost each	5.00	6.00	—
Overhead allocation	7.41	7.41	—
Gross margin each	$(0.41)	1.59	—
Gross margin total	$(1,435)	$15,900	$14,465

Now the Product Beta margin has become negative, with a fully
burdened loss of $1,435. Acorn therefore stops selling Product Beta.
Overhead expenses do not decline as a result of this product cancellation, so now the entire overhead cost is allocated to Product Charlie,

Continued

at a rate of $10.00 per unit ($100,000 overhead expense/10,000 units). The result is shown in the next table.

	Product Charlie
Units sold	10,000
Price each	$15.00
Variable cost each	6.00
Overhead allocation	10.00
Gross margin each	$(1.00)
Gross margin total	$(10,000)

Based on the new cost allocation, Acorn cancels Product Charlie as well and now finds itself out of business! It has gone from a profitable company to a bankrupt one, because it included fixed overhead costs in its product cancellation decisions.

Immediate Liquidation Option

In some cases, financial analysis reveals that some products are unprofitable, but management chooses to keep those products for a limited period of time in order to use up remaining stocks of inventory. If so, determine how much money the company would receive by selling off the remaining stocks to a third party right now rather than waiting for them to be used up in production of the product. Selling off the remaining stocks may be a better option if the underlying product is minimally profitable and does not sell well, since one can instead convert the stock immediately into cash.

Key Product Concerns

Another consideration is that an unprofitable product may be of critical importance to customers. If so, it may be useful to offer an upgrade path to another (presumably more profitable) product that provides them with the required level of functionality. If there is no obvious replacement, the product cancellation process is likely to be greatly prolonged until a new upgrade product can be readied for service.

Even if a product is clearly unprofitable, it may be needed by a key customer who orders other, more profitable products from the company. If so, combine the profits of all sales made to that customer to ensure that the net combined profit is sufficiently high to warrant the retention of the unprofitable product. If this is not the case, consider canceling the unprofitable product and negotiating with the customer for a price reduction on other products in order to retain the customer.

Another cancellation issue is the presence of dependent products. There may be ancillary products that are supplements to the main product and that provide additional profits to the overall product line. For example, the profit margin on a cell phone may be negative, but there may be a sufficiently high profit level on extra cell phone batteries, car chargers, headsets, and phone covers to more than offset the loss on the initial product sale. In these cases, the margins on all ancillary products should be included in the profitability analysis.

Dropping an Entire Product Line

The point has already been made that only variable costs should be considered when making the decision to cancel a product. The reason is that associated overhead costs are rarely eliminated when a single product is canceled. However, this is no longer the case if an entire product line is canceled. There may very well be a production facility, advertising campaign, and product manager associated with a full product line, so all of these costs will be eliminated if the line is canceled. Thus, the range of impacted costs increases as the scope of the potential cancellation expands.

Example

Chestnut Company manufactures a broad range of hardwood furniture products, which it divides into product lines by type of hardwood. Its Imperial line is comprised solely of mahogany wood, whose popularity has declined significantly over the past decade. The Imperial line is produced solely from Chestnut's Wellesley facility, which also manufactures the company's StarBright children's products and CleanAway bathroom cabinets on the same equipment used for the Imperial line.

The Imperial line generated a gross margin of $183,000 during the past year. Since the Wellesley facility also manufactures other products, its cost cannot be directly associated with the Imperial line. However, a more detailed analysis of overhead costs reveals that these annualized expenses would be eliminated if the Imperial line were canceled:

Continued

Advertising campaign	$35,000
Customer support staff	32,000
Marketing brochures	4,500
Obsolete inventory	22,000
Procurement staff	93,000
Product manager	85,000
Warranty claims	15,000
	$286,500

The overhead of $286,500 is greater than the Imperial line's gross margin of $183,000, resulting in a net loss of $103,500. Chestnut's president therefore makes the decision to terminate the entire Imperial product line, which eliminates all of the overhead items just noted.

Another way of looking at a product line cancellation is that it allows a company to concentrate more of its marketing funds on the remaining product lines. If targeted effectively, the extra marketing expenditure can disproportionately increase sales for the remaining product lines, thereby leading to an incremental increase in profits.

Timing of Product Cancellations

The discussion thus far has assumed that an analyst must root through a vast array of products that have been sold for many years, searching for those few items that should be canceled. A better approach is to constantly review products that have just been launched and monitor their sales and margins on a monthly basis. If they do not achieve their profit potential, then an immediate kaizen costing review should take place to see if the product's performance can be improved. If this cannot be achieved, or if revenue levels are inordinately low, then the product should be canceled as soon as possible.

By eliminating products sooner rather than later, a company keeps its staff focused on either the continuing sale of its best products or the development of those new products that appear to have the best profit potential. It *does not* spend time on products that return little or no profit.

Finally, the frequency of product profitability reviews will be greatly dependent on product life cycles. If products have very short life cycles, then sales levels will drop rapidly once products enter the decline phase of their life cycles, potentially leaving the company with large stocks of excess inventory. In these situations, it is critical to conduct frequent reviews in order to keep a company's investment in working capital from becoming excessive.

Reasons to Keep Unprofitable Products

There are also two nonfinancial reasons for retaining unprofitable products that must be considered before cancellation:

1. A company may want to offer to customers a full range of product offerings, so they can purchase anything they need from the company, without having to go to a competitor. This may require the retention of a product whose absence would otherwise create a hole in the corporate product line.
2. It may be necessary to offer a product in a specific market niche in order to keep competitors from entering a market that the company considers to be crucial to its ongoing viability.

Add New Products

When adding a new product, management may be startled to find that profits actually decline as a result of the introduction. This happens when the new product eliminates an older product that yielded more *throughput per minute*. *Throughput* is the margin left after a product's price is reduced by the amount of its totally variable costs. *Throughput per minute* is a product's throughput, divided by the amount of processing time that it uses in the company's bottleneck operation. Since the bottleneck operation has only a limited amount of processing time, a high-throughput product that requires minimal processing time in the bottleneck will yield more profit to the company than an equally high-throughput product that requires more processing time. An example is shown next.

Example

ColorView Corporation's engineers have designed a new, lower-cost 32-inch LCD television to replace the existing model. The characteristics of the two products are:

	32″ LCD Television (New)	32″ LCD Television (Old)
Price	$400	$400
Totally variable costs	$340	$355
Throughput	$60	$45
Overhead allocation	$35	$35
Profit	$25	$10
Required bottleneck usage	10 minutes	6 minutes
Throughput per bottleneck minute	$6.00	$7.50

Continued

A traditional cost analysis would concluded that the new model is clearly better, since it costs less to build, resulting in a profit $15 greater than the old model. However, the new model achieves less throughput per minute, because its larger total throughput is being spread over a substantial increase in the required amount of time on the constrained resource. By replacing the old model with the new model, ColorView arrives at these results for a bottleneck operation that is available for 8,000 minutes of production time per month:

	Throughput $/Minute of Bottleneck	Required Bottleneck Usage (minutes)	Units of Scheduled Production	Bottleneck Utilization (minutes)	Throughput per Product
32" television (new)	$6.00	10	800	8,000	$48,000
32" television (old)	$7.50	6	1,333	7,998	$59,985
				Variance	$(11,985)

Thus, the new model's reduced throughput per minute results in a total monthly profit reduction of $11,985, because it requires too much of the bottleneck operation's processing time.

ColorView's management decides to revise the new LCD television so that it reduces the required bottleneck usage per unit to just five minutes, though at an incremental cost increase of $20, which reduces its total throughput to $40 per unit. The results are shown next.

	Throughput $/Minute of Bottleneck	Required Bottleneck Usage (minutes)	Units of Scheduled Production	Bottleneck Utilization (minutes)	Throughput per Product
32" television (new)	$8.00	5	1,600	8,000	$64,000
32" television (old)	$7.50	6	1,333	7,998	$59,985
				Variance	$4,015

Even though the total throughput of the new product is lower than the throughput of the product it is replacing, more units can be produced on the bottleneck operation, so the total profit increases. This new product introduction might possibly have been canceled by the accountants, on the grounds that the per-unit margin has declined; only by reviewing the additional impact on the bottleneck operation does it become apparent that the new product will yield greater total profits.

Outsource Products

A common decision is whether to outsource the manufacture of a product. The usual analysis focuses on the reduced margin that the company will earn, since the supplier likely will charge a higher price (in order to include a profit) than the company can achieve if it keeps the work in-house. From a pure cost reduction standpoint, then, very few products will ever be outsourced. However, the correct view of the situation is whether the company can earn more throughput (as defined in the last section) on a combination of the outsourced production and the additional new production that will now be available through the bottleneck operation. The next example illustrates the concept.

Example

ColorView Corporation produces four sizes of LCD televisions, for which it has 30,000 minutes per month of processing time available on its bottleneck operation. The current production situation is illustrated in the next table. The products are sorted within the table in declining order by throughput per minute. The fourth column shows the number of units of scheduled production, followed by the number of units that could be produced if sufficient bottleneck capacity were available.

	Throughput $/Minute of Bottleneck	Required Bottleneck Usage (minutes)	Units of Scheduled Production	Bottleneck Utilization (minutes)	Throughput per Product
32″ LCD television	$8.00	5	1,600/1,600	8,000	$64,000

Continued

	Throughput $/Minute of Bottleneck	Required Bottleneck Usage (minutes)	Units of Scheduled Production	Bottleneck Utilization (minutes)	Throughput per Product
20″ LCD television	$6.25	6	800/800	4,800	30,000
50″ LCD television	$5.15	10	1,200/1,200	12,000	61,800
42″ LCD television	$4.00	12	433/1,500	5,196	20,784
			Total planned bottleneck time	29,996	—
			Maximum available bottleneck time	30,000	—
			Total throughput		**$176,584**

One of ColorView's key suppliers has offered to take over the entire production of the 50″ LCD television and drop ship the completed goods directly to the company's customers. The catch is that the company's throughput per unit will decline from its current $51.50 to $30.00. ColorView's analyst constructs the next table, which includes the reduced throughput from outsourcing the 50″ LCD television, but with no usage of the bottleneck operation. Instead, additional bottleneck usage by the 42″ LCD television (having the next lowest throughput per minute) is increased to make use of the remaining available bottleneck minutes.

	Throughput $/Minute of Bottleneck	Required Bottleneck Usage (minutes)	Units of Scheduled Production	Bottleneck Utilization (minutes)	Throughput per Product
32″ LCD television	$8.00	5	1,600/1,600	8,000	$64,000
20″ LCD television	$6.25	6	800/800	4,800	30,000
50″ LCD television	$5.15	10	1,200/1,200	—	36,000
42″ LCD television	$4.00	12	1,433/1,500	17,196	68,784
			Total planned bottleneck time	29,996	—
			Maximum available bottleneck time	30,000	—
			Total throughput		**$198,784**

> The result is a higher profit for ColorView, because it is still earning some throughput on the outsourced television, while producing more units of the next most profitable product, during the production interval created on the bottleneck operation.

Another consideration in the outsourcing decision is the reduction in purchasing volumes across the entire company. If a major product line is outsourced, and it shares parts with other products that the company still produces, then it is likely that the purchasing staff will have to accept higher prices from suppliers, given the company's reduction in purchasing volume. This issue has a lesser impact if materials used for the outsourced product are obtained from a different group of suppliers.

Product Rework Costs

The production staff may devote an inordinate amount of time to the repair and rework of products. These costs frequently are not tracked well and so drop into overhead costs without being charged back to the products in question. The first step in dealing with rework costs is to develop a better timekeeping system so that management can see which products are piling up rework costs. This simple step tells management where to direct its quality improvement efforts.

A common result of the improved rework cost reporting system is that specific components will be shown to have unusually high failure rates. The engineering and procurement staffs can then work on increasing the quality of these components, through substitutions, tighter tolerances, or redesigns. Thus, greater expenditures to improve quality ultimately should reduce the total cost spent on rework.

Conversely, rework cost reporting also tells the company where *not* to pursue further cost reduction efforts. If a component is already breaking, then further reducing its durability will only increase rework costs even more.

Another result of more accurate cost tracking is that some products may no longer earn a profit, due to all of the additional rework costs. This does not necessarily mean that those products should be canceled—it is entirely possible that a continuing quality improvement campaign will eliminate rework problems and return the products to profitability. If there continues to be a rework problem, this may call for the redesign of the product to eliminate the issue causing the problem. Actually canceling the product should be considered only after these intermediate steps have been attempted and discarded.

Custom Product Costs

It is extremely difficult to earn a respectable profit on the sale of customized products. The sales process is more extensive, there is a greater risk of using incorrect specifications, customer support time increases, procurement costs are high, and more staff training is needed. Also, there is an increased risk of inventory obsolescence, since parts may be custom-ordered for a specific customer request and then not used.

Of particular concern for a highly customized product is the need for extensive sales support. The sales staff may make numerous sales calls to discuss product configurations with clients, which may continue throughout the production process. Further, the sales staff subsequently may fall into the role of customer support representatives in order to deal with any customer issues once they receive the completed product, which takes salespeople away from the generation of new orders.

Example

GoCart Company manufactures customized food carts on wheels, which its customers move to high-traffic locations for the sale of hot dogs, hamburgers, and other types of fast food. GoCart sells four basic sizes of food cart, along with custom graphics and awnings. It also allows customers to modify the placement of kitchen equipment within each cart.

The sales staff works from a centralized location in Chicago. Upon receipt of a customer deposit, the sales staff travels to the customer to obtain a rough draft of the ordered carts. The GoCart design staff then creates design specifications and artwork for customer approval, which the sales staff brings to the customer as part of a second on-site visit. All further sales contacts are made from the company's headquarters location. The sales staff is compensated entirely through commission payments that are a percentage of the invoiced price, and which they receive upon final cash receipt from the customer.

GoCart is losing a great deal of money on its cart sales, but there does not appear to be much room for a price increase. Accordingly, management focuses on costs instead. The company controller investigates the travel cost of the sales staff, and finds that it spends an average of $1,500 on each customer visit, for a total of $3,000 per order. The sales staff has no incentive to reduce its costs, since it is compensated based on revenue only, not net income. Also, the sales staff keeps handling customer calls throughout the production process and until the customer sends payment to the company, since they are paid a commission only once the company receives final payment from the customer.

The company's average gross margin on each food cart is $1,500, so the $3,000 average travel cost associated with each order means that every single-cart order loses $1,500, and a two-cart order only breaks even.

GoCart's management institutes four changes to rectify the situation:

1. It does not allow customers to modify the standard cart configuration unless they place a minimum order of five carts.
2. It changes the commission payment date to be based on the invoice date rather than the cash receipt date; this encourages the sales staff to hand off customer calls to the customer support staff, thereby giving them more time to pursue new orders.
3. It places a limit of one sales visit for each order of less than five carts, with all other contacts being by phone.
4. Management creates a new commission structure where larger orders earn the sales staff a larger commission percentage.

By making these changes, GoCart will likely lose some single-cart orders, which were not earning a profit anyway, and positions itself for higher-volume orders over which it can more easily spread its salesperson travel expenses.

Another issue with custom products is that returned products cannot be resold easily to another customer. Instead, they may need to be disassembled into their component parts and rebuilt to the specifications of another customer. To avoid this scenario, consider having customers pay up front for the entire cost of the product, and do not allow product returns. A variation on this approach for large-dollar orders is to require a series of deposits, with all payments being made before the company delivers the product to the customer. The timing of these deposits should roughly correspond to the company's expenditures for the components and labor needed to construct the product.

A particular danger for a company dealing with customized products is the gradual buildup of obsolete inventory. It may need to buy a large variety of special-purpose components, some of which must be bought in quantities that leave some excess on the shelf. Also, if a product is rejected by a customer, the completed product or its disassembled parts will find their way into the warehouse. These inventory items may be listed on the company's books for years after the original project was completed, so that management does not see their underlying expense for some time.

A good way to handle inventory obsolescence in a custom product environment is to review the cost of new items added to inventory immediately, as soon as a custom project has been completed, and add their expense to the final profit report for the project. Further, these items should be brought to the attention of the company's materials review board immediately, which is tasked with dispositioning inventory that is no longer needed.

Product Metrics

There are a number of metrics that can be used in the examination of product costs. Good areas for analysis include the investment in finished goods inventory, approved parts usage in new products, revenue from new products, progress toward achieving target cost goals, and warranty claims. These areas and more are encompassed by the next metrics:

- *Finished inventory turnover.* A company may be building more product than it can sell or is experiencing a sudden slowdown in sales that is causing excess finished goods inventory levels. Either condition is spotlighted by the number of finished goods inventory turns, where a low number of turns indicates an excessive inventory level. The calculation is the most recent month's product revenue, divided by the dollar amount of month-end finished goods on hand, and then multiplied by 12.
- *New product breakeven time.* This is the period of time required before the development cost of a new product has been paid back by the margin on subsequent sales of that product. This metric is most useful for products having a short life cycle. If the breakeven time encompasses nearly all of a product's life cycle, then the company needs to shorten its development cycle through such methods as process streamlining and incremental product enhancements. The calculation is the total cost of product development, divided by the *cumulative* gross margin, to be recalculated as each month of new sales is completed.
- *Number of products per design platform.* If a company designs too many product platforms, it runs into problems with having too many production lines, each of which is tooled to manufacture one platform only.

This also results in a vast array of components for all of the products, plus a great deal of design time needed to update each platform. It is better to have a large number of products based on the smallest possible number of platforms. The calculation is to divide the total number of distinct products by the total number of design platforms.

- *Percentage of existing parts reused in new products.* If a company encourages its designers to construct new products using an approved standardized list of components, then it can concentrate its supplier purchases and achieve volume discounts. The calculation is to divide the number of approved parts in a new product's bill of materials by the total number of parts in the bill.

- *Percentage of sales from new products.* The engineering department should be encouraged to create not simply vast numbers of new products but rather precisely targeted ones that are most likely to generate maximum revenues. This behavior can be encouraged by tracking the percentage of sales from products created within the past 12 months, three years, and five years. The calculation is to divide new product sales by total company sales during the selected measurement period.

- *Ratio of actual to target cost.* In a target costing environment, the finalized product cost should match or be lower than the target cost originally determined based on a joint evaluation of the engineering and marketing departments. The ratio of actual to target costs can also be measured throughout the design process, to determine progress toward the cost goal. The calculation is to divide the total of actual expected product costs by the total amount of target costs. A footnote should accompany this metric, stating the expected production volume at which the costs are stated (since component costs can change drastically if production volumes vary).

- *Warranty claims percentage.* The engineering staff needs to know if there are unusually high failure rates among its products. A simple metric for determining this is the warranty claims percentage. The calculation is the total number of warranty claims received, divided by the total number of products sold. There can be a significant time lag between the point when a product is sold and when it is returned under warranty. To obtain a measurement that properly relates the amount of units sold and the number of warranty claims, the measurement period should comprise several months.

In particular, consider a combination of the percentage of sales from new products and the ratio of actual to target cost. These two metrics focus on the revenue and profits generated by new products, and so drive at the core issues in the product development process.

Summary

Target costing is the single most important aspect of product analysis, since costs are "baked in" to a product during the design stage and can be reduced only to a modest extent thereafter. Once a product is launched, its performance should be carefully monitored to see if it is achieving targeted revenue and profit levels. If not, and if any underlying issues cannot be corrected, then it is best to cancel the product as soon as possible rather than letting it linger and further occupy valuable employee time.

The addition of new products or the outsourcing of existing ones should be examined in light of their use of any bottleneck operation. Either action should increase the amount of profit flowing through the bottleneck operation, or else they should not be allowed. This assessment calls for complete knowledge of the margins associated with each existing product and their use of the bottleneck operation.

Finally, customized products are generally hazardous to the health of a company, given their exceptionally large use of resources, and should generally be avoided unless a company has an excellent knowledge of the costs associated with each customer order.

CHAPTER 4

Production Cost Reduction

Introduction

The traditional production process has been one involving long production runs to drive down per-unit product costs, a large investment in inventory to create buffers throughout the plant, and a blizzard of efficiency projects everywhere to continually drive down costs. These concepts are largely incorrect, resulting in a ponderous organization that is not capable of switching to new products on short notice and that is smothered in so much inventory that underlying problems are completely hidden from view.

In this chapter, we describe a much leaner production facility that operates with minimal inventory and where fast feedback loops are used to spot and correct problems as soon as possible. The impact on production costs is highly favorable.

Throughput Analysis

When reviewing the production area for cost reduction possibilities, throughput analysis is an extremely important tool, to the extent that it overrides many other concepts described in this chapter. In essence, it holds that total production output will increase only if the bottleneck (constrained) operation is properly managed; improvements to any other part of the production area are irrelevant. Also, the throughput (sales minus totally variable expenses) coming from production will be maximized if products having high throughput and reduced usage time on the bottleneck operation have priority in being produced.

Based on these concepts, cost reduction at the bottleneck operation is generally a bad idea, since it may reduce the efficiency of that operation. If anything, more money should be poured *into* the bottleneck operation in order to maximize throughput. Thus, throughput analysis is an excellent tool for determining where *not* to cut costs. This is such a large topic that it is addressed separately in Chapter 12, "Throughput Analysis." The reader should consider reading that chapter before proceeding with this one.

Product Line Complexity

Before delving into the details of the production area for potential cost reductions, it is worthwhile simply to review the number of types of products being manufactured. If production is focused on a relatively small product line, then the production volume will likely be higher on a per-product basis, so there will be a quicker accumulation of learning and costs will tend to decline faster. This logic is based on the experience curve concept, under which costs are expected to decline by anywhere from 10 to 30 percent for every doubling of cumulative output.

Conversely, if production volumes are scattered across a broad array of products, then production volumes will be subscale, and there will be a slower accumulation of learning that causes costs to decline more slowly. Consequently, a cost reduction method at a strategic level is to concentrate production upon fewer products and product lines.

Production Flow

The system used to manage the flow of production through a manufacturing facility is crucial to its ability to reduce costs. In general, a "push" system tends to accumulate more costs than a "pull" system.

A good example of a push system is a material requirements planning (MRP) system, where a production planner decides on how much of which products to manufacture. MRP software then calculates how much material is needed, and the production team creates the products.

A pull system is typified by a just-in-time system, where a customer order triggers a production order to manufacture the exact amount of product listed in the customer order. This order then ripples back through the production facility, with each work center making only enough of each component needed to create the customer's order. Thus, the presence of a customer order "pulls" manufacturing work through the facility.

The pull system results in less inventory, both between workstations and in the warehouse. There should be no finished goods inventory on hand because everything produced is immediately shipped to customers. There is less inventory between workstations because production runs at each workstation are extremely short.

The push system results in more inventory because production orders are placed based on a forecast, which always varies somewhat from actual demand. This results in some leftover finished goods accumulating in the warehouse.

Cellular Manufacturing

A common arrangement of machines on the shop floor is by functional group, where all machines of one type are kept in one place. By doing so, jobs requiring a specific type of processing can all be routed to the same cluster of machines and loaded into whichever one will become available for processing next. The emphasis of this approach is on keeping every machine fully utilized. However, by doing so, there tend to be large batches of work-in-process inventory waiting in front of machines, because this approach calls for the completion of a job at the last workstation before the entire job is moved to the next workstation. The large amount of inventory involved masks the presence of improperly manufactured parts, of which an entire batch may have been created before anyone notices them at the next workstation. It also requires the existence of a sizable production planning staff, since work flows must be preplanned for all machines in the factory. Further, work in process usually must be moved considerable distances across the factory in order to reach the next workstation, which introduces the risk of damage to the parts as well as the added materials handling expense.

These problems with large inventories and scrap can be significantly reduced through the use of cellular manufacturing. Under this technique, a small cluster of machines are set up in close proximity to one another, each one performing a sequential task in completing a specific type or common set of products. Usually, only one or a few employees man each cell and walk a single part all the way through the cell before moving on to the next part. By doing so, there is obviously no work in process in the cell at all, besides the part on which machining is currently being performed. Also, it becomes quite evident when a part is improperly manufactured, since subsequent machining steps cannot be completed. With no work in process to hide scrap, employees can take action at once to fix the problem. Further, by slowing down the fastest machines in the cell to the speed of the slowest machine, there is no way for inventory to build up in front of the slowest machine.

In addition, product families (those having similar parts) typically are assigned to the same cells, so the people working in those cells gain considerable experience producing the same items, which tends to improve product quality. Also, cells creating parts for the same finished product are grouped close together, resulting in the minimum amount of inventory movement between cells. Finally, the production planning staff only has to arrange for materials to arrive at the beginning workstation of a cell, rather than planning movements to each machine within the cell, which greatly reduces the amount of inventory planning staff.

Consequently, cellular manufacturing reduces costs in a number of areas by reducing inventory, minimizing scrap rates, shrinking the amount of inventory planning labor, and improving worker experience levels.

Continuous Flow

A key aspect of the preceding cellular manufacturing section was the continual flow of work within a manufacturing cell, which has the dual advantages of minimal work-in-process inventory and immediate detection of any conditions potentially causing scrap. The concept of continuous flow should be followed wherever possible in the production area. This can involve areas that are not specifically configured as cells as well as between cells.

Continuous flow requires constant adjustments to maintain because cells will regularly be rearranged to match long-term changes in the product mix, and the volume of production will vary, which creates inventory buildups in front of localized bottlenecks.

Monument Equipment

Managers like to purchase the latest, largest, and most complex machines. By doing so, they obtain equipment with a higher rate of throughput, typically resulting in a lower cost per unit. However, after having made the considerable investment in this equipment, they also find that any downtime for maintenance results in no production at all, since they could not afford to purchase backup equipment. Also, because of the size and expense of the machine, they are inclined to have long production runs in order to justify the investment, resulting in excess inventory levels. Thus, having the biggest and best equipment results in large "monument" operations that do not yield a very flexible manufacturing process.

The solution is to invest in multiple smaller machines. By doing so, there is equipment available to take on immediate production needs while other similar equipment is unavailable due to repairs. Also, because of the general reduction of complexity in lower capacity machines, it is easy to reconfigure them for different types of production, so they can be used for many short production runs to match their use more closely to demand, thereby avoiding excess inventory. Finally, these less complex machines are easier to maintain and require less-skilled maintenance technicians to do so.

However, the use of high-capacity machines still makes sense when a company has enormously long production runs, especially when competition is so intense that reducing the cost per unit to the absolute minimum is mandatory. From a practical perspective, a company will experience varying levels of demand for its product mix and will need to acquire a range of low- to high-volume equipment to match that demand.

Quick Changeovers

A long-held belief in cost accounting is that product costs are lower when there are long production runs because the setup cost of the production run is then spread over a large number of products. The fallacy in this belief is that a company may not be able to sell the entire output from a large production run immediately, so finished goods languish in the warehouse, losing value and piling up storage costs. Also, a large production run may contain a quality problem that is not discovered for a long time, resulting in the scrapping of a great deal of product.

The solution is to have much shorter production runs, potentially as low as a single unit; however, the cost of equipment changeover makes this solution cost prohibitive. To succeed, one must greatly reduce the equipment setup time. A quick changeover generally follows these six steps:

1. Determine which changeover steps can be completed before the last production run has been completed (known as external activities), and schedule them toward the end of the preceding production run.
2. Determine which changeover steps can be performed only when the process is stopped (known as internal activities) and convert as many as possible into external activities.
3. Simplify the remaining internal activities. A common focus is on the elimination of fasteners and adjustments.
4. Streamline the external activities.
5. Document the new process.
6. Conduct additional iterations.

A number of iterations likely will be required before a changeover is fully optimized. Full optimization has likely been reached when a changeover no longer has any errors, tool shortages, late adjustments, oversight by experts, excessive operator movement during the changeover, or attachment points requiring more than one turn to fasten.

Assembly Line Configuration

The typical assembly line is composed of a single straight conveyor down which parts flow, with raw materials at one end and a finished product at the other. This classic production method tends to suffer from a high product defect rate because the assembly line may be so long that people causing incorrect assembly problems at one end of the line are completely out of touch with people at the other end who are discovering the problems. A common result is that quality inspectors are added to the end of the line, who report to management on mistakes found, resulting in investigation a few days later; in the meantime, errors will continue until a manager finds and resolves the problem.

A better solution is the serpentine line, in which the conveyor is compressed into a connecting series of U shapes like a snake. By using this approach, assembly workers are much closer together and can communicate far more easily. When a person at one end of this line finds a mistake, it is usually quite possible to talk to everyone on the line, determine the problem at once, and correct it on the spot. The result is a much lower scrap rate, which in turn results in a lower investment in raw materials.

A common concern with serpentine lines is how to handle product flow around corners, of which there are many in this line configuration. A number of conveyor alternatives exist, though they are more expensive than a simple straight conveyor. Another issue is the reconfiguration of the assembly area to accommodate a serpentine line, which may require a long-term, gradual realignment of equipment in accordance with a master facility plan.

Assembly Line Length

Assembly lines typically contain a fair amount of space between workers, which gives them a spacious feel. Unfortunately, it also leaves a considerable amount of room on the conveyor for extra work-in-process inventory. The amount of excess inventory is the total work in process moving between workers on the assembly line that is not currently being modified by the workers. In many cases, this can constitute three-quarters or more of the total inventory moving down the assembly line.

The solution is to shorten the assembly line, which eliminates all work-in-process inventory that would otherwise have been moving between employees. The ideal line length should result in just one unit of work-in-process inventory per assembly worker.

The objection to this approach is that the extra work in process is really a buffer between workers, which is needed in case of worker speed differences, thereby keeping all employees working at maximum speed at all times. Though a valid objection, the industrial engineering staff can be called on to review the work flow and devise work efficiencies to reduce worker speed differences, thereby eliminating the need for work-in-process buffer stock.

Container Sizes

When an employee completes work on an item, he or she typically places it in a container for transport to the next downstream workstation. That container stays next to the workstation until the employee has completely filled it, at which point it is moved to the next workstation. If the container is a large one, a considerable amount of work-in-process inventory can build up before it is time to move the container. If there are a great many workstations in use, each one using the same size container, the total work in process created by the size of the container can be considerable. Not only does this represent a significant inventory investment, but there is also a greater risk of scrap losses, since an entire container must be filled with potentially faulty parts before the employee at the next workstation has a chance to review the parts and discover any problems.

Simply reducing the size of the containers can mitigate both problems. For example, if every storage container in the production area is cut in half, this automatically reduces the work-in-process level by one-half. The process can theoretically be continued until each container holds just one item or the containers are completely eliminated.

The main objection to this practice is that the containers represent a work buffer between workstations, so there is always enough work to do even if the feeding workstation stops production for some reason. Solving this problem requires either an acceptance that some machines will be underutilized or a great deal of attention to balancing machine capacities throughout the factory.

Source Inspection

A considerable source of cost is inspection stations that are set up at various points in a production process. The cost of inspection involves not only the wages of the inspection personnel but also the cost of destruction that attends some types of testing. Also, this is not necessarily the most efficient form of testing, since a number of production steps may have occurred between the point where the failure originated and the location of the inspection station; all of the work subsequently performed on the product between the point of failure origination and testing is waste.

A better approach that reduces costs is to have workstation operators inspect incoming goods before conducting further processing, as part of their standard work routine. This source inspection, when repeated at every workstation, will immediately catch failures before subsequent processing, which also creates a shorter feedback loop for determining and fixing the underlying problem.

It is especially important to inspect goods immediately in front of the bottleneck workstation, so that it does not waste time working on flawed goods that must subsequently be scrapped or reworked. If it were to do so, the throughput of the entire process would decline. (See Chapter 12.)

Source inspection does not necessarily mean that designated inspection stations will be eliminated entirely. They still may be needed when there is a significant financial impact associated with product failure or of putting customers at risk. Also, some types of testing require specialized equipment and training and so cannot be performed by workstation operators.

Control Chart Analysis

Every machine is set up to operate with a certain range of tolerances. Any product manufactured within those tolerances is acceptable, and anything outside of it (known as the upper and lower control limits) must either be scrapped or reworked to bring it back within the pre-established tolerance.

Entitlement is the amount of variation that is naturally built into a process. It is the amount of variation to be expected even when all special causes of variation have been identified and eliminated. A good ongoing cost reduction project is to spot activity in a machine's current performance that exceeds the outer boundaries of its entitlement performance and to address the underlying problems causing those results. This analysis can be done with a control chart, such as the one shown in Exhibit 4.1. The exhibit shows the completion time for the assembly of a product. All of the completion times are within the upper and lower boundaries to be expected with normal variation.

The situation changes in Exhibit 4.2, where the control chart reveals a steady, gradual increase in the central tendency of the process, which implies the presence of something that is imposing a cumulative effect on the process. This is evidence that some event out of the ordinary has occurred that has shifted the plotted performance. In this case, the assembly time is gradually increasing, which clearly requires further investigation. Common causes of trends include machine wear and tear, machine temperature changes, and operator training levels.

A control chart can also reveal a series of increasing or decreasing observations, or *runs*, such as those shown in Exhibit 4.3. A run also calls

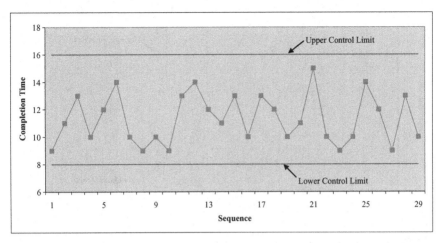

EXHIBIT 4.1 Control Chart with Normal Variation

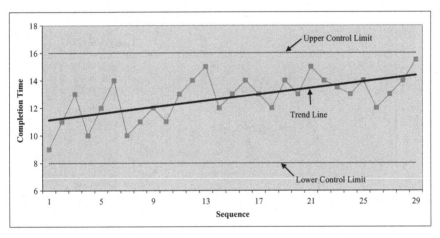

EXHIBIT 4.2 Control Chart Containing a Trend

for investigation, since it indicates such issues as improper equipment calibration during a changeover or faulty equipment that may be in need of maintenance.

A control chart can also reveal a sudden shift in the center of variation, as is shown in Exhibit 4.4. This indicates a permanent change in the process. It usually calls for the most prompt investigation of all, since all subsequent production may be outside the control limits of the process. A shift may be caused by such factors as a new operating policy or procedure, new operator, new machine, or new materials.

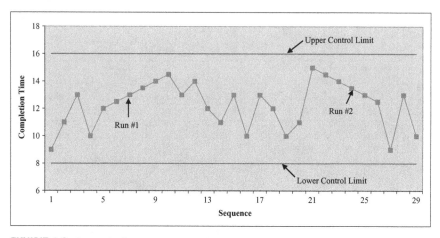

EXHIBIT 4.3 Control Chart Containing Runs

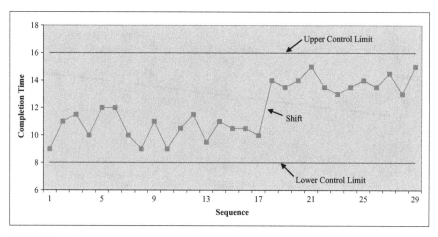

EXHIBIT 4.4 Control Chart Containing a Shift

Some customers may require unusually tight tolerances for products they commission. If so, the natural variation of a machine or process may result in a number of parts being outside of the customers' tolerance limits. In such cases, a company will have great difficulty in obtaining good product within the new tolerance limits and so should charge the customers a premium price in exchange for the higher scrap rate that it will experience.

Mistake Proofing

Manufacturing is typically a series of complex work steps, and there are abundant opportunities for mistakes to arise anywhere in or between these steps. Some mistakes will occur repeatedly, which indicates an opportunity for mistake proofing. There are a potentially infinite number of ways to implement mistake proofing. For example, a machine operator may be required to use a standard checklist during a quick changeover in order to avoid missing a step. Or a part may be designed so that it can fit into a larger assembly only if positioned in a certain way. Another example is in data entry, where some fields must be entered within certain range limits before the computer will accept an entry. One of the classic forms of mistake proofing is the use of a different-width gas pump tube for diesel fuel, so that a person cannot accidentally put diesel fuel into a car that only runs on gasoline.

A mistake-proofing program starts with an analysis of which mistakes occur repeatedly; then a team descends on the offending area to examine the source of the problem. This may involve the use of an Ishikawa diagram, as described earlier in Chapter 1, "The Cost Reduction Process," to determine the underlying cause of the mistake. The team then implements the change and monitors the mistakes report to see if the problem recurs.

Operating Instructions

If a manufacturing facility's employees are mostly new hires, or if training levels are low, or if there is a considerable amount of employee turnover then the level of production process knowledge will be low and therefore efficiency will be low. One solution is to create detailed operating instructions for each workstation, which can include such additional items as preventive maintenance tasks and work-in-process quantity ranges to maintain. These instructions form the basis for new operator training as well as refresher training. They are particularly useful for new employees, who are most likely to refer to such information and profit from it more frequently than an experienced workstation operator.

Operating instructions can also cause errors if they are not properly updated. Whenever a processing change or machine setting is changed, the alteration must be reflected in the operating instructions. Otherwise, a machine operator who punctiliously follows the instructions may subsequently generate a large amount of product that must be scrapped.

Expediting

There are times when an order absolutely, positively has to be shipped by a certain date, but the order is well down in the work queue or there are not enough parts on hand to construct it. No matter: Just assign an expediter to walk the order through the shop. The trouble is the rippling waves of confusion this activity breeds. Inventory already allocated for other uses suddenly disappears into the maw of expedited jobs, causing stock shortages for any number of other jobs, not to mention the additional machine changeovers required to restore machines to their prior operational status. Further, hordes of expediters are needed to watch over the orders being rushed through the production process. Finally, all these interruptions cause total production volume to drop precipitously.

Breaking the expediting habit can be surprisingly difficult. It will result in some customers not receiving orders as fast as possible, especially early on when the production planners are trying to settle down a production process muddled by previously expedited orders. Also, even one expedited order can cause unwanted ripple effects throughout the organization, so one must go cold turkey when eliminating expediting. One solution is to reserve some excess capacity in the production schedule for last-minute orders, though this may still require the sudden, unplanned loss of inventory intended for other uses. The best alternative is to drive purchasing lead times down as much as possible in order to make valid, short-term ship dates available to customers, thereby allowing for reasonably fast ship times.

Maintenance Planning

The haphazard administration of maintenance activities results in unplanned machine downtime, which plays havoc with the production schedule. Also, the maintenance staff spends time in reactive mode, incurring overtime to fix problems and having repair parts sent in by overnight delivery service. All of these issues are extremely expensive. A better approach is preventive maintenance, where equipment is brought down on a scheduled basis for the minor adjustments and repairs needed to keep it operational longer. At these times, the maintenance staff examines the equipment for additional problems, orders repair parts well in advance, and schedules the extra maintenance in conjunction with the production planners.

This high degree of maintenance planning vastly reduces unscheduled downtime, so actual production levels are more likely to meet the production plan.

Maintenance planning should focus in particular on the bottleneck operation. It is entirely possible that the throughput lost from equipment downtime at the bottleneck may even justify the hiring of a full-time maintenance staff just to monitor that single operation, even if it appears that the staff is not especially well utilized.

Machinery Standardization

There can be a significant cost associated with maintaining spare parts and conducting extra operator training for a broad range of machines. Each machine requires different operating instructions, different maintenance and operator training, and also a separate store of spare parts.

If a company requires multiple machines to perform the same function, then it should try to acquire the same brand and model of machine. By doing so, it can simplify its training requirements and keep a smaller total amount of repair parts in stock than would have been the case for a more diversified range of machines. Further, if it buys assets in sufficient quantities, it may be able to negotiate a volume price discount on the machinery.

Machinery standardization is of particular importance to those companies that prefer to buy secondhand equipment at lower prices. They may think they are getting a good deal at the point of purchase, but they should calculate the total lifetime cost of owning a disparate set of equipment before committing to own a medley of machines.

Machinery Assignment

When an item is scheduled for production, it is usually assigned to whichever machine is available next. The setup person then spends considerable time making minor adjustments to the equipment and making test runs to ensure that the item is being produced within tolerance. During this testing period, the machine is producing a considerable amount of scrap. The reason for extended test runs is that no two machines are exactly alike, due either to minor tolerance differences or to variations in wear and tear. Thus, even with extensive setup notes, it is not possible to exactly configure a machine to run correctly on the initial settings. The solution is to schedule the same part to be run on the same machine as much as possible. Setups can then be fully documented and used repeatedly with minimal need for additional test runs.

Metrics

Cost reduction in the production area centers on the effectiveness of the operation in generating the highest possible level of throughput. Several metrics that address effectiveness are listed in Chapter 12, including constraint utilization, the ratio of throughput to constraint time consumption, and the throughput associated with scrap. In addition to these measures, we note next additional metrics to address manufacturing cell capacity levels, production yield, unscheduled downtime, and the effectiveness of production at the bottleneck operation.

- *Degree of unbalance.* This is the amount of productive capacity in a production cell that cannot be utilized because of the presence of a production bottleneck. This measure is used by the industrial engineering staff and production manager to determine which bottleneck operations within cells should be improved or supplemented so that the degree of unbalance is reduced. The calculation is to divide the maximum capacity of the work cell bottleneck operation by the maximum capacity of the next most restrictive work cell operation.
- *First-time yield.* A workstation is performing correctly if it processes all of the units coming into it, without damage. A high first-time yield is a good indicator of a process from which processing errors have been stripped out successfully. The calculation is the number of good units produced by a process, divided by the total number of units going into a process.
- *Manufacturing effectiveness.* The utilization level at a bottleneck operation may be quite high, but this does not necessarily mean that the hours being used at the operation are effectively translated into more shipments to customers. For example, the hours used might be for rework, for production that is later scrapped, or for testing or setup. If a significant proportion of the production hours used at a bottleneck operation consist of these activities, then profits will not be maximized. The calculation is to divide the total standard throughput hours shipped in the reporting period by the total number of bottleneck hour consumed.
- *Unscheduled downtime percentage.* If a machine is stopped for unscheduled maintenance downtime, it can seriously reduce a factory's production capabilities. To calculate the percentage of unscheduled downtime, divide the total minutes of unscheduled downtime by the total minutes of machine time.

Summary

Production area cost reductions generally center on the minimization of work-in-process inventory, rapid feedback loops to spot and correct mistakes, and the creation of an agile facility that can quickly switch to creating new products on short notice. This chapter touched on all of these target areas, with discussions of manufacturing cells, production flow concepts, quick changeovers, source inspections, and the like.

The overriding factor in dealing with production cost reductions is the impact of any change on the throughput of the entire operation. A production department, perhaps to a greater extent than any other department, should be judged on its ability—as an entire system of production—to generate throughput. Localized cost reductions may severely damage the entire department's ability to generate throughput. Consequently, an analyst needs to consult with the production team about the impact of a proposed cost reduction on throughput before enacting *any* change.

CHAPTER 5

Payroll Cost Reduction

Introduction

In many companies, payroll is either the largest or second-largest expense (after the cost of goods sold). As such, it deserves serious attention for cost reduction analysis. In fact, if payroll were to be ignored in many companies, then there would be few expenses left to target for cost reduction.

However, many people consider a workforce reduction to be reprehensible, on the grounds that a company has an implied employment contract with its employees, which they uphold on their part through efficiency improvements and so on. If a company begins to reduce its staffing levels, this would reduce morale and lead to a general drop in efficiency that reduces the cost reduction impact of the layoffs.

Given these concerns, the next sections go beyond the basic analysis needed for a workforce reduction and also address alternatives to a reduction as well as methods for managing payroll expenses on an ongoing basis, so that there will be less need for a workforce reduction.

Analysis for a Workforce Reduction

It is extremely dangerous simply to enact an across-the-board payroll cut across a number of departments. By doing so, a company will undoubtedly cripple a number of areas that directly contribute to its ability to create a profit. There is a high risk of losing talented employees as well as those with strong institutional knowledge and those who provide crucial capacity at bottleneck operations. These losses are particularly likely in the complete absence of any analysis, since then the basis for a layoff decision is likely to be political.

Instead, a manager should conduct the analyses itemized here and in the next sections, as well as the throughput analysis described in Chapter 12, "Throughput Analysis." The result should be a well-considered cost reduction that bears a closer resemblance to a surgical paring than the nuclear bomb approach of a general cost reduction.

The first step in payroll cost reduction is to determine the cost directly attributable to each employee. Many companies understate this cost because they do not consider the full range of expenses that an employee incurs. Exhibit 5.1 shows a good format for this calculation. From left to right, it shows base-level annual compensation, followed by all related payroll taxes and net benefit costs. It then continues with several additional expenses that can be directly traced to each employee. The social security tax is applicable only below a certain maximum wage level, which is noted in the lower left corner of the exhibit. The 401(k) pension withholding for each employee is not an expense but is included in order to show the company 401(k) match, which *is* an expense. The exhibit is sorted in alphabetical order by employee last name.

The percentages across the bottom of the exhibit are particularly instructive. They show that the base-level compensation represents approximately 80 percent of the total compensation associated with each individual, so it is worthwhile to add the additional information noted in the table in order to obtain a more comprehensive picture of expense by employee.

The exhibit is by no means sufficient for making a layoff decision, for it only aggregates cost by person—it does nothing to show the role of each person, or if anyone individually generates a profit. Nonetheless, some companies will decide on whom to lay off with only this information, on the theory that the most expensive employees should be the first ones to go. Instead, they should follow through the additional exhibits to glean more information.

Exhibit 5.1 does not include any allocation of overhead costs, on the assumption that overhead costs will not disappear if an employee is laid off. For example, laying off just one person will not eliminate the cost of the floor space that person used to occupy, nor will it lead to the direct reduction of any expenses in the human resources staff that administers that person's pension plan, and so on.

However, overhead costs *should* be considered if a sufficient number of positions are eliminated to also trigger an immediate overhead reduction. Exhibit 5.2 uses the same format as Exhibit 5.1, but now the assumption is that by laying off entire groups of employees, a block of clearly identifiable overhead expenses can be eliminated. In the exhibit, employees are now sorted by store location, so that the elimination of an entire group of employees and their associated overhead costs can be clumped together.

EXHIBIT 5.1 Sonoma Silversmiths Employee Cost Roll-up

Employee Name	Annual Pay	Social Security	Medicare	401(k) Withhold	50% 401(k) Match	Medical	Medical Deducts	Annual Phone	Annual T&E	Total Cost
Andrews, Bill	$ 42,750	$ 2,651	$ 620	$ 4,000	$ 2,000	$ 14,185	$ (5,242)	$ 1,200	$ 5,000	$ 63,163
Brennan, Charles	$ 125,000	$ 6,622	$ 1,813	$ 16,500	$ 8,250	$ 17,265	$ (6,780)	$ —	$ —	$ 152,169
Cantor, David	$ 80,000	$ 4,960	$ 1,160	$ 7,250	$ 3,625	$ 6,175	$ (1,225)	$ 1,200	$ 8,500	$ 104,395
DiMaggio, Earnest	$ 77,500	$ 4,805	$ 1,124	$ 2,500	$ 1,250	$ 17,265	$ (6,780)	$ 1,450	$ 500	$ 97,114
Entenmann, Franklin	$ 142,500	$ 6,622	$ 2,066	$ 16,500	$ 8,250	$ 17,265	$ (6,780)	$ 1,200	$ 18,500	$ 189,623
Fairview, George	$ 37,500	$ 2,325	$ 544	$ 500	$ 250	$ —	$ —	$ 1,200	$ 1,250	$ 43,069
Gorman, Hercules	$ 225,000	$ 6,622	$ 3,263	$ 16,500	$ 8,250	$ —	$ —	$ 1,200	$ 32,750	$ 277,084
Henderson, Ian	$ 85,000	$ 5,270	$ 1,233	$ 4,000	$ 2,000	$ 17,265	$ (6,780)	$ 1,200	$ 1,750	$ 106,938
Innes, Julie	$ 73,000	$ 4,526	$ 1,059	$ —	$ —	$ —	$ —	$ —	$ —	$ 78,585
Jackson, Kari	$ 119,000	$ 6,622	$ 1,726	$ 14,250	$ 7,125	$ 6,175	$ (1,225)	$ —	$ —	$ 139,422
Klerk, Larry	$ 170,000	$ 6,622	$ 2,465	$ 16,500	$ 8,250	$ 14,185	$ (5,242)	$ 1,450	$ 800	$ 198,530
Lincoln, Mandy	$ 95,000	$ 5,890	$ 1,378	$ 9,000	$ 4,500	$ 6,175	$ (1,225)	$ 1,200	$ 4,250	$ 117,168
Masters, Nancy	$ 62,500	$ 3,875	$ 906	$ 1,000	$ 500	$ 14,185	$ (5,242)	$ 1,200	$ —	$ 77,924
	$ 1,334,750	$ 67,410	$ 19,354		$ 54,250	$ 130,140	$ (46,521)	$ 12,500	$ 73,300	$ 1,645,182
Percent of total	81%	4%	1%		3%	8%	-3%	1%	4%	100%
Tax percentage		6.20%	1.45%							
Maximum cap		$ 106,800	None							

EXHIBIT 5.2 Sonoma Silversmiths Employee Cost Roll-up with Overhead

	Annual Pay	Social Security	Medicare	401(k) Withhold	50% 401(k) Match	Medical	Medical Deducts	Annual Phone	Annual T&E	Total Cost
Napa Store:										
Andrews, Bill	$ 42,750	$ 2,651	$ 620	$ 4,000	$ 2,000	$ 14,185	$ (5,242)	$ 1,200	$ 5,000	$ 63,163
Entenmann, Franklin	$ 142,500	$ 6,622	$ 2,066	$ 16,500	$ 8,250	$ 17,265	$ (6,780)	$ 1,200	$ 18,500	$ 189,623
Jackson, Kari	$ 119,000	$ 6,622	$ 1,726	$ 14,250	$ 7,125	$ 6,175	$ (1,225)	$ —	$ —	$ 139,422
Klerk, Larry	$ 170,000	$ 6,622	$ 2,465	$ 16,500	$ 8,250	$ 14,185	$ (5,242)	$ 1,450	$ 800	$ 198,530
Lincoln, Mandy	$ 95,000	$ 5,890	$ 1,378	$ 9,000	$ 4,500	$ 6,175	$ (1,225)	$ 1,200	$ 4,250	$ 117,168
Masters, Nancy	$ 62,500	$ 3,875	$ 906	$ 1,000	$ 500	$ 14,185	$ (5,242)	$ 1,200	$ —	$ 77,924
										$ 785,830
									Annual Rent:	$ 156,000
									Annual Utilities:	$ 28,000
										$ 969,830
Santa Rosa Store:										
Brennan, Charles	$ 125,000	$ 6,622	$ 1,813	$ 16,500	$ 8,250	$ 17,265	$ (6,780)	$ —	$ —	$ 152,169
Cantor, David	$ 80,000	$ 4,960	$ 1,160	$ 7,250	$ 3,625	$ 6,175	$ (1,225)	$ 1,200	$ 8,500	$ 104,395
DiMaggio, Earnest	$ 77,500	$ 4,805	$ 1,124	$ 2,500	$ 1,250	$ 17,265	$ (6,780)	$ 1,450	$ 500	$ 97,114
Fairview, George	$ 37,500	$ 2,325	$ 544	$ 500	$ 250	$ —	$ —	$ 1,200	$ 1,250	$ 43,069
Gorman, Hercules	$ 225,000	$ 6,622	$ 3,263	$ 16,500	$ 8,250	$ —	$ —	$ 1,200	$ 32,750	$ 277,084
Henderson, Ian	$ 85,000	$ 5,270	$ 1,233	$ 4,000	$ 2,000	$ 17,265	$ (6,780)	$ 1,200	$ 1,750	$ 106,938
Innes, Julie	$ 73,000	$ 4,526	$ 1,059	$ —	$ —	$ —	$ —	$ —	$ —	$ 78,585
										$ 859,353
									Annual Rent:	$ 172,000
									Annual Utilities:	$ 32,500
										$ 1,063,853

The cost reduction decision point is no longer the individual employee but rather an entire company location.

Thus far, the analysis has only addressed the cost of each employee or group of employees; it does not incorporate any revenue that employees may generate directly, such as in a service environment. Without this information, a company may lay off its most expensive employee, without considering that the same person also generates a great deal of revenue for the company. Adding revenue by store to Exhibit 5.2 makes that exhibit an extremely useful tool for deciding whether to shut down an entire store, though one should also consider if a location is in a start-up phase and is not yet showing its maximum earning potential.

Exhibit 5.3 shows a breakdown of both revenue and cost for employees, so that profitability can now be ascertained on an individual level. The exhibit compresses the level of expense detail, thereby making room for revenue and profit information. The exhibit includes a column for a commission expense, which is subtracted from the revenues to arrive at a net revenue amount for each employee.

The trouble with Exhibit 5.3 is that it only displays employee profitability for an entire year; it does not show a trend line of profitability over a shorter period of time, so there is no way to see if anyone has lapsed into a loss situation that offsets an earlier state of profitability. Exhibit 5.4 provides this information on a rolling 12-month basis, so the reader can easily spot trends. The report is sorted in increasing order of profitability for the final month *only*, which brings employees with current losses to the top of the chart. In addition, the bottom row of the exhibit lists the number of business days in each month, which usually correlates to the amount of revenue earned in each month. Thus, a profit downturn can sometimes be explained simply by the number of days in a month, and so is not the fault of the employee.

Example

The president of Sonoma Silversmiths has decided to eliminate one of the company's jewelry designers as a cost-saving measure. The controller, Paula Revere, runs the employee profitability calculation shown in Exhibit 5.3. This report shows that the two designers, Hercules Gorman and Mandy Lincoln, have been unprofitable during the past year. Ms. Revere decides to drill down deeper into the data and formulates the profitability trend line shown in Exhibit 5.4. This exhibit highlights the results for the two silversmiths with shading. In this report, it is

Continued

apparent that Mandy Lincoln's profits have declined steadily through the year, and she is now generating no revenue at all. Conversely, Hercules Gorman was losing a considerable amount early in the year, broke even midway through the year, and is now earning a profit. Thus, the full-year results in Exhibit 5.3 were hiding the fact that Mr. Gorman is now earning a comfortable profit. Consequently, Ms. Revere recommends that Mr. Gorman be retained and Ms. Lincoln be laid off.

The employee profitability trend line is useful not only for determining which positions to eliminate but also for seeing which positions are profitable enough to support a pay increase.

Example

The director of the custom design division of Sonoma Silversmiths contacts the controller, Ms. Revere, to point out that David Cantor, a mid-grade jewelry designer, is about to be hired away by a competitor. Should the company offer a pay boost to Mr. Cantor to retain him? Ms. Revere accesses the spreadsheet shown in Exhibit 5.3, and sees that Mr. Cantor earns the company a profit of $10,085 per year, before any overhead allocation. Based on his base cost of $104,395 shown in Exhibit 5.3, this is a profit percentage of slightly under 10 percent. This leaves very little room for a pay boost, so she recommends that the company allow Mr. Cantor to leave without making a counteroffer.

While the information in Exhibits 5.3 and 5.4 are a considerable improvement over basic employee cost information, they do not incorporate any payroll costs that are purely overhead in nature or that generate revenue as a group rather than individually. Exhibit 5.5 shows a template for this more advanced (and realistic) level of information.

In Exhibit 5.5, the directly billable employees are listed at the top, followed by a group of employees who are working on projects that have fixed-fee billings. As such, their costs are accumulated and offset against the total fixed-fee billings that they generate. Finally, all overhead positions are noted at the bottom of the exhibit.

The Exhibit 5.5 format is most useful in a service environment, where the bulk of all employees are in some way associated with customer billings. This approach is less useful in a production or distribution environment, where the association between employees and revenues is more tenuous.

EXHIBIT 5.3 Sonoma Silversmiths Employee Profitability Calculation

Employee Name	Revenues		Net Revenues	Expenses			Total Cost	Profit	Profit %
	Annual Revenues	Commission		Annual Pay	Payroll Taxes	Benefits			
Andrews, Bill	$ 101,890	$ 4,076	$ 97,814	$ 42,750	$ 3,270	$ 17,143	$ 63,163	$ 34,651	35%
Brennan, Charles	$ 234,750	$ 9,390	$ 225,360	$ 125,000	$ 8,434	$ 18,735	$ 152,169	$ 73,191	32%
Cantor, David	$ 119,250	$ 4,770	$ 114,480	$ 80,000	$ 6,120	$ 18,275	$ 104,395	$ 10,085	9%
DiMaggio, Earnest	$ 142,120	$ 5,685	$ 136,435	$ 77,500	$ 5,929	$ 13,685	$ 97,114	$ 39,321	29%
Entenmann, Franklin	$ 267,040	$ 10,682	$ 256,358	$ 142,500	$ 8,688	$ 38,435	$ 189,623	$ 66,736	26%
Fairview, George	$ 71,020	$ 2,841	$ 68,179	$ 37,500	$ 2,869	$ 2,700	$ 43,069	$ 25,110	37%
Gorman, Hercules	$ 203,150	$ 8,126	$ 195,024	$ 225,000	$ 9,884	$ 42,200	$ 277,084	$ (82,060)	-42%
Henderson, Ian	$ 173,350	$ 6,934	$ 166,416	$ 85,000	$ 6,503	$ 15,435	$ 106,938	$ 59,479	36%
Innes, Julie	$ 123,950	$ 4,958	$ 118,992	$ 73,000	$ 5,585	$ —	$ 78,585	$ 40,408	34%
Jackson, Kari	$ 225,290	$ 9,012	$ 216,278	$ 119,000	$ 8,347	$ 12,075	$ 139,422	$ 76,856	36%
Klerk, Larry	$ 274,040	$ 10,962	$ 263,078	$ 170,000	$ 9,087	$ 19,443	$ 198,530	$ 64,549	25%
Lincoln, Mandy	$ 92,650	$ 3,706	$ 88,944	$ 95,000	$ 7,268	$ 14,900	$ 117,168	$ (28,224)	-32%
Masters, Nancy	$ 129,740	$ 5,190	$ 124,550	$ 62,500	$ 4,781	$ 10,643	$ 77,924	$ 46,626	37%
	$ 2,158,240	$ 86,330	$ 2,071,910	$ 1,334,750	$ 86,763	$ 223,669	$ 1,645,182	$ 426,728	21%

EXHIBIT 5.4 Sonoma Silversmiths Employee Profitability Trend Line

	Jan	Feb	Mar	Apr	May	Jun	Jul	Aug	Sep	Oct	Nov	Dec	Total
Lincoln, Mandy	$8,810	$8,810	$8,810	$8,810	-$4,880	-$4,882	-$4,882	-$9,764	-$9,764	-$9,764	-$9,764	-$9,764	-$28,224
Cantor, David	$840	$760	$880	$880	$800	$880	$880	$840	$880	$880	$760	$800	$10,085
Fairview, George	$2,093	$1,893	$2,192	$2,192	$1,993	$2,192	$2,192	$2,093	$2,192	$2,192	$1,893	$1,993	$25,110
Andrews, Bill	$2,888	$2,613	$3,025	$3,025	$2,750	$3,025	$3,025	$2,888	$3,025	$3,025	$2,613	$2,750	$34,651
DiMaggio, Earnest	$3,277	$2,965	$3,433	$3,433	$3,121	$3,433	$3,433	$3,277	$3,433	$3,433	$2,965	$3,121	$39,321
Innes, Julie	$3,367	$3,047	$3,528	$3,528	$3,207	$3,528	$3,528	$3,367	$3,528	$3,528	$3,047	$3,207	$40,408
Henderson, Ian	$4,957	$4,485	$5,193	$5,193	$4,721	$5,193	$5,193	$4,957	$5,193	$5,193	$4,485	$4,721	$59,479
Masters, Nancy	$3,886	$3,515	$4,071	$4,071	$3,700	$4,071	$4,071	$3,886	$4,071	$4,071	$3,515	$3,700	$46,626
Klerk, Larry	$5,379	$4,867	$5,635	$5,635	$5,123	$5,635	$5,635	$5,379	$5,635	$5,635	$4,867	$5,123	$64,549
Entenmann, Franklin	$5,561	$5,032	$5,826	$5,826	$5,297	$5,826	$5,826	$5,561	$5,826	$5,826	$5,032	$5,297	$66,736
Brennan, Charles	$6,099	$5,518	$6,390	$6,390	$5,809	$6,390	$6,390	$6,099	$6,390	$6,390	$5,518	$5,809	$73,191
Jackson, Kari	$6,405	$5,795	$6,710	$6,710	$6,100	$6,710	$6,710	$6,405	$6,710	$6,710	$5,795	$6,100	$76,856
Gorman, Hercules	-$23,090	-$23,090	-$23,090	-$23,090	-$11,545	$0	$0	$0	$0	$0	$5,850	$15,995	-$82,060
Business Days	$30,471	$26,209	$32,602	$32,602	$26,195	$42,000	$42,000	$34,987	$37,118	$37,118	$36,575	$48,851	$426,728
	21	19	22	22	20	22	22	21	22	22	19	20	252

114

EXHIBIT 5.5 Sonoma Silversmiths Company-Wide Employee Profit Calculation

Directly Billable Positions	Expenses			Revenues				
	Annual Revenues	Commission	Net Revenues	Annual Pay	Payroll Taxes	Benefits	Total Cost	Profit
Andrews, Bill	$ 101,890	$ 4,076	$ 97,814	$ 42,750	$ 3,270	$ 17,143	$ 63,163	$ 34,651
Brennan, Charles	$ 234,750	$ 9,390	$ 225,360	$ 125,000	$ 8,434	$ 18,735	$ 152,169	$ 73,191
Cantor, David	$ 119,250	$ 4,770	$ 114,480	$ 80,000	$ 6,120	$ 18,275	$ 104,395	$ 10,085
DiMaggio, Earnest	$ 142,120	$ 5,685	$ 136,435	$ 77,500	$ 5,929	$ 13,685	$ 97,114	$ 39,321
Entenmann, Franklin	$ 267,040	$ 10,682	$ 256,358	$ 142,500	$ 8,688	$ 38,435	$ 189,623	$ 66,736
Fairview, George	$ 71,020	$ 2,841	$ 68,179	$ 37,500	$ 2,869	$ 2,700	$ 43,069	$ 25,110
Gorman, Hercules	$ 203,150	$ 8,126	$ 195,024	$ 225,000	$ 9,884	$ 42,200	$ 277,084	$ (82,060)
							Total billable staff profit	$ 167,034
Fixed Fee Billable Positions								
Northrop, Olin				$ 85,000	$ 6,503	$ 15,435	$ 106,938	$ (106,938)
Paulson, Richard				$ 73,000	$ 5,585	$ —	$ 78,585	$ (78,585)
Randall, Steven				$ 119,000	$ 8,347	$ 12,075	$ 139,422	$ (139,422)
Stephenson, Thomas				$ 95,000	$ 7,268	$ 14,900	$ 117,168	$ (117,168)
								$ (442,112)
							Fixed fee billings	$ 425,000
							Less: commissions	$ (17,000)
							Net fixed fee billings	$ 408,000
							Net profit (loss) on fixed fee billings	$ (34,112)
Overhead Positions								
Revere, Paula (controller)				$ 85,000	$ 6,503	$ 12,485	$ 103,988	$ (103,988)
VanVleet, Xavier (reception)				$ 32,500	$ 2,486	$ 4,950	$ 39,936	$ (39,936)
							Total overhead staff cost	$ (143,924)

Example

Sonoma Silversmiths has recently accepted several fixed-fee projects, to which it has assigned four personnel on a full-time basis. The controller, Ms. Revere, reviews the results of this endeavor as displayed on Exhibit 5.5. The fixed-fee group is generating a loss, so Ms. Revere decides to discuss the company's fixed-fee pricing strategy with the sales manager to see if a margin increase can be incorporated into future bids. Also, the controller notes that the profit of $167,034 generated by the directly billable staff is still sufficient to cover the cost of company overhead positions of $143,924. Thus, there is an additional viable alternative of completely eliminating the fixed-fee business and laying off all staff associated with that work, which will improve overall company profitability.

Thus far, the analysis of a cost reduction has focused primarily on whether an employee contributes to profitability—but there are certainly other factors to consider. Here are some considerations:

- *Skill set.* An employee may have a skill set that is difficult to find and that is critical to the operation of the company. However, this attribute can be taken too far by an employee who essentially holds a company hostage. This is a particular problem if the employee is mostly underutilized and is being retained only because of a unique skill. In this case, see if there are contractors who also have the required skill and can provide it on an as-needed basis.
- *Institutional knowledge.* Some employees may have an exceptional knowledge of company processes and an unusual ability to fix process problems. This may reflect inadequate process documentation and cross-training, both of which can eliminate this issue from consideration during a workforce reduction.
- *Bottleneck capacity.* If an employee operates a bottleneck operation but is not fully utilized, that position probably should be retained on the grounds that overall profitability will drop by more than the cost of the employee if he or she were to leave. This topic is addressed in more detail in Chapter 12, "Throughput Analysis."
- *Protected groups.* Under federal rules, a company cannot be seen to target any ethnic group, gender, age group, or protected class during a workforce reduction. Thus, the human resources staff should be asked to conduct this review for all planned reductions. The easiest

way around this problem is to offer early retirement to all or a large subset of employees, so that the employees themselves determine if they shall leave.

- *Early retirement modeling.* If a company offers early retirement to a block of its employees, then it should estimate the skill sets most likely to be lost through retirement and how those losses will impact its future ability to conduct business.

A final consideration is whether a workforce reduction is intentional or not. A company may find that there is an unusual level of employee turnover in one part of its business, which in turn requires significant expenditures to recruit and train replacement employees. This turnover level may, for example, be caused by bad management, an unsafe work environment, or excessively low pay levels. If so, it is worth the effort to explore the reasons for the unusual turnover and then correct them.

Clearly, a great deal of analysis should be conducted before enacting a workforce reduction. One should understand the full cost of each position or group of positions, any related profitability, and the precise impact of a person's departure on the ability of a company to operate. The next sections provide a number of alternatives if it appears that alternatives to a workforce reduction must be used.

Cost of a Workforce Reduction

A workforce reduction is designed to save money, but it may do the reverse in the short term, since there are a number of expenses associated with it. Here are several expenses to consider, followed by several ways to mitigate them:

- *Severance package.* The most minimal severance package is simply severance pay, but it can also include a number of other costs, such as benefits continuation, the use of a company phone or computer, and outplacement services. Severance pay typically is linked to the number of years of employee service, so the payout can be severe if the workforce reduction includes personnel with high seniority.
- *Accrued vacation.* If an employee has not used any portion of his or her earned vacation, the company must pay it to the employee at the time of the workforce reduction. The company should have been accruing this expense as part of its normal financial statement closing procedure, so it is only a cash outflow, not an additional expense.
- *Stock grant acceleration.* If an employee is part of a stock grant program, the program likely will have an award acceleration clause,

where vesting in the shares is accelerated in the event of a change in control of the company. If the employee is being laid off because of the change in control, it is likely that he or she will receive the stock grant at termination. If so, the company must record a noncash expense at the time of vesting to reflect the recognition of all remaining expense associated with the stock grant.

- *Unemployment insurance.* If a company continually lays off its employees, they in turn will draw down the state's unemployment fund, which the state government must replenish by increasing the company's unemployment contribution rate in the following year.
- *Potential lawsuits.* There is always a risk that some employees will sue the company for wrongful termination. Even if there is no likelihood of a payout, the company still must pay legal fees to defend its position. If a company has a history of being sued by employees after their termination, then it may be cost effective to make a severance payment conditional on employee agreement not file a claim against the company.

The severance and vacation expenses just noted can be mitigated to some extent by paying them out based on an average of an employee's pay for the past few years rather than on the final pay level (which is presumably higher). This pay calculation should be fully documented in the employee manual.

A company's unemployment insurance costs can increase unnecessarily if former employees make unwarranted unemployment claims. The company should challenge these claims. Its success in doing so will increase if it documents all disciplinary actions and has clearly stated policies and procedures for employee terminations. It may also make sense to monitor state payments to all unemployment claimants, to spot overpayments that would otherwise be charged back to the company as part of its unemployment insurance rate in the following year.

There are two other ways to make modest reductions in a company's state unemployment insurance costs:

1. If there are two or more company subsidiaries located in a state that permits joint unemployment insurance accounts, it may be possible to reduce this tax by combining their unemployment experiences and then using a lower blended rate that applies to all of the entities.
2. It may be cost effective to make an additional unemployment tax payment during the current year, in order to reduce the rate for the following year. In many cases, the additional payment reduces the potential next-year tax much more than the amount of the payment.

In addition to these tangible costs, there are also several potentially serious intangible costs associated with a workforce reduction. One is the loss of institutional memory. Some long-term employees have a superb knowledge of how processes "really" work and how to resolve problems in ways that are not presented in formal corporate procedures. When these people are lost through a layoff, there can be a significant drop in corporate efficiency that may take a considerable amount of time to rebuild.

The second intangible cost is a loss of trust in management. This may appear in the form of more unionization activity, fewer improvement suggestions, less willingness to work overtime, and higher turnover. One way to combat this problem is to be extremely open about the reasons for a workforce reduction so that employees are not blindsided by any actual reductions.

The third intangible cost is the time required to alter and perfect work processes once a workforce reduction has occurred. This is a common situation; with fewer people being asked to handle a larger workload, it makes sense to spend time wrapping processes around a different group of people than the group for whom the processes were originally designed. This will likely require some retraining time. Further, it may call for the intentional elimination of some control points, which may eventually yield occasional losses from process failures.

The fourth intangible cost relates to recruiting. Recruits will be less likely to accept offers from a company that has a recent history of layoffs, especially if those layoffs appear to target newer employees. This is less of a factor in high-unemployment regions. However, if a direct competitor has avoided layoffs, it will have a recruiting edge that eventually may lead to a noticeable improvement in its competitiveness.

In addition to these expenses, cash outflows, and intangible losses, there is also the possibility that a company's financial position will right itself in the near term, requiring that the positions just eliminated must now be refilled. If so, these additional expenses must be considered:

- *Recruitment.* This can include the cost of a recruiter's fee, an employee referral bonus, advertisements, drug testing, a hiring bonus, and reimbursement for relocation expenses.
- *Orientation and training.* Someone must give new hires an orientation session and possibly also additional training on company procedures and systems. If these tasks are handled by an outside training supplier, then it represents an outright expense; if handled internally, it is an opportunity cost to the employees so designated.
- *Market premium paid.* Depending on the market demand for a position, it is entirely possible that a company may need to pay more for a replacement than it was paying for the employee who previously occupied the position.

- *Lower initial productivity.* If a junior-level person is hired, there will likely be a significant time period before that person becomes efficient in the position. If a more senior-level person is hired, then that person's greater compensation cost merely offsets the reduced level of inefficiency that would have been experienced with a more junior person.

Given these considerations, a company expecting a short business downturn and fortified with sufficient cash should consider leaving the workforce in place, or with only a minor reduction in staffing. However, if the downturn is of uncertain duration and liquidity is questionable, then a company may have to act quickly and cut deeply, irrespective of any attendant costs.

Alternatives to a Workforce Reduction

Given the costs noted in the last section, many companies will try to avoid an outright workforce reduction. However, there are still prospects for reducing payroll costs. These techniques are available:

- *Review overtime pay.* In an uncontrolled environment, employees can record overtime on their timesheets and be paid for it. To avoid this, there should be a formal supervisory review of all overtime hours claimed, which can be triggered by an automated timekeeping system. Better yet, an analyst should review the reasons why the bulk of the overtime hours were incurred and see if there are any alternatives that can avoid the future incurrence of this cost. For example, if overtime is being incurred to complete a project, are people working to meet a deadline that could have been extended?
- *Use vacation time.* By encouraging its staff to take unused vacation time, a company still incurs a cash outflow to pay for the vacations, but this may also soak up a considerable amount of unused vacation time, so that employees will be more available later, when they may be needed for revenue-generating activities. This is an extremely short-term alternative, since employees may have only a few weeks of accrued vacation. A company using this alternative should reasonably expect that business will pick up in the near future.
- *Delay new hires.* If there is a reasonable expectation that business will improve shortly, then hold off on making offers to new hire candidates. If offers have already been extended, then consider delaying their start dates while paying them a stipend and moving expenses. The stipend is still less expensive than a full rate of pay and may be tolerable to the new hires for several months.

- *Attrition.* The most noninvasive form of workforce reduction is simply to not replace employees when they retire or leave the company for other reasons. This is a long-term solution, since employee departures may occur over quite a few years before a company has reduced its headcount to its targeted level. Also, the skill sets leaving the company may not be the ones that a company wants to lose, so this option may call for a considerable amount of retraining of the remaining staff.
- *Delay or reduce scheduled pay raises.* If a medium-term business downturn is expected, then management can authorize a significant delay in scheduled pay raises or reduce the amount of raises that will be granted. This approach should be shared by all, to gain acceptance, and may be accepted without too much backlash for the duration of the downturn. A variation is to make the pay freeze mandatory for a designated pay grade, with compensation changes still being available on a limited basis below that level. This directs the pay freeze toward those employees who are in a better fiscal position to handle it.
- *Require unpaid days off.* There may be cases where occasional unpaid days off for the entire workforce will resolve financial difficulties. If so, reduce the sting for employees by allowing them to pick which days to take off. For example, the days off may coincide with school vacations or be adjacent to federal holidays.
- *Shorten the workweek.* If there is not enough work for a large part of the company, then the company can elect to shorten the workweek for some period of time, with reduced pay to match the shorter work period. This alternative works best for a single-day reduction from a five-day to a four-day workweek, since the result is a 20 percent pay cut for everyone in the company. A further reduction to a three-day workweek will likely result in such a significant total pay reduction that many employees will be forced to find work elsewhere. An interesting offshoot of this shortened workweek is that, if customer orders subsequently increase, the company has the option of retaining the four-day workweek but adding longer hours per day. This yields a gradual increase back to full-time status.
- *Shorten working hours.* It is generally better to shorten the workweek rather than the number of working hours per day so that employees do not have to commute to and from work five times a week in exchange for reduced pay. However, in a retail environment, it may make sense to determine when the bulk of customers are shopping and then contract store hours to match. There is a risk of lost sales by shrinking store hours, so this approach is profitable only when there are very few sales clustered near the start or end of a store's current business hours.

- *Use unpaid leaves of absence.* An unpaid leave of absence only encour ages employees to look for new jobs and likely will result in a very high turnover level in the near term. However, if the company offers to continue paying benefits to employees during their leaves of absence, they may be more inclined to stay out of work longer and still return to the company at the end of their leaves of absence.

- *Offer paid sabbaticals.* If the business downturn is expected to be lengthy, management can offer a sabbatical with a moderate rate of pay to those employees judged to have sufficient seniority. The amount paid can be viewed as a retainer for consulting services, which the company can exercise by occasionally calling in employees on sab- batical to assist during high-volume periods. This approach works best when applied to senior-level staff whom the company values and would like to have back, and may be acceptable if offered along with continuing benefits and access to basic company services, such as a cell phone and a company e-mail address.

- *Freeze pay.* The workforce may accept a complete pay freeze for a limited period of time if they understand that the situation is caused by economic conditions that put the company at risk. This approach works best if everyone is included in the pay freeze. A less drastic alternative is to combine the pay freeze with an increase in incentive pay, so that employees still can improve their compensation by taking actions that improve the company's profitability.

- *Implement a pay cut.* A more drastic alternative is to mandate a pay cut. If implemented, this should be universal, so that no charges of favoritism can be levied. Further, the pay cut should be even greater for the management team, which creates a solid reason for the man- agement group to work the company back into profitability.

If the company enacts either a shorter workweek or fewer working hours during the business day, then this will also reduce the amount of vacation and sick hours accrued, so there is a cumulative cost reduction effect.

The trouble with these alternatives to a workforce reduction is that they are mostly short term—employees cannot subsist on below-market compensation for an indefinite period of time; they will soon find jobs elsewhere. Thus, using an alternative to a workforce reduction works best during short downturns in a company's revenues, when there is a reason- able expectation of recovery. However, if there appears to be a significant, long-term revenue reduction in store, outright layoffs are probably the correct method to effect significant cost reductions.

If the payroll cost reduction techniques noted here appear too onerous, an alternative is to sell off entire business units. By doing so, the buyer gains ownership of the legal entity, along with responsibility for any future workforce reductions. If the business unit in question is not profitable, then this is a less desirable option, on the grounds that the sale price likely will be based on its earnings. However, if the buyer finds value in the intellectual property or other aspects of a business unit, irrespective of its financial condition, then the resulting sale price may make this a viable alternative to a large workforce reduction. Also, if the buyer can reposition the business unit in order to improve its profitability, there may be no need to institute any payroll cost reductions.

Manage Payroll Expenses at the Hiring Stage

For the many reasons already noted, companies are reluctant to engage in a workforce reduction—and yet there are times when it is simply not economically feasible to do otherwise. To be kept from being placed in this uncomfortable situation, consider shifting the cost reduction analysis around to the *hiring* process, so that fewer employees are hired initially. If staffing levels are kept low and well utilized from the start, it is much less likely that a workforce reduction will be needed at a later date.

New Hire Modeling

One possibility is to increase headcount slower than revenues, as an ongoing and company-mandated practice. Under this approach, management assumes that employees will become more efficient over time, so that revenues per employee (or some similar measure) will continually climb as the company expands. However, this alternative works best at a strategic level and less so at a tactical level, where managers need to fill specific slots and have little patience with such a high-level concept. Nonetheless, this notion can be incorporated into the annual budgeting process as a factor to be considered when budgeting for new staff positions.

A variation on this concept is to model what positions will no longer be needed within the workforce if there is a drop in revenues or profits, and use this analysis when deciding which positions to fill; there will be greater reluctance to fill a position that the company may have to turn around and eliminate if business declines. Of course, this approach can also turn into a self-fulfilling prophecy, since a company will always be correctly positioned for a business *down*turn but never ready for a business *up*turn. The result is a greater likelihood of slow growth, in exchange for less risk in a down market.

Mandatory Delays

One of the issues with hiring a new person is doing so from only a brief consideration of the underlying need for doing the hire. A company may find, after a few months, that the tasks for which an employee was hired are not that critical, or that activity levels have declined to the point where the person is no longer needed. To sidestep this issue, consider requiring a mandatory delay before authorizing a new hire, either for an entirely new position or to replace a departing employee. This delay can be for several months and perhaps up to a half year, thereby giving sufficient time for managers to fully weigh the need for a new hire. However, as just noted, this approach will limit a company's ability to respond to a business upturn.

If the decision is made to hire a new person, then there should be an exceedingly thorough review process for new hires. This can include extensive background checks and drug testing as well as multiple interviews and possibly also a review by a psychiatrist. The reason for such an up-front (and expensive) effort is to avoid a prolonged (and more expensive) termination of an employee who does not fit in. Thus, the cost of the hiring process, no matter how high, is still much less expensive than the cost of termination.

Investment Case

An alternative to a mandatory hiring delay is to require an investment case to be created for every new hire, or at least for every new hire to be made on short notice. The business case should itemize all potential revenue and profit to be gained from the new hire as well as the reasons why other hiring scenarios (such as using a contractor or part-time hire) will not work. The investment case should be analyzed by the human resources staff, to obtain their opinion regarding its assertions.

Other Alternatives

Another way to test the need for a new hire is to first start with a short-term employment contract or part-time staffing. This approach allows a company to "try the position on for size" and potentially drop it after a short testing period. This approach is best suited for lower-level positions where there is large pool of candidates who might accept such work. This is more difficult for highly technical positions, such as engineers, where there are fewer available candidates.

The initial rate of pay at which a person is hired is crucial to the subsequent amount of pay increases issued to that person. Ideally, the initial pay level is that amount below which it is difficult to locate competent candidates and must leave sufficient room for multiple years of upside pay changes. Ideally, at the point of hire, the human resources staff can create a general profile of how many years it will take, at a predetermined pay rate increase, to attain a market rate that approximately matches a new hire's expected rate of improvement in expertise. If a candidate insists on an extremely high initial rate of pay, the company is placed in a difficult position for future hiring and should consider continuing to search for a less-expensive person.

In rare cases, a recruit will demand a pay package that includes a guaranteed cost of living adjustment (COLA). A COLA clause is an extremely foolish perquisite to grant, since it guarantees continuing pay increases to an employee without the corresponding offset of any effort by the employee to improve performance. It also calls for a continuing series of expense increases for so long as the employee works for the company. Thus, a company should seriously consider avoiding hiring anyone who demands such a clause.

Summary

In summary, a company can use expected efficiency improvements to budget for fewer hires in relation to revenues as well as implement delayed hiring, investment cases, thorough investigations, and pay analysis to manage payroll expenses appropriately at the hiring stage.

Combat Institutionalized Pay Increases

A management team may spend an inordinate amount of time combating price increases from its suppliers and yet accept routine cost of living adjustments for all of its employees without a murmur. This does not need to be the case. There are a number of methods available for combating institutionalized pay increases.

Merit-Based Pay

The original rate of pay at which an employee was hired should have been based on that person's qualifications—in other words, his or her expected performance. Subsequent to that time, any additional pay changes should also be based on performance. This means that the pay system should be skewed in favor of merit-based payments to high performers. Conversely, if an employee does not perform well, then his performance is considered to have not changed since the last performance review, and so there is no need to enact a pay increase. This approach will improve a company's chances of retaining its top talent while those whose pay stagnates will be more likely to leave the company in search of higher compensation elsewhere. A compensation system structured under this methodology should allow for a very large range of compensation changes over the high- and low-performing employees rather than a mandated incremental pay increase for all employees.

A performance review system should be in place that supports this merit-based payment system. Such a system involves the use of a consistently applied ranking process. If employees rank near the bottom, then they are given an additional period of time in which to improve their performance. If they cannot improve their performance, then they are counseled out of the company.

A variation on merit-based pay is the increased use of stock options instead of base pay. This approach may not cut expenses, but it does conserve cash. Stock options give the holder the right to acquire company stock at a predetermined price, which can yield a significant profit to the holder if the company's stock price increases during the period when the options can be exercised. However, this is a viable option only for a publicly held company, since there must be a market for the company's stock in order to determine its value. Also, an individual's job performance does not necessarily have a significant impact on company financial results, so there is no clear correlation between individual performance and the resulting stock option payout. Consequently, stock options should be used only in publicly held companies, and only for senior executive employees whose activities can directly impact the stock price.

Another alternative is to increase the proportion of pay tied to performance bonuses, so that a company's total pay automatically declines during slower economic periods. This may be quite acceptable to employees, as long as the performance bonus plan also allows them to increase their total compensation during periods of heightened profitability.

A good foundation for performance bonuses is operational profitability at the division level, without any allocation of corporate overhead. It is most easily tied back to employee performance, avoids the results of other divisions over which employees have no control, and also avoids financing costs that are not related to operational results.

Turnover Investigation

If a company's compensation levels drop too far below market rates, then it may be necessary to increase pay levels gradually to the point where employee turnover is reduced to a modest level. This does *not* mean that there should be a sudden massive increase in pay levels to attain instant comparability to market rates. Instead, the human resources staff should create a target pay level for each position where there appears to be a turnover problem and calculate the amount of pay increase needed to attain that level over several years. It is extremely important to track the turnover metric continually as the pay increases are enacted gradually over time; by doing so, a company has the option of canceling further pay increases at any point when the metrics reveal that the turnover level has declined to the target level; any further pay increases at that point would be superfluous.

The use of pay raises simply to avoid excessive levels of employee turnover should be examined with great care. Is there really an excessive level of employee turnover? A company should investigate its turnover level in comparison not only to other companies in its industry but also locally. For example, a company in the fast-food industry always will have a high rate of turnover, unless it pays its employees well above the market rate. Also, turnover in the local market will be low in a depressed economy, irrespective of pay levels. Increasing pay to reduce turnover is an even less valid strategic in a down economy, when many employees are more concerned with not being laid off than with the size of their next pay raise. Exploring these issues may result in a decision not to increase pay levels.

Further, a company should use exit interviews to determine the exact cause of each employee departure, which may have nothing to do with obtaining a higher rate of pay elsewhere. It could be caused by family planning or because a spouse has obtained a job in another state or because an employee wants to make a career change. Thus, a simple assumption that turnover is caused by low pay is incorrect and requires further investigation into base-level causes.

Initial Pay Rate Alternatives

If there is a hot labor market for a particular position, such as a computer programmer, a company may be forced to start a person at a startlingly high pay rate. In subsequent years, the company is then forced to either keep adding to this high base level of compensation or to issue one-time bonuses instead. An alternative to this uncomfortable pay scenario is to outsource work while waiting for job demand to ease. This may call for paying high outsourcing fees for several years, but the payoff is when pay levels gradually decline to the point where outsourced work eventually can be cut off and replaced with in-house staff. This strategy is a long-term one and calls for a considerable amount of patience by management.

If a company elects to hire someone at a very high rate of pay, it can avoid continuing pay increases by switching to annual bonuses. This effectively freezes an employee's pay until such time as the market rate of pay gradually increases to encompass the employee's compensation level. If there is employee resistance to this approach, consider sharing market-based pay information with them and the rate of change in pay rates so that they can estimate for themselves when their rate of pay is no longer beyond the top end of the compensation range.

Bureaucracy

A final method for combating institutionalized pay increases is to bring the full weight of the company's bureaucracy to bear on the issue. If a manager wishes to issue a large base pay increase, this calls for a correspondingly large number of approvals, possibly right up to the company president. However, the approval process for one-time bonuses can be much easier, so managers have an incentive to favor bonuses over pay increases.

Summary

In short, a company's pay systems and overall mind-set for granting pay changes is that a base-level compensation increase should be treated as an exception, not a right. Further, a detailed review of the reasons for employee turnover may help avoid a decision to raise employee pay levels across the board. Finally, selective use of the corporate bureaucracy can make the pay raise process difficult enough for managers to steer them instead to one-time bonus grants.

Restructure Commissions

Another way to tie compensation to performance is to shift a greater proportion of employee compensation to commissions, which are inherently performance based. Thus, a high-performance employee automatically earns more while a less aggressive employee will earn less. However, this concept can be taken too far, especially if salespeople have such a strong commission incentive that they push unnecessary sales onto customers. Also, the commission plan should be adjusted to reward high-margin sales with higher commissions and lower-margin sales with correspondingly lower commissions. Otherwise, a company may find itself giving up the majority of its gross margin to its sales staff.

The timing of commission payments can be altered to ensure that payments are made only once cash is received. This approach is especially useful in cases where it appears that the sales staff is selling to customers in poor financial condition. If this is not the case, then it is easier for the accounting staff to calculate commissions when sales are invoiced rather than paid.

Another cost-reduction possibility is to create a written policy that, if a salesperson leaves the company, she will be paid a commission only on those sales that have been invoiced through the date of her departure. Otherwise, a salesperson might expect to continue receiving commissions on sales prospects that she developed or on customer orders that have not yet been shipped.

The problem with shifting compensation into commissions is that it is not easily applicable outside of the sales department. Other employees may have some incidental relationship with sales (such as those who assist with writing sales proposals), but if there is no direct linkage between landing a sale and earning a commission, there will be no reason for the targeted employee to change behavior.

Thus, it is generally worthwhile to shift some compensation into a performance-based commission plan, as long as it will not result in low-margin sales or annoyed customers and targets only those individuals who can increase total corporate sales.

Restructure the Workforce

Another way to reduce payroll costs is to restructure the workforce so that the sum total of all labor expended within the company is reduced. The most obvious examples of this are using part-time employees, outsourcing work, cross-training, and job restructuring.

Part-Time Employees

Part-time employees are very useful for seasonal or peak demand situations. In these cases, hiring full-time staff to handle a momentary surge in business leaves the company with an excess supply of in-house labor that will be wasted outside of the surge period. If the company plans to use part-time employees during these periods, then consider paying them somewhat more than the market rate. By doing so, they have more of an incentive to remain in the available labor pool and may choose repeatedly to work for the company when needed. This concept can be extended by including part-time staff in employee newsletters and other employee programs. By using the same part-time employees, the company can avoid the cost of training entirely new employees. Further, the company can evaluate part-time employees for eventual hiring into full-time positions, which reduces recruiting costs.

Part-time employees may also be appropriate for entry-level positions. This concept works when there is a high level of turnover among first-year employees, as is frequently the case in the retail sector. Using part-time staff in these positions allows the company to avoid extending benefits to people who will likely be gone in a few months anyways.

Outsourcing

Outsourcing is used frequently for highly skilled technical jobs, specialized work that a company needs only occasionally, or to address peak period overloads. All of these alternatives are appropriate ones for restructuring the workforce. Prime candidates for outsourcing are highly skilled but significantly underutilized positions within the company. Functional areas where this opportunity frequently arises are information technology, internal auditing, legal, marketing, and investor relations—essentially anywhere where there is a comparatively small staff of specialists providing support services.

However, outsourcing can be taken too far. It is not wise to outsource positions that are considered to be a core competency of the company, since shifting the work to a supplier may create a competitor, or at least someone who now has the ability to raise prices with relative impunity. In this latter case, a good rule is to never outsource when there are only a small number of identifiable suppliers.

Cross-Training

Every company contains a plethora of jobs where the skill set is sufficiently specialized that only one or a few people are sufficiently trained to perform each job. In these cases, if the trained employees are overwhelmed with work or are away on vacation, then the company must either use part-time staff or outsource the work. A less expensive alternative is to cross-train employees to handle those aspects of each other's jobs that are most likely to experience capacity constraints. By doing so, much more work can be handled by existing staff.

Of particular note when using cross-training is to emphasize cross-training only on those tasks *likely to experience capacity constraints.* This focus can significantly reduce the amount of time spent on cross-training. A good way to determine the need for cross-training is to examine expenses for outsourced work and part-time staff and determine exactly what tasks they were used for.

Cross-training results in a more practiced workforce, so there are reasonable grounds for enacting modest pay increases to reflect their higher knowledge level. Doing so encourages other employees also to apply themselves to cross-training. However, this pay boost should be structured as a periodic bonus rather than an addition to an employee's base pay. By using a bonus structure, employees must recertify on their new skills every year in order to continue to earn the bonus. Otherwise, their skill levels may drop while they continue to earn the higher level of base pay.

Task Analysis

Another way to restructure the workforce is to conduct periodically a detailed review of the specific tasks that higher-paid employees are performing. If some tasks can be safely completed by lower-paid employees, then restructure these jobs to focus the work of the highly compensated staff on the more difficult tasks to which they are more suited. This restructuring can yield a net compensation reduction by eliminating some highly paid staff in favor of adding lower-paid staff.

Summary

There are significant opportunities for restructuring the workforce in many companies. Use part-time employees for peak-period and high-turnover work and use outsourcing for low-volume, specialized tasks. Cross-training is especially useful for maximizing the utilization of the existing in-house staff, while a periodic tasks analysis can yield some shifting of low-skill work away from highly paid employees. These opportunities should be pursued on an ongoing basis, to make the existing workforce as cost effective as possible.

Hire Contractors

A company typically employs a contractor because there is a short-term need for that person's services. If there are discussions about hiring the individual on a permanent basis, the company should first consider the worst-case scenario of whether there will be any use for the person if business declines or if the specific task for which he is being hired turns out to require less time than currently estimated. In many cases, this analysis will yield a decision not to hire the contractor.

An additional issue is the appropriate compensation level to pay a person who has likely been charging the company quite a high hourly rate as a contractor. The human resources staff should consult their database of pay scales to determine the appropriate rate at which the contractor should be hired. Ideally, the compensation should be nowhere near the top of the pay scale, so there is room to increase compensation in later years.

Unfortunately, contractors may want to convert their current hourly rate into a directly comparable salary. For example, a $150 hourly contractor rate becomes a salary of $312,000 (assuming the $150 is multiplied by 40 working hours in a 52-week year). This is clearly a catastrophic rate of pay for the company, which must also tack on the cost of payroll taxes and benefits.

Consequently, it is generally better not to hire contractors directly into the company if they insist on annualizing their current rate of pay, and especially if there is a reasonable risk that they will subsequently be underutilized.

Other Types of Payroll Cost Reduction

The next three points address additional miscellaneous areas in which payroll costs can be reduced.

Bonus Plan Participants

If a company has a bonus plan, it is entirely likely that the group included in the plan has gradually increased in size over the years. However, not many positions in the company have an impact on company cash flow, which should be the primary reason for issuing a bonus. Instead, as the bonus plan has expanded over time, more marginal reasons for granting bonuses have likely been included in the plan. A reasonable cost reduction step is to closely examine the group of employees included in the bonus plan, with the objective of reducing the number of participants to just those whose actions will directly impact cash flow. Further, any bonus plan performance criteria not related to cash flow improvement should be eliminated. Thus, the plan should be tightly restricted and paid out only based on quantitative criteria that are directly beneficial to the company.

Step Costs

An area rarely considered when adding staff is the step cost of also adding more support personnel. The human resources and payroll departments need to add staff periodically when the number of employees they are supporting becomes too large. Consequently, management should monitor the utilization levels of these areas as headcount is added elsewhere in the company and try to hold staff counts below the next step cost point for as long as possible. This can be done by using contractors and outsourced services for as long as it is economical to do so.

Common Review Dates

The process of reviewing employee compensation and adjusting it based on a variety of factors is a time-consuming one. Many companies conduct this review on an annual basis, 12 months following each person's hire date. Given the random distribution of employee hiring throughout the year, this means that the human resources staff must deal with pay adjustments throughout the year. A more efficient approach is to schedule all pay reviews to be effective as of the same date, once a year. This completely eliminates pay reviews from the human resources work schedule for the remainder of the year and also reduces the risk that anyone's review will be inadvertently missed.

Worker Adjustment and Retraining Notification Act

If a company is planning to carry out a large workforce reduction, it should be aware of the Worker Adjustment and Retraining Notification Act (WARN). This act requires employers to provide 60 days' notice of either a plant closing or a mass layoff. An employer must abide by WARN if it has at least 100 employees, not counting any employees who have worked fewer than 6 months in the last 12 months and not counting employees who work an average of fewer than 20 hours a week. Federal, state, and local government entities are not covered by the act.

A covered employer must give notice if it plans to close a facility that will result in a loss of at least 50 employees. Or a company must give notice if it is planning a mass layoff that will not result in a plant closing but will result in an employment loss of 500 or more employees, or from 50 to 499 employees if they comprise at least one-third of the company's active workforce. Job losses within any 90-day period will count together toward these threshold levels, unless the company can demonstrate that the workforce reductions during that interval are the result of separate and distinct actions and causes.

A company can be exempted from the WARN notice provision if a plant closing or layoff is caused by business circumstances that were not reasonably foreseeable at the time notice would otherwise have been required, or if it is the result of a natural disaster.

If a company does not provide the notice mandated by WARN, it is liable to each affected employee for an amount including back pay and benefits for the period of the violation, up to 60 days.

Payroll Cost Metrics

Any number of metrics can be used to track the performance of individual employees. However, the list is quite a bit smaller for tracking, at a general level, the number of employees in relation to the size and activity level of a company. The metrics are:

- *Sales per person.* This is one of the most closely watched of all performance measures. It is based on the assumption that employees form the core of a company's profitability, and so high degrees of efficiency in this area are bound to result in strong profitability. (See the next metric for an alternative view.) The calculation is annualized revenue divided by the total number of full-time equivalents (FTEs) employed by the company. An FTE is the combination of staffing that equals a 40-hour week.
- *Profit per person.* This measure is useful for those companies with a high proportion of personnel costs to other costs, such as consulting or other service businesses, where changes in the efficiency of the staff have a direct impact on the profitability of the company. It is least useful in highly automated entities or distributorships, where the proportion of labor costs to total costs is quite small. This is a more comprehensive measure than sales per person, since it accounts not only for the ability of the staff to bring in sales, but also for their ability to wring a profit from those sales. The calculation is the annual net profit divided by the total number of FTEs.
- *Ratio of support staff to total staff.* If a company employs a high proportion of billable employees, such as a consulting firm, a prime determinant of profitability is its ability to operate with the lowest possible proportion of support staff to the total number of employees. In this situation, tracking the ratio of support staff to total staff is a good way to monitor overhead costs. The calculation is to divide the average number of support staff FTEs during the past 12 months by the average number of all FTE employees during the same period.

In addition, consider tracking employee turnover by supervisor. A poor supervisor may be causing valuable employees to leave the company, thereby calling for more recruiting and training expenditures for additional new hires. To spot this problem, track employee turnover by supervisor on a trend line and in comparison to other supervisors in the same functional area. The calculation of this metric for each supervisor's staff is the number of FTEs who resigned during the past 12 months divided by the average number of FTEs during the same period.

Summary

Given the high proportion of total expenses that payroll comprises, the astute manager must keep it in check. However, reducing payroll is a serious matter, since it can cut away much of a company's key talent as well as its ability to generate additional revenue. However, if applied intelligently and using the concepts and analyses discussed in this chapter, it is possible to selectively pare away some payroll expenses and keep others from growing at an excessive rate.

Part of this effort is highly detailed, requiring continuing analysis of compensation plans, market rates, and individual performance levels. In addition, successful payroll cost reduction requires a long-term strategy of determining where a company wishes to selectively target its funds for robust growth and how this is going to impact payroll within the various functional areas of the company.

CHAPTER 6

Benefits Cost Reduction

Introduction

A company's benefits package can be a very significant part of its total expenses, but in many companies benefits are not really viewed as expenses. Instead, because of the need to hire and retain top-quality employees, the benefits package is considered a key asset that must be maintained if not increased. While a rich package can certainly be an exceptional tool in the race to acquire the best and brightest, it is also sometimes viewed as an entitlement that is absolutely, positively never reduced.

The correct view of a benefits package is that, irrespective of its worth, it is still an expense and therefore must be carefully managed. This means not only bargaining down benefit providers whenever possible and whittling away at some less-necessary items but also strategically concentrating a company's available cash into those benefits that are most valuable to the workforce.

The cost reductions noted in this chapter only express a broad range of *potential* actions; they are not a recommendation for wholesale cutting that will leave a company's benefits package a mere skeleton of its former self. The correct way to use these actions is to review the benefits package with great care and then selectively reposition funding and pare extraneous expenses only to such an extent that the benefits package as a whole still meets the company's requirements.

The remainder of this chapter breaks down and discusses cost reduction opportunities for each component of a benefits package.

Benefits Administration

Most of the cost savings to be gleaned from the benefits area apply to specific types of benefits. However, it is also possible to strip some costs out of the *administration* of benefits.

Forms and FAQs

One cost-saving measure is to convert all benefits-related forms and manuals to PDF files that can be posted on the corporate intranet site. In addition, the Web site can include a list of frequently asked questions (FAQs) and answers; both items prevent employees from having to contact the human resources staff for information.

Benefits Standardization

There should be a single benefits package to be used throughout the company and a single set of procedures for administering it. By taking this approach, the human resources staff needs to be trained on only one benefits package. Also, it may be possible to centrally administer benefits from a single location, which reduces the amount of administration personnel who need to be involved in outlying locations. Thus, benefits standardization can significantly streamline the administrative staff.

Benefit Deductions

A company can offer a large number of benefits to its employees, many of which require some sort of deduction from payroll. For example, a company can set up deductions for employee medical, dental, life, and supplemental life insurance as well as flexible spending account deductions for medical insurance or child care payments and 401(k) deductions for contributions and loans. If there are many employees and many deduction types, the payroll staff can be overwhelmed at payroll processing time by the volume of changes continually occurring in this area. Also, whenever there is a change in the underlying cost of insurance provided to the company, the company commonly passes along some portion of these costs to employees, resulting in a massive updating of deductions for all employees who take that particular type of insurance. This not only takes time away from other, more value-added payroll tasks but also is subject to error, so that adjustments must later be made to correct the errors, which requires even more staff time.

There are several ways to address this problem. One is to eliminate the employee-paid portion of some types of insurance. For example, if the cost to the company for monthly dental insurance is $20 per employee and the related deduction is only $2 per person, management can elect to pay for the entire cost rather than burden the payroll staff with the tracking of this trivial sum. Another alternative is to eliminate certain types of benefits, such as supplemental life insurance or 401(k) loans, in order to eliminate the related deductions. Yet another alternative is to create a policy that limits employee changes to any benefit plans, so they can make only a small number of changes per year. This eliminates the continual changing of deduction amounts in favor of just a few large bursts of activity at pre-scheduled times during the year.

A very good alternative is to create a benefit package for all employees that requires a single deduction of the same amount for everyone or for a group (such as one deduction for single employees and another for employees with families); employees can then pick and choose the exact amount of each type of benefit they want within the boundaries of each benefit package without altering the amount of the underlying deduction. This last alternative has the unique advantage of consolidating all deductions into a single item, which is much simpler to administer. Any of these approaches to the problem will reduce the number or timing of deduction changes, thereby reducing the workload of the payroll staff.

Online Enrollment

If a company offers its employees many benefits that involve a number of service providers, then there will be a correspondingly large number of forms to fill out. This can occupy a considerable amount of staff time. If the company is a large one, it may make sense to have the software development group create online forms that employees can fill out. These forms can have automatic error-checking routines to ensure that all submissions are correct. Using these forms, the administrative staff only has to accumulate the submitted information and forward it to the service providers. This approach effectively shifts nearly all paperwork issues from the administrative staff to employees.

Benefit Alternatives

Some employees obtain the bulk of their insurance benefits through their spouse's employer. If so, they may prefer an alternative to their standard benefits package. A common trade-off is to give them extra vacation time. By doing so, the company exchanges the "hard" cost of benefits avoided for vacation time that can potentially be scheduled so that it does not require additional paid staff to fill in during an absence. This is a clear win for both parties.

Disability Insurance

Long-term disability and short-term disability insurance is an important benefit, but most employees do not consider it to be within the core benefit package, which is composed of health insurance, a pension plan, and vacation time. Accordingly, a company should certainly make this insurance available to employees but does not need to absorb the cost. Also, when an employee pays for the cost of this insurance, the resulting benefits are not taxable; this is a massive benefit to employees and should be pointed out to them. If the company were to pay for the premiums, then any resulting disability payments would be taxable.

Life Insurance

Life insurance is a benefit that most employees consider to be tangential to the core benefit package. Consequently, there is some room available for reducing its cost.

The typical life insurance benefit is to provide for each employee life insurance in the amount of one year's wages. This amount will therefore naturally increase over time as an employee's wages rise. The life insurance premium charged will also increase as employees become older. Thus, a company must deal with two factors that naturally increase the cost of this benefit: wage increases and age. Of the two factors, premium increases caused by age form a much larger component of cost increases.

A simple way to reduce cost increases is to put a cap on the amount of life insurance granted to each employee. If employees wish to increase life insurance beyond that point, then they can buy additional insurance through the company—but the company will not pay for it.

An alternative is to simply eliminate life insurance altogether as a company-paid benefit. This approach is most acceptable with a younger or unmarried workforce, which would not normally purchase such insurance on its own.

Medical Insurance

The largest of the benefits expenses is nearly always medical insurance. In this section, we address a variety of methods for gaining control over the cost of medical insurance or at least for reducing its rate of growth. Over time, a company will likely need to consider all of the changes noted here, if only to keep the cost of medical insurance from overwhelming it.

Plan Consolidation

A company may have a number of subsidiaries, each one with its own medical insurance provider. If so, the company is not taking advantage of volume pricing, which it can achieve by forcing all subsidiaries into a single, nationwide plan. This approach does not always work for more remote company locations, since the coverage of a national plan may not be available to them. Thus, a practical resolution is to cluster as many locations as possible into a national plan and obtain separate insurance for outlying locations.

Plan Structure

There may be different groups within a company that want different levels of medical coverage. A younger staff may be content with a lower-cost plan that provides just basic insurance, while an older group may have considerable interest in a plan with richer benefits. If this is the case, it can be very expensive to cater to the group wanting the richer plan and implement a richer plan for *everyone*, since the plan will apply to the other group that does not need the extra benefits. To avoid this issue, consider doing the reverse: offer a low-cost medical plan as the standard corporate plan but have an upgrade option to a richer plan. Those employees using the richer plan must pay for the premium difference between the two plans. Thus, the company does not pay for the extra expense, while the plan is still available to those employees wanting to access it.

Another possible type of plan stratification arises when a company has high employee turnover within the first year of employment, as is common in the retail environment. In this case, the company can offer a very low-cost medical plan during the first year of employment and then make a richer plan available after the first year. This approach reduces participation in the richer plan, but only at the expense of people who are not likely to have any longevity with the firm.

An alternative to stratified plans is to offer only a catastrophic insurance plan that covers major medical expenses and then pay an extra amount directly to employees. The staff can use the additional payment to acquire their own insurance policies or to use them in any other way they choose. By taking this approach, the company is less tied to insurance premium inflation, since the amount it pays employees does not have to directly correlate to the cost of insurance.

Yet another variation is to offer no medical insurance at all. This approach does not work well when competing firms are offering it but can work very well if the company simply compensates by paying well above market rates for employee wages. By doing so, some people with outside access to medical insurance will be more than happy to swap medical insurance for a significant pay boost. The company also completely avoids the cost of health plan administration. This approach tends to attract employees who already have access to medical insurance, such as through a spouse or as a retirement benefit.

A final variation is to self-insure, under which a company pays into an insurance fund that pays for claims and carries over excess funding into future years. This approach works best if the company also obtains catastrophic coverage to cap its liability and also uses a third-party administrator to deal with claims. The primary benefits of using self-insurance are that the company will no longer have the uncertainty of locating an insurer and that it does not have to pay for the profit component of an insurer's premiums. Self-insurance can be less expensive over the long term but does require careful administration to mitigate risks.

Copays, Deductibles, and Lifetime Limits

A major tool for reducing medical insurance costs is increasing the copay. This is the proportion of the doctor's fee that an employee must pay as part of a doctor consultation. Charging a higher copay presumably makes an employee think twice before going to the doctor and also shifts part of the insurance cost to the employee. If there is currently no copay at all or a very minor one, a company can generate significant savings by imposing a variety of copays for different types of treatment. It may also be possible to charge a higher copay for visits to specialists; by doing so, employees have an incentive to first visit a primary care physician, who tends to be less expensive.

Another cost reduction possibility is to increase the amount of deductibles, whereby employees pay a higher percentage of the medical service costs provided to them. This will work only within limits; there will be a backlash if multiple employees require services that involve a hefty deductible.

Insurance providers will also quote lower premiums if a policy includes lifetime limits on expenditures. These limits cap the insurers' liability and transfer the risk to employees. These limits are usually quite high (in the range of $1 million to $5 million), and employees will not normally reach them except in catastrophic situations. However, in this case, the company must balance cost reduction against providing an adequate level of medical protection to employees. Major medical events, such as organ transplants, cancer, and open heart surgery, can exceed the lifetime limits and prevent employees from obtaining medical care precisely when they need it the most.

Of the cost reductions noted here, copays and deductibles are an annoyance to employees, but lifetime limits can cause them a severe financial shock.

Prescriptions

The use of copays can be extended to a multitiered approach with branded medications. Under this system, employees pay a lower copay if they accept a generic alternative to a prescription drug and a higher copay if they insist on receiving a branded version instead. Some companies have taken the extra step of *requiring* the use of generic drugs whenever they are available. Since the cost differential between generic and branded drugs can be enormous, this tiered system saves insurers a great deal of money, which they pass back to the company in the form of lower premiums.

It is less expensive for a mail-order pharmacy to fill prescriptions. However, the nature of their business requires a fulfillment delay of several days, which does not make it a viable option for prescriptions that are needed on a more pressing basis. For all other prescription requirements, which are of the long-term maintenance variety, a company can either require mail-order fulfillment or at least encourage it with an unusually low copay.

Another cost reduction option is called *step therapy*. Under this program, employees and their doctors are required to begin with less expensive treatments for certain medical conditions and then escalate to more expensive treatments if the first stage of treatment is ineffective.

A final option is for a company to pay only a fixed amount for prescriptions relating to certain conditions. If an employee's doctor prescribes an inexpensive medication, then the employee may find that the company's payment covers the entire cost of the medication. However, if the doctor prescribes a more expensive alternative, the employee would have to pay for the difference between the price of the drug and the company's payment.

Thus, some prescription alternatives shift the cost to the employee, and other are designed to encourage the use of less expensive drugs or methods for delivering them.

Spousal Coverage

It is possible to not allow coverage to a spouse if that person is eligible for insurance through his or her employer. By doing so, the company is shifting insurance expense not onto its employees but rather onto another company.

A more aggressive way to address a spouse's medical coverage is through a medical opt-out policy, under which a company pays its employees a small amount for every month in which they obtain their medical insurance elsewhere, such as through a spouse. Thus, the company is shifting the bulk of the insurance liability for *all* members of an employee's family onto another company.

Dental and Vision Coverage

Dental and vision coverage are similar to short-term and long-term disability coverage, in that they are important but not considered part of the core benefits package. Thus, it may be possible to shift either the entire cost directly to employees or else quite a large proportion of the cost.

Pensions

The pension plan is generally considered to be a core benefit, after medical insurance. As such, most employers realize that they must offer it—but they still have some leeway in regard to associated expenditures. Some cost reduction possibilities are presented next.

Defined Benefit Pension Plans

It is highly inadvisable to offer employees a pension plan that offers a fixed set of defined benefits, on the simple grounds that such payments are partially based on investment returns over a long period of time, and such returns are completely outside of the company's control. If investment returns drop below initial projections, then the company must make up the difference in payments to employees, which can be extremely expensive.

A much better alternative to the defined benefit pension plan is the defined *payment* pension plan, where the company only guarantees that it will contribute a fixed amount into the pension plan. Once the payment is made, the company is under no obligation to make additional payments.

401(k) Matching

A common feature of a 401(k) plan is for the company to match some percentage of the contributions made by employees. This can be a full 100 percent match of employee contributions or some lesser percentage. Also, a company may place a cap on the total match that the company offers. For example, a matching program might be for 50 percent of any employee's contributions to the plan, with a cap of 6 percent of an employee's wages.

The matching program may be valued highly by employees, but it can also be a substantial liability for the company. Therefore, the terms of the matching program should be reviewed at least annually. Some questions to ask during this review are:

- How many employees are using the 401(k) program?
- Are employees tailoring their contributions to maximize the match?
- Do employees indicate that the match is a key reason for remaining with the company?
- How does the matching program compare to that of competitors?

If it appears that employees are not maximizing their use of the program and it is not critical for retention, then consider scaling back the various provisions of the matching program.

401(k) Matching Vesting Duration

When a company decides to match some portion of the funds that its employees are contributing, it also needs to decide on the vesting period over which employees will earn the right to the matching funds. For example, five-year vesting would give employees ownership of 20 percent of matching funds in each of five successive years. If they leave the company prior to a vesting date, then they lose the remaining unvested matching funds. It is very much to the company's benefit to require vesting. By doing so, any unvested funds that are given up by departing employees are now available for matching the savings of remaining employees, which reduces the company's matching obligation. A side benefit is that vesting gives employees an incentive to stay with the company until they have earned their matching funds—this can have a modest positive impact on employee turnover.

401(k) Safe Harbor Matching

A 401(k) matching program requires periodic discrimination testing to ensure that highly compensated employees (HCEs) are not receiving an excessive proportion of the company's matching funds. If they are, then the HCEs must scale back their contributions and likely take back some of the contributions they have already made. This process is irritating for the HCEs and also requires the expense of periodic testing by third parties.

Management can instead authorize the use of safe harbor matching, under which the company is required to match each employee's contribution, dollar for dollar, up to 3 percent of the employee's compensation, and 50 cents on the dollar for the employee's contribution that exceeds 3 percent of the employee's compensation. An alternative is to contribute an amount equal to 3 percent of compensation to each employee's 401(k) account. The matched funds must vest immediately. This approach usually decreases the additional consulting and reporting assistance that would otherwise be needed to conduct and remediate nondiscrimination testing. However, the cost of the contribution and immediate vesting may more than offset any savings, so this concept should be thoroughly analyzed before enacting any changes.

401(k) Automatic Enrollment

Automatically enrolling employees in the corporate 401(k) plan has long been considered a benefits best practice because it enhances employee participation in the plan. However, is this really a best practice from the point of view of the company? By automatically enrolling employees, a company may find that it is incurring the cost of administering a large number of small-balance accounts. Also, if the company is matching some portion of employee payments into the plan, then it is also incurring an extra matching cost for each person it has automatically added to the plan (and who might not otherwise have enrolled). Offsetting these costs, increased participation allows HCEs to put more money into the plan—but this also carries with it an increased matching liability for the company. In short, review the cost impact of automatic enrollment before installing such a system.

401(k) Administration Fees

Any company sponsoring a 401(k) plan can expect to pay a variety of administrative and management fees to third parties to collect and invest funds on behalf of the plan. Depending on the amount of funds invested, the company may also be paying for an audit of the plan. The company can pass along some or all of these fees to the plan participants, either as a line item on employee investment statements or as a reduction of their investment returns. Because there may be some pushback from employees over such a pass-through, it works better if there are a large number of plan participants, so that the fees can be spread around enough to reduce the total cost for any one individual.

401(k) Loan Fees

When an employee borrows money from her own 401(k) retirement funds, the plan administrator typically charges the company a fee for the transaction. The company should shift this charge to the employee taking out the loan, since the transaction is to the benefit of the employee, not the company. Also, an employee may add together the interest rate and loan fee and find that it is less expensive to borrow funds elsewhere, which eliminates all administrative burdens from the company for handling any loan-related paperwork.

401(k) Service Provider Fees

Service providers can charge a variety of fees for their handling of a 401(k) plan, which can include a fixed fee, a per-participant fee, and a percentage of the funds under management. As the amount of money under management gradually increases, the service provider will earn more in fees. This presents an opportunity to the company, which can press the provider to accept a lower fee structure, thereby dropping its total fees back to where they were on a per-person basis when the provider originally provided a quote.

It is always easier to leave a 401(k) plan with the same service provider for as long as possible. However, if its fees appear to be too high and it is resisting a fee reduction, then consider putting the plan up for bid. Creating a competitive bidding environment may force the current provider to reduce its fees; if not, then the company can always engage another provider to handle the business.

Seasonal Bonuses

A company may issue bonuses to its employees in connection with various holidays or personal events, such as Christmas, Thanksgiving, or the birth of a child. However, the company receives nothing in return for these bonuses, and in fact they are rarely even documented in the corporate list of official benefits. Thus, there is virtually no payoff to the company in return for its payment of such bonuses.

While one option is to completely eliminate these bonuses, an alternative approach is to redirect the funds into a performance-based plan, such as a drawing based on submissions of improvement suggestions. This approach yields some gain to the company and still provides a payout to the staff.

Sick Time

Under no circumstances should a company allow employees to cash in their sick days. This creates an incentive for employees to show up sick at the office and potentially infect other employees rather than stay at home and use their sick days.

It is also not a good idea to allow for the unlimited roll forward of accrued sick time. By doing so, employees are once again encouraged to not use sick time in favor of gaining a payout when they retire; this is a doubly bad idea because employee pay will likely be at its maximum level just prior to retirement, so the payout will also be maximized. However, a modest amount of roll forward is allowable to guard against downtime caused by major illnesses.

Some companies require a note from a doctor to prove that an employee is entitled to take sick time. However, this requirement can actually *increase* the total cost of sick time; now an employee has to visit the doctor and incur the cost of the consultation in order to obtain the note for what may be a common illness that would not normally have required a consultation.

A better alternative than sick time is paid time off (PTO), into which both sick time and vacation time can be lumped. With PTO, employees can use it for any purpose, with no portion of it segregated for sick time. Because sick time is no longer broken out, the company's administrative time for tracking it is eliminated.

Snacks

When a company provides free snacks and drinks to its employees, it may soon find itself facing a startling expense; a few employees tend to look on free snacks as literally a free lunch, thereby escalating the cost out of proportion to management's original intentions. To avoid this issue, consider using vending machines that require at least a modest fee for each snack or drink. This is essentially the same as a copay for insurance— employees will think twice before getting more food.

Training

Training can be considered a benefit, since it enhances the skill level of employees, which they can use to obtain pay increases. A company should maximize the return on its trading investment by paying considerable attention not only to the content of the training it provides but also to the method of training delivery. Several cost reduction options are described next.

Training Assessments

Companies have a bad habit of providing a standard set of training classes to everyone performing a specific job function. What they do not do is assess in advance whether anyone *needs* the training. Such an assessment will likely find that the training is hopelessly basic for many employees and excessively advanced for others. Thus, implementing an assessment will yield a determination of *exactly* what types of training are needed, by individual. This may not yield an outright cost reduction, but it most assuredly will tailor training needs to employees—which improves staff efficiency over the long term.

Training Delivery

Consider having a small number of employees receive training and then have these employees train the remainder of the staff. Two benefits of this approach are having a small cadre of well-trained employees who can provide training at any time as well as a significant reduction in the cost of using outside trainers. However, some employees may not be good trainers, and in fact impede the learning experience for their students. Thus, this approach depends on the teaching skill of selected employees.

Another training alternative is to use instructors who provide online training. Under this method, employees do not need to leave their offices in order to obtain training. This method has the advantage of completely avoiding all travel expenses, both by the employees and by the trainers. However, because of the ongoing interruptions that are likely to arise when someone is training on-site, it is best to keep training sessions relatively short.

If there are a large number of employees to be trained on essentially the same material, consider videotaping a training session and posting it on the company's intranet site. Employees can then review it whenever their schedules allow as well as go over the materials repeatedly, if needed.

Training for a Software Package

A great deal of training is provided specifically at the point of introduction of a new software package, usually a comprehensive accounting or enterprise resources planning system. If so, the supplier will likely charge a substantial fee for training large numbers of company employees. However, because the supplier is already making a great deal of money on the high-margin software sale, it may be amenable to providing the training either for free or for a substantial discount.

Some software packages come with self-training modules, so that employees can select only those modules directly pertaining to their needs and can repeatedly access the modules whenever they need refresher training. Many of these modular programs also include a manager oversight capability, to see who is using the modules and how they are scoring on the associated tests.

Expense Sharing

Employees may sometimes insist that a training program in a distant location (most likely a resort) is critical to their ongoing education and job performance. The company has no way of knowing if this claim is correct, but it can make employees back up their claims with some of their own money. This calls for a company policy where the company pays a certain percentage of the trip cost while the remainder is reimbursed by the employee.

Training Measurement

The method used to administer training will likely impact employee comprehension of the training materials, so measure employee knowledge of the materials both before and after training sessions to see which training method yields the best results. Poor results may call for adjustments to the subject matter and accompanying training materials as well.

Vacation Time

Vacation pay is typically based on an increasing scale, where employees earn progressively more vacation time for each year of employment. This system tends to result in a disproportionately large amount of vacation expense for the company as employee tenure increases—not just because of the increased vacation time, but also because their rates of pay presumably increase too.

The double factors of increased vacation accrual and increased pay rates at which vacation is taken presents a problem in regard to a company's vacation carry-forward policy. If the carry-forward policy is unlimited, then an employee could theoretically never take any vacations and let the vacation time accrue for years; when the employee leaves, the company is obligated to pay for the accrued vacation based on the employee's final rate of pay, which is usually the highest possible rate at which the vacation time can be paid.

There are several ways to avoid this liability. One option is a use-it-or-lose-it policy, whereby employees must take earned vacation time within a predetermined period of time or else they lose the accrued vacation. This concept does not work in some government jurisdictions, where accrued vacation time cannot be taken away from an employee. If so, an alternative is to allow only a certain amount of vacation time to be accrued, after which no further amounts will accrue until the employee starts drawing down earned vacation time.

A possible source of cost reduction is in environments where there is a great deal of employee turnover during the first year or two of employment, such as in the retail industry. In this case, it may be possible to offer an unusually low vacation accrual for an employee's initial year or two, after which the accrual increases substantially. This approach reduces the vacation expense associated with new employees while offering a long-term incentive to that small cadre of employees who choose to remain with the firm for the long term.

Wellness Programs

A long-term cost reduction opportunity is to create a corporate wellness program with the intent of making modest outlays in the near term in order to improve employee health, which pays off in the form of fewer sick days, reduced hospital admissions, fewer emergency room visits, and generally fewer insurance claims. Here are some potential components of a wellness program:

- Have a nurse administer flu shots on-site.
- Institute a smoking cessation program.
- Offer free annual screenings.
- Offer time off to attend major health events.
- Pay for a disease management service, which provides screenings and nurse follow-ups to ensure that employees with chronic conditions are taking their medications and seeing their doctors at predetermined intervals.
- Pay for an on-site Weight Watchers program during business hours.
- Pay the entire cost of flu shots.
- Put snacks in the snack machines that meet some minimum health standard for ingredients.

Workers' Compensation Insurance

There are a number of techniques for bringing about modest reductions in the cost of workers' compensation insurance. These are discussed next.

Job Classifications

One of the key determinants of the cost of workers' compensation insurance is the job classifications into which all employees are slotted. An employee designated in a high-risk classification will cost far more in insurance premiums than someone in a clerical position. Consequently, review the classifications for all employees once a year, just before the insurance is due for its annual renewal. If an insurance auditor wants to reclassify an employee into a higher-risk classification, then this is worth the time of the human resources staff to protest the designation.

Employee Screening

It is of considerable importance to conduct a drug test, background check, and felony search for every job candidate who is being considered for employment. By doing so, a company may spot someone who has a history of workers' compensation fraud or who has indicators that may lead to false workers' compensation claims. The cost of this screening is far less than the savings from a single workers' compensation claim.

If a company has a large workforce and there are numerous workers' compensation claims, then it can be cost-effective to hire an on-site nurse and route all such cases through that person. The nurse can conduct an immediate evaluation of probable claim types, provide initial care, and dispatch employees to a medical care facility. These actions can mitigate the size of a company's workers' compensation claims.

The incidence of employee injuries may be impacted by their use of illegal drugs. To see if this is the case, institute a policy of requiring post-accident drug testing. If a test is positive, then the company has grounds for terminating the employee, thereby preventing any future workers' compensation claims from arising.

Other Alternatives

If an employee has a legitimate workers' compensation claim and is unable to perform his job, then consider having him come into the office and perform some less stressful tasks that will not interfere with his recovery from the original injury. This will likely require the participation of a doctor and the cooperation of the injured employee.

If a company is experiencing large numbers of claims in a specific work area, it should consider outsourcing the work performed in that area. While this may seem like an extreme solution, larger claims can be very expensive, and will eventually drive up a company's insurance premiums dramatically. When the alternatives to outsourcing are ongoing insurance payments, extensive staff retraining, and the purchase of safety equipment, outsourcing may not seem like such a bad alternative.

Miscellaneous Perquisites

A company may pay for a variety of additional perquisites, usually at the behest of a senior manager or owner who has a personal interest in it. These miscellaneous items can include season tickets to any number of sporting events, passes to major golf tournaments, a company condominium in a resort area, and so forth. It may be difficult to cancel these items entirely, given the level of management support, but here are some ways to mitigate the cost:

- *Downgrade tickets.* It may be possible to downgrade sports tickets to a development league, rather than premium major league seats. For example, AAA baseball tickets for excellent seats are inexpensive, and the games can be quite competitive.
- *Chargeback expense.* The sales manager is frequently behind the use of event tickets, in order to invite and have quality time with customers. This may be an entirely valid reason, but be sure to charge the cost of these tickets to the sales department so that their total cost is as visible as possible. Better yet, include their cost in the calculation of the sales manager's bonus compensation.
- *Annual review.* Miscellaneous perquisites tend to be buried in general corporate expenses and renewed with minimal management oversight, year after year. To avoid this, compile all such perquisites in a single summary-level document, including the annual cost of each one, and review it with senior management. They may not cancel any of the expenses, but they will at least be aware of them.

Free Benefits

There are a few minor benefits that a company can obtain on behalf of its employees for no cost at all, and so are certainly recommended for that reason. Examples of these benefits are free membership in the local credit union and discounts for employees with local merchants, national retail chains, and car dealerships. There are more of these opportunities available for larger firms, since they can direct hundreds or even thousands of employees toward local businesses.

A "free" benefit is not really free if the company must continually allocate administrative time to it, so consider taking on these benefits only when there is just an initial application to process.

Metrics

The cost reduction possibilities noted in this chapter are so detailed that they do not lend themselves well to any metrics, which are inherently designed to be aggregated at a high level. The first metric noted next is useful for gaining a general impression of the overall level of benefits offered, while the second can be used at a detail level to determine progress toward training goals.

1. *Ratio of benefits to wages.* When engaged in benefits cost reduction, the management team can compare the proportion of benefits to wages for competing firms, to see if the company is still offering benefits that are approximately similar. The calculation is to add together the cost of all discretionary benefit costs, minus the cost of any related deductions from employee pay, and divide this amount by the total of all wages, salaries, and payroll taxes.

    A shortcoming of the ratio is that it assumes all companies being compared have the same ability in wringing the best benefits package from the same expenditure. This is certainly not the case, since a company using the suggestions in this chapter will likely create a better set of benefits than another company spending the same amount of money. Thus, a company with well-managed benefits will likely achieve a lower ratio of benefits to wages than a competitor while still having approximately the same level of benefits.

2. *Proportion of training hours completed by employee.* A company should not merely set a high-level goal of a certain number of hours of training per year for its employees. Some positions require far more training than others, and this may vary based on the experience and prior training of the individual employee. Thus, it is best to track the proportion of training hours that each employee has completed in relation to the total hours contained within her specific training plan.

Summary

It is possible to whittle away at every feature of a benefits program, which can save a company a startling amount of money. However, the result may also be a penurious program that is so skimpy in comparison to the benefits of competitors that a company will find itself with increased turnover and a more difficult time attracting new recruits. Thus, cost cutting in the benefits area should be considered more of a careful tree pruning with scissors than clear-cutting with a chain saw.

Another consideration when dealing with the cutting of benefits is to initially not have any benefits requiring cutting. There is a significant impact on morale when benefits are reduced, whereas there is less likely to be any impact if there is simply no benefit to begin with. This argument does not apply to base-level benefits, such as medical insurance, since employees expect such items to be present in some form. However, more tangential benefits are not necessarily expected. Thus, the *real* analysis is on the front end of a benefit: Does a company need it to begin with? If not, then it is far better never to implement it than to cut it back on some later date.

PART II

Procurement Cost Reduction

CHAPTER 7

Procurement Cost Reduction

Introduction

Procurement is usually a time-consuming and seriously inefficient series of steps for obtaining goods and services. Under the guise of maintaining tight control over purchase transactions, the function is buried under a series of manager approvals and a blizzard of paperwork. This presents two opportunities from the perspective of cost reduction.

1. There is a significant cost associated with the procurement process itself, which can be reduced through process streamlining.
2. Streamlining the procurement process gives the purchasing staff more time for spend analysis, which can yield large additional cost reductions.

This chapter examines the procurement process flow and shows how to shunt many transactions away from the standard procurement process and streamline the remainder. The chapter also deals with the general concepts of supplier consolidation and supplier relations—both of which are crucial to finding the lowest procurement costs that can be maintained over the long term.

A key part of procurement cost reduction is spend management, which involves consolidating all of a company's purchasing information into a single database, enhancing the information stored within it, and combing through it for cost saving opportunities. Spend management is a sufficiently large topic that it is addressed in Chapter 8, "Spend Analysis." The discussion of procurement cost reduction concludes with Chapter 9, "Maintenance, Repairs, and Operations Analysis." This final chapter addresses ways to cut costs in areas where there are a broad array of purchased items, frequently having low purchasing volumes.

Standard Procurement Process Flow

A typical procurement transaction involves many approval steps, takes an inordinate amount of time, and crosses department lines regularly. These factors result in perhaps the most confused paperwork flow of any transaction with which a company must deal.

A purchasing request can begin in any department when an employee fills out a purchase requisition for an item, gets it signed by a manager, and brings it to the purchasing department. That department then adds more information to the requisition, such as the account number to be charged and the supplier to be used. This last item may require considerable time if the purchasing department puts all items over a certain price level out to bid.

The purchasing department then creates a purchase order and has it signed by a manager. These documents are numerically sequenced, and the purchase order stock is usually locked away when not in use. Copies of the purchase order go to the supplier as well as to the accounting and receiving departments, and another copy is filed in the purchasing department (usually with a copy of the requisition).

Once the ordered part has arrived, a receiving clerk inspects it and marks down the receipt in a receiving log. This log provides evidence that the item has been received, and it is needed by the accounting department as backup for paying the supplier; therefore, a copy of the log is sent to the accounting department.

The supplier then sends the company an invoice for the item just received. The payables clerk compares the quantity listed on the invoice to that on the receiving report and purchase order to ensure that payment is being made only for the item ordered and received. The prices, discounts, and terms of shipment are also reviewed to ensure that no overpayments are made. The purchase order, receiving document, and invoice frequently do not match and so must be reconciled. The payables clerk becomes an investigator, checking with the payables department for incorrect terms and prices, the receiving department for the amount received, the shipping company for evidence of shipment, and (most often) with management to see whose in-box currently contains the invoice, which may require multiple layers of management approval. While this investigation goes on, the payables staff may accumulate a large number of unverified supplier invoices, which can build into a considerable backlog of work.

After all documents for a purchase have been reconciled, the payables clerk authorizes payment to the supplier. A check is printed, signed, and mailed. All documents are stapled together, along with a copy of the check remittance, and filed away. A stripped-down version of this payables process, excluding management approvals and document filing, is shown in Exhibit 7.1.

One of the biggest problems with the accounts payable reconciliation process is that the payables clerk is often deluged with conflicting information from many sources. For example, the incidental information on the supplier invoice may not match the information on the purchase order—the tax rate or shipping and handling prices may vary. The purchase order quantity frequently varies from the amount received (and invoiced). The received amount is frequently miscounted or not recorded in the receiving log at all. If damaged goods are returned or there are overages, the supplier must be debited or credited for these variances. Finally, there may be a legal contract associated with the payment that must be consulted for such items as scheduled price increases and methods of delivery. In short, the payables clerk faces a monumental task that must be performed for even the smallest, most insignificant items; in fact, cheaper parts tend not to receive as much attention from the purchasing and receiving personnel as expensive items.

Procurement documents are very likely to become lost because they are transferred across departmental boundaries so frequently. As shown in Exhibit 7.2, departmental transfers occur for all management approvals, purchase requisitions, purchase orders, and receiving logs. Every time such a transfer occurs, it is possible that a document will be delayed or lost.

It is evident that the traditional procurement cycle is an inordinately slow one that requires a massive amount of paper shuffling, delays, and error checking—all of which increase the process cost. And yet the use of purchase orders is considered a key control for many purchasing situations. The solution is to restrict purchase orders to specific types of transactions only while also improving the procurement process flow. We address these solutions in the next sections.

Procurement Cards

An analysis of the dollar value of each procurement transaction will reveal that a disproportionate amount of labor is devoted to very small purchases that are not worth all the approvals, purchase requisitions, purchase orders, supplier invoices, matching, and payment with individual checks. Instead, institute the use of corporate procurement cards. These credit cards allow employees to purchase small-dollar items directly from suppliers. The advantage is that a large number of transactions are reduced to a small

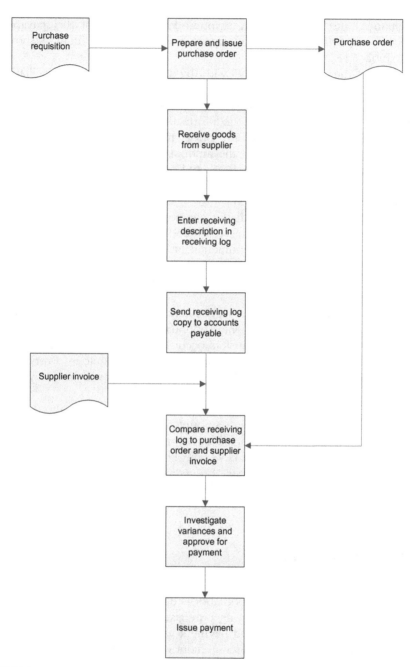

EXHIBIT 7.1 Typical Procurement Process

EXHIBIT 7.2 Payables Paperwork Movement across Departments

	Accounting	Receiving	Purchasing	Legal	Management
Purchase requisition	√		√		√
Purchase order	√	√	√		√
Invoice	√				√
Receiving log	√	√			
Supplier debits/ credits	√	√			
Contract information	√		√	√	

number of monthly credit card payments. A typical purchasing and payables transaction costs about $30 to process; by switching to corporate credit cards, the cost per transaction drops to less than $1. Also, some procurement cards include a cash-back feature, where the return payment increases with the volume of usage; thus, a cost reduction occurs simply by shifting more purchases to procurement cards.

Example

The Black Bag Luggage Company's controller, Mr. Tumi, wants to introduce corporate purchasing cards and needs to present a cost/benefit analysis to the purchasing manager. Mr. Tumi finds that the annual fee of each of 20 corporate purchasing cards is $20. He also conducts an analysis of all company purchases and finds that 20 percent of all purchase orders are for purchases of less than $100, with an average purchase price of $52. Of those purchases, 75 percent are from five local supply companies, all of which accept credit cards as payment for goods. The company issued 28,000 purchase orders in the previous year, totaling $33,600,000. An activity-based costing analysis has shown that the average purchase order, including all related activities, requires $30 to complete. A local internal auditor trade association has conducted a confidential survey of employee theft using corporate purchasing cards and concluded that improper use increased the cost of items purchased with corporate purchasing cards by 0.5 percent. Is it worthwhile to use corporate purchasing cards? The analysis is shown next.

The following table is part of the feature box.

Continued

Cost of Using Corporate Purchasing Cards

Number of corporate purchasing cards	20
Annual fee per card	× $20
Total annual fee for cards	$400
No. of purchase orders	28,000
Percentage under $100	× 20%
No. of purchase orders under $100	5,600
Percentage of under-$100 purchase orders (POs) allowing credit	× 75%
No. of under-$100 POs allowing credit	4,200
Average amount of under-$100 POs	× $52
Amount of POs converted to credit cards	$218,400
Expected percentage of improper credit purchases	× .5%
Total amount of improper credit purchases	$1,092
Total cost of using corporate purchase cards	$1,492

Cost of Not Using Corporate Purchasing Cards

No. of POs	28,000
Percentage under $100	× 20%
No. of POs under $100	5,600
Cost to process a PO	× $30
Total cost to process under-$100 POs	$168,000

The analysis reveals that the costs associated with using corporate purchasing cards are minuscule compared to the savings resulting from their use. Based on the example, the conversion would pay for itself in less than three days.

Evaluated Receipts System

The most advanced level of procurement efficiency is to pay suppliers based on production records. This system is called *evaluated receipts*. The key item here is to avoid the review by receiving personnel of incoming shipments. Instead, the parts are moved directly to the manufacturing area, where they are used immediately. Then the amount of each part (as listed on the bill of materials) is multiplied by the number of products completed to arrive at the total number of parts the company has received from the supplier. This unit total is then multiplied by the cost per unit, as noted in the purchase order, thus arriving at a total amount to pay the supplier. Of course, the system must also include reporting for items damaged during production, so that the supplier is paid for these items as well. The use of payments based on production records is possible only in a well-run just-in-time (JIT) manufacturing system, because the payment scheme will not work unless these factors are present:

- *Only enough parts are delivered to manufacture the product.* If excess parts are delivered, additional accounting is required to determine the number of units for which to pay the supplier; in this case, it would be easier to determine from purchase order information than from production records.
- *Production is rapid.* If it takes an inordinate amount of time to manufacture a product, the supplier must wait too long for payment, since payments are based on finished products.
- *Only one supplier supplies each part.* It is very difficult to pay suppliers when more than one supplies the same part. When payments are determined based on the parts included in a finished product, there is no way to tell which supplier delivered an included part.
- *The bills of material are totally accurate.* If they are not, suppliers will not be paid for the correct quantity of parts delivered.
- *Product changes are minimal.* If the quantity of a part used in the product is constantly changed because of design iterations, it is very difficult to determine the correct number of parts for which to pay the supplier.
- *Bulk purchases are not needed.* If bulk purchases are required for key items that can be procured only in volume, because of pricing, packaging, distances traveled, and so forth, then they must be paid for by some other means than production records, since it may be some time before the company would otherwise issue payment.

An evaluated receipts system is shown in Exhibit 7.3.

Example

The chief financial officer (CFO) of the Shine Bright Lamp Company is interested in paying suppliers from the information contained in the company's production records rather than from supplier invoices. The CFO's assistant, Mr. Dunwoody, is asked to construct a cost/benefit analysis of the project. He notes that one-half of all payments based on supplier invoices could be switched to payments based on production records. This would allow the company to cut its accounts payable department in half. The department has a staff of six, who are paid an average of $35,000 each. In addition, Mr. Dunwoody finds that the programming cost of paying from production records is substantial—four programmers will be required to design, create, and test the needed software over a period of six months. The company's average rate of pay for programmers is $82,000. Also, the 18 key suppliers that will be affected by this change must be visited and informed of the new

Continued

payment method. The company will send two programmers to the supplier locations to discuss the changes in their systems that will be required. Those two people must visit suppliers full-time for six months. Also, the purchasing manager will visit all 18 companies in advance during a one-month road trip to prepare the suppliers for the change. The purchasing manager earns $90,000 per year. Total travel costs for the programmers and purchasing manager will be $60,000. Finally, the company's bills of material (BOMs) are not yet accurate enough, so an engineer must be hired who will review the BOMs on a continuing basis. The salary of the engineer is expected to be $70,000. Should this project be implemented? The analysis is shown next.

The following table is part of the feature box.

Cost of Payment from Production Records

Cost/year of programmer	$82,000
No. of programmers	× 6
Six months' work	× .50
Total programming cost	$246,000
Cost/year of purchasing manager	$90,000
One month's work	× 8.3%
Total purchasing manager cost	$7,470
Total travel cost	+ $60,000
BOM engineer salary	±$70,000
Total implementation cost	$383,470

Benefit of Payment from Production Records

Cost/year of payables clerk	$35,000
Clerical positions eliminated	× 3
Total savings	$105,000

It is evident from the preceding information that the payback period for this project would be too long for many companies. The economics of the case study would have been better if a larger number of payables clerks were made redundant (which is why this system is usually implemented only by large companies) or if a just-in-time manufacturing system were already in place. With a just-in-time system, BOMs are already extremely accurate, and there are fewer suppliers. For example, if there were half the number of suppliers and no need for an extra BOM engineer, the project cost would have dropped by about $100,000. In short, efficient manufacturing systems make it much easier to justify an evaluated receipts system.

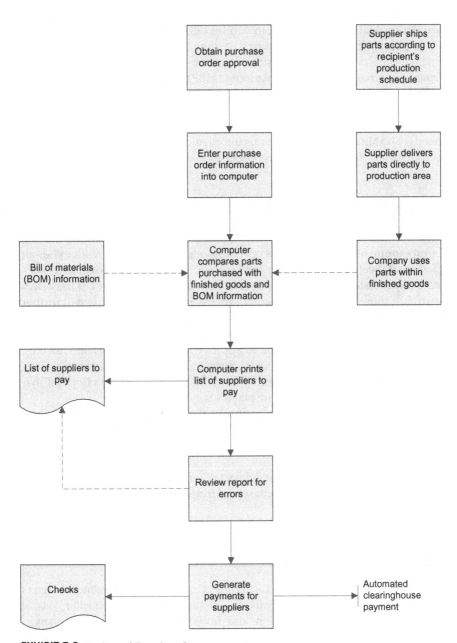

EXHIBIT 7.3 Evaluated Receipts System

An evaluated receipts system can be difficult to install, given the need for a preexisting JIT manufacturing system. An alternative that eliminates manual purchase order processing is to issue purchase orders automatically from a material requirements planning (MRP) system. Simply described, an MRP system compares the production schedule to on-hand inventory balances, subtracts out any inventory that is reserved for other uses, and generates a list of materials that must be purchased for future scheduled production needs. The MRP system can use this information to generate purchase orders automatically and can even send them electronically to suppliers.

Additional Procurement Process Flow Changes

Thus far, we have streamlined small-dollar purchases by instituting the use of procurement cards as well as cost of goods sold purchases with either an evaluated receipts system or an MRP system. These two improvements substantially reduce the amount of paperwork that the purchasing staff must deal with, but there are three additional process improvements that will further reduce the cost of procurement and subsequent payment processing:

1. There is no need for anyone to approve a purchase requisition, as long as there is a strong downstream approval process for purchase orders.
2. There is no need for anyone to formally review and sign checks if that same approval process is in place for purchase orders.
3. There is no need for a formal approval of a supplier's invoice, as long as the invoice references a purchase order that has already been approved.

Thus, we eliminate the time delays built into three separate approvals— but this works only if the purchase order approval control is robust.

Example

A reengineering team at A.L. Skrupp Corp. has recommended that purchase requisition approvals be eliminated. The controller, Ms. Boldrup, reviews the situation and finds that the average company manager can review, sign, and forward a purchase requisition in two minutes. The average time required to find a manager who can sign the requisition is one day. Discussions with a sampling of company managers reveal that they typically reject 2 percent of all purchase requisitions sent to them for approval. They are later called on to sign off on completed purchase orders that contain the same information. The somewhat annoyed purchasing manager informs Ms. Boldrup that it takes 45 minutes of purchasing department time whenever it converts a purchase requisition into a purchase order; if an unapproved requisition is later rejected in purchase order form by a manager, then that is a waste of 45 minutes of purchasing time. The average company buyer earns $22.00 per hour. The average company manager earns $40 per hour. The purchasing department receives 82,500 purchase requisitions per year. Should the A.L. Skrupp Corporation eliminate manager sign-offs on purchase requisitions? The analysis is presented next.

The following table is part of the feature box.

Cost of Retaining Purchase Requisition Approvals

Cost/hour of manager	$40
Minutes/hour	/ 60
Cost/minute of manager	$0.67
Time to review requisition	× 2 min.
Cost/requisitions of management review	$1.34
No. of requisitions per year	82,500
Total cost of management review	$110,550

Cost of Eliminating Purchase Requisition Approvals

No. of requisitions approved/year	82,500
Percentage of requisitions not approved	× 2%
No. of requisitions not approved	1,650
Time to create purchase order	× .75 hr
Total time to create purchase orders	1691,238 hrs
Cost/hour of buyer	$22.00
Total cost of creating unneeded POs	$27,236

The analysis reveals that reviewing all purchase requisitions is costing the company a startling amount of management time, which is four times more expensive than the added cost to the purchasing department caused by extra requisitions being converted into purchase orders. An objection to this analysis is that the company does not actually realize any cost savings, since the managers will still be paid by the company, while the purchasing department may have to add a buyer to handle the extra purchase requisitions. However, this practice keeps some clerical work away from the management group, which will therefore have more time for value-added activities.

Another string of procurement improvements comes from the treatment of supplier invoices. If a purchase order was already issued that authorizes the invoice, then the company should pay from the PO rather than the invoice. The receiving staff logs in the quantity received, the computer system multiplies the number of units received times the unit cost listed in the PO, and it issues a payment. This approach works best if the supplier's sales tax information is included in the PO, so that the system can automatically generate sales tax information. By taking this approach, a company can eliminate the supplier invoice, except in cases where there is no supporting PO.

Example

In an effort to cut costs, the CFO of Daisy Baby Foods wants to start paying suppliers from purchase orders rather than from supplier invoices. As the controller, you are assigned the task of creating a cost/ benefit analysis. You find that the requirements definition, programming, testing, and documentation work related to the changeover will require the time of three programmers for half a year. The average programmer is paid $68,000. In addition, the mailing and staff costs associated with notifying key suppliers of the changeover will be $25,000. Training time for the staff that will be using the new system will cost about $17,000. You also estimate that two accounts payable clerks will be needed even after the new system is installed because there will still be a limited number of supplier invoices arriving that do not have related POs; in addition, the clerks must resolve payment disputes with suppliers, which will occur no matter what payment method is used. Despite these issues, the new system should allow the company to reduce the accounts payable department by four positions; the average salary of those positions is $35,000. Is this a cost-effective project? The analysis is presented next.

The following table is part of the feature box.

Cost to Implement a Payment System Based on Purchase Orders	
Cost/year per programmer	$68,000
No. of programmers required	× 3
Six months' work	× .50
Total programming cost	$102,000
Mailing and notification cost	+ $25,000
Training cost	± $17,000
Total implementation cost	$144,000

Cost Reductions with New System

Cost/year of payables clerk	$35,000
Clerical positions eliminated	× 4
Total salary-related savings	$140,000

The one-time cost to install the purchase order–based payment system is $144,000 versus annual savings of $140,000, which is a payback of just over one year.

The volume of orders running through the procurement process can also be reduced by standardizing orders for commonly purchased items. This can be achieved with a standard order form or an electronic store. Employees enter their orders by either means, and the purchasing staff forwards the orders directly to a preferred supplier after reviewing them for excessive quantities. Since these types of orders involve moderate dollar amounts but very large transaction volumes, the risk of losing large amounts of money with improper orders is minimal, and the volume of payables transactions is noticeably reduced.

Supplier Consolidation

Once the purchasing process has been streamlined, as was described in the preceding sections, the next step is to pursue cost reduction activities. A significant cost reduction technique is to reduce the number of suppliers with which a company does business. By concentrating its orders with a smaller number of suppliers, it can use higher purchasing volume to negotiate price reductions, rebates, and discounts. This concept is addressed in more detail in Chapters 8 and 9. The following subtopics address various supplier consolidation issues at a general level.

Bottom 10 Percent

Besides concentrating order volume, another reason to consolidate suppliers is to eliminate the worst-performing ones. These are the suppliers that deliver the wrong items late and with low quality. Even if these suppliers offer what appear to be rock-bottom prices, the total cost of doing business with them is much higher, because the company is endlessly dealing with receiving inspections, product returns, and the processing of credits.

Consequently, having a separate program to identify and eliminate a company's lowest-rated suppliers can also reduce costs.

This approach calls for the creation of a supplier report card system, where suppliers are rated based on a variety of factors. The information should be summarized and tracked on a trend line and reported both to management and the suppliers. If a supplier has been warned about poor performance and does not improve, then the company should withdraw its business entirely and place the offending supplier on a no-buy list.

Eliminating a large number of suppliers at once is a difficult task (see the next section, "Risk of Switching"). To make it more manageable, the purchasing staff should identify the bottom 10 percent of its supplier base and constantly monitor them to see which ones should be replaced. The number actually replaced will be controlled by the company's ability to gradually shift business to other suppliers, which may involve as little as 1 percent of all suppliers in a single year.

Risk of Switching

Consolidating orders with a small number of suppliers can certainly reduce costs. However, switching from an existing supplier to an entirely new one is a different matter entirely. In that case, the company switches from the certainty of the existing supplier's performance (whether it is good or bad) to the complete uncertainty of a new one. In addition, the company may need new procedures for dealing with the new supplier as well as the construction of a new performance scoring system and a review of the supplier by the company's industrial engineering team regarding product quality issues. In short, switching to an entirely new supplier can be perilous; the purchasing staff should handle only a small number of such switches at a time, so that it is not overwhelmed if a new supplier relationship falls apart.

Total Cost Analysis

When the purchasing staff considers switching to a new supplier or consolidating its purchases with an existing one, it cannot evaluate the supplier based solely on its quoted price. Instead, it must also consider the *total acquisition cost*, which can in some cases exceed a product's initial price. The total acquisition cost includes these items:

- *Material.* The list price of the item being bought, less any rebates or discounts.
- *Freight.* The cost of shipping from the supplier to the company.

- *Packaging.* The company may specify special packaging, such as for quantities that differ from the supplier's standards and for which the supplier charges an extra fee.
- *Tooling.* If the supplier had to acquire special tooling in order to manufacture parts for the company, such as an injection mold, then it will charge through this cost, either as a lump sum or amortized over some predetermined unit volume.
- *Setup.* If the setup for a production run is unusually lengthy or involves scrap, then the supplier may charge through the cost of the setup.
- *Warranty.* If the product being purchased is to be retained by the company for a lengthy period of time, it may have to buy a warranty extension from the supplier.
- *Inventory.* If there are long delays between when a company orders goods and when it receives them, then it must maintain a safety stock on hand to guard against stock-out conditions and support the cost of funds needed to maintain this stock.
- *Payment terms.* If the supplier insists on rapid payment terms and the company's own customers have longer payment terms, then the company must support the cost of funds for the period between when it pays the supplier and it is paid by its customers.
- *Currency used.* If supplier payments are to be made in a different currency from the company's home currency, then it must pay for a foreign exchange transaction and may also need to pay for a hedge, to guard against any unfavorable changes in the exchange rate prior to the scheduled payment date.

These costs are only the ones directly associated with a product. In addition, there may be overhead costs related to dealing with a specific supplier (see "Sourcing Distance" later in the chapter), which can be allocated to all products purchased from that supplier.

Product Family Consolidation

A particularly opportune prospect for consolidation is when a company is buying materials within the same product family from several different suppliers. If all of these materials are consolidated with a single supplier that is already providing some of them to the company, there is a greater likelihood of cost savings for the supplier, which presumably can be passed along to the company. The reason for the cost savings is that the supplier can use the same materials and processes to construct the necessary components and so has a minimal learning curve to ramp up its production.

Supplier Relations

If a company simply imposes a price reduction on a supplier, then the supplier's profits are reduced, which it may counteract by eventually reducing the quality of its products. Consequently, a company needs to find ways to reduce its purchased costs that retain the financial viability of its suppliers. This section addresses several supplier relations techniques that can yield benefits to both sides.

Access to Demand Records

A supplier does not know which items its customers will order, or the timing or quantities of their orders. Instead, it engages in sales forecasting, which may not be very accurate, and it likely has excess inventory stocks because of its reliance on those forecasts. This may result in inventory write-offs due to obsolescence.

A company can eliminate some of these costs for a supplier by giving it direct access to the company's production planning database. The supplier can then see *exactly* what the company needs to order from it over the short term and can insert this highly accurate information into its own forecasting system. The net result to the supplier should be a reduction in its inventory investment and reduced obsolescence costs.

Structure of Price Reductions

If a company demands price reductions from a supplier in exchange for an increased volume of orders, the supplier can grant either a price reduction or a rebate. The safest type of price reduction from the perspective of the supplier is to enforce its list price for all products, but to issue rebates once a company achieves various order volume levels. By doing so, the supplier does not put itself at risk of granting a lower price and then not having the company deliver the order volumes that it had initially promised. This should be acceptable to the company, though it should also monitor its order volumes to ensure that it receives rebates in a timely manner.

Scheduled Price Reductions

A company may attempt to insert a series of scheduled price reductions into longer-term contracts with its suppliers. While this is great for the company, it leaves suppliers with an obligation to somehow reduce their costs in order to still earn a profit. Otherwise, the company is merely robbing the supplier's profits and will likely have a financially weakened supplier by the end of the contract period. If the company wants these price reductions, then it should commit its industrial engineers to working jointly with their counterparts at the supplier to reduce costs out of the products being supplied to the company.

Process Reviews

A company can have review sessions with its major suppliers to examine the testing and inspection activities that the suppliers impose on products shipped to the company. If the company is also testing and inspecting the same products, then there is an opportunity to eliminate some duplication. Either the supplier can reduce its activities in this area (and reduce its prices to the company accordingly) or the company can eliminate the duplication and save labor in-house.

A company can even assist its suppliers with their subtier of suppliers, leveraging volume with a smaller number of suppliers, sharing forecasts, and so forth. Even if there is no specific agreement to share the resulting cost reductions with the company, assisting at this level creates an economically more robust supplier, which, one hopes, makes it a more reliable and effective business partner.

Solicit Advice

The typical relationship between a company and its suppliers is of the command-and-control variety, where the company does the telling. However, it can try the reverse approach and do some asking instead. Specifically, it can share with suppliers its manufacturing and assembly instructions for each product and ask if they have any design changes that can improve on the company's instructions. This approach implies that good relations exist between the parties, so that suppliers will feel like they are reasonably assured of receiving continuing orders from the company if they share their expertise. The company gains, because it can plumb the special expertise of its suppliers.

Key Account Manager

If a company does a significant volume of business with a supplier, then the purchasing manager should ask the supplier to designate one of its employees to be a key account manager for the company. This key account manager will be rated by the supplier based on his ability to retain the company's business and so will be more likely to see matters from the company's perspective—perhaps to the extent of taking the company's side in requesting cost reductions. This person can also assist in presenting the supplier's viewpoint to the company, and so in effect acts as an ambassador in both directions.

Payment Options

If a company has a larger amount of available funding than its suppliers, it can offer faster payment to them in exchange for price discounts. This may work well for suppliers, if the discount requested by the company is lower than their borrowing costs. In some cases, a supplier cannot obtain any funding, which makes this a superb opportunity for both parties.

An alternative is supply chain financing. Under this solution, a company sends its approved payables list to its bank, specifying the dates on which invoice payments are to be made. The bank makes these payments on behalf of the company. However, in addition to this basic payables function, the bank also contacts the company's suppliers with an offer of early payment, in exchange for a financing charge for the period until maturity. If a supplier agrees with this arrangement and signs a receivables sale contract, then the bank delivers payment from its own funds to the supplier, less its fee. Once the company's payment dates are reached, the bank removes the funds from the company's account, transferring some of the cash to those customers electing to be paid on the prearrangement settlement date and transferring the remaining funds to its own account to pay for those invoices that it paid early to suppliers at a discount.

This arrangement works very well for suppliers, since they may be in need of early settlement. In addition, they receive a much higher percentage of invoice face value than would be the case if they opted for a factoring arrangement with a third party, where 80 percent of the invoice is typically the maximum amount that will be advanced. Also, the amount of the discount offered by the bank may be quite small (much less than if the supplier were offering an early payment discount), if the company is a large and well-funded entity having excellent credit. Finally, the arrangement is usually nonrecourse for the supplier, since the arrangement with the bank is structured as a receivables assignment.

Supply chain financing is less useful when payment terms are relatively short, since there is not much benefit for suppliers in being paid just a few days early. However, it is an excellent tool when standard payment terms are quite long.

Summary

Successful cost reduction involves a great deal of cooperation between a company and its suppliers—a company cannot simply impose price reductions without paying the price of high supplier turnover, weakened suppliers, and possibly lower product quality. Instead, the two parties need to share information and swap advice as well as mutually arrive at pricing structures and financing arrangements that fit the needs of both parties.

Additional Cost Reduction Considerations

The next issues should be considered when dealing with suppliers in a variety of situations—at long distance, for long-term contracts, for reverse auctions, and for performance-based fee structures.

Sourcing Distance

There has been a general trend for years to shift manufacturing overseas, because of the extraordinarily low labor costs in other parts of the world. While the cost reductions appear to be massive, sourcing overseas also requires new costs to manage suppliers, transport goods back to the company's markets, and travel to and from supplier locations. In addition, transit times are longer because of the greatly extended length of the supplier pipeline, so a company must invest in the extra inventory that is continually in transit. Further, restocking times are longer, which calls for additional safety stock. Thus, sourcing in a distant location will typically add between 20 and 30 percent to the cost of a product, before deducting the reduced cost of labor in that location.

Supplier Contract Duration

In some industries, such as telecommunications, there is a long-run trend toward lower costs, so suppliers constantly try to get their customers to sign up for long-term contracts; this gives the suppliers an increasing profit percentage over the course of the contracts, as revenues hold firm while costs decline. This situation is not the case in all industries, but where there is a clear declining cost trend, a company would be well advised to opt for short-term contracts. By doing so, it can easily switch suppliers to take advantage of the cost decline.

Reverse Auctions

A company's purchasing staff uses reverse auctions to get suppliers to compete for its business, with the lowest bidders winning. (This concept is the reverse of a normal auction, where bidders drive the price *up*.) A company wanting to engage in a reverse auction usually contracts with a market maker that locates new suppliers, organizes the auction using a request for quote, and provides auction information back to the company. During the auction period, bidding suppliers log onto an auction site and input their quotes to provide the requested goods or services.

To start using reverse auctions, it is best to start with a few low-risk commodities that the purchasing staff is comfortable with switching around among suppliers. It may also be acceptable to start with those commodities that are not currently being actively managed, since there are more likely to be unrealized savings available in these areas. If the results of these auctions are good, then the purchasing staff can gradually roll out the concept to include other products for which a number of competing alternatives are available.

In order to keep a number of suppliers interested in bidding on an ongoing basis, a company needs to spread around its orders (unless one supplier is being *extremely* aggressive on pricing). By doing so, there will be a reasonable pool of bidders in the future that keep the auctions competitive.

The reverse auction process may at first seem to reduce costs, but it introduces some new costs and risks that can offset the savings. For example, the company may need to spend time and money inspecting the first products shipped to it by a new winning bidder, to ensure that they meet the company's acceptance criteria. Also, the company runs the risk that the new supplier will not meet delivery or quality standards, which may result in a scramble to shift back to the former supplier on very short notice.

Reverse auctions do not work well when non-price attributes (such as tight tolerances or low failure rates) are critical to the buying decision. When this is the case, a company may find that it accepts the *highest* bid, since the winning bidder scored best on the alternative characteristics. Because reverse auctions are based on prices, they are clearly not a suitable forum for these types of products.

Percentage Fees

In some industries, such as advertising and investment banking, it has become the norm to charge clients based on a percentage, rather than for hours worked. For example, an advertising agency may bill its clients a percentage of their television advertising, while an investment banker charges a percentage of the funding procured for a client. These fee structures can yield inordinately high payments and so should be replaced with hourly or fixed fees where possible.

However, percentage fees cannot be avoided in some cases. For example, an investment banker is very unlikely to work for an hourly rate.

The best alternative in such a case is to allow a graduated success fee, so that the supplier makes more money if the company makes more money. For example, an investment banker may agree to a 4 percent fee for all funds raised below $10 million, a 6 percent fee for the next $10 million, and an 8 percent fee for all funds raised above $20 million.

Metrics

The first two of the next metrics are designed to monitor a company's use of procurement cards, which are critical for reducing the volume of purchase orders that are issued. The third metric shows the volume of payments being processed through an evaluated receipts system, and could easily be converted to track orders being generated through an MRP system; in either case, the metric is useful for showing the amount of cost of goods sold that is not being routed through the purchasing staff. The final metric monitors the volume of a company's remaining expenditures that are authorized with purchase orders.

1. *Proportion of procurement card usage.* Using procurement cards reduces the amount of paperwork required of the purchasing staff. The target procurement card usage should be close to 100 percent for all purchasing transactions under $100 (though a higher cutoff figure can be used). The calculation is to divide the number of credit card purchasing transactions by the total number of purchasing transactions below the designated cutoff limit.

2. *Percentage of purchase orders below a minimum value.* A company should endeavor to purchase low-dollar items without purchase orders (usually with procurement cards or standard order forms), thereby reducing the workload of the purchasing, receiving, and payables departments. A company should create a threshold below which no purchase orders should be issued. Any such issuances can be reported by the computer system and reviewed periodically by management.

3. *Percentage of total payments from evaluated receipts.* If a company is moving to payments based on completed production information, then a key performance measure is the percentage of total payments made from production records. When backed up by a detailed report that lists the suppliers not paid in this manner, this information can be used by management to target additional suppliers to be paid under this system.

4. *Percentage of payments with purchase orders.* If a company is trying to move in the direction of paying suppliers from POs instead of from supplier invoices, then this is the accounts payable measure to track.

The calculation is to summarize the total number of payments per month and divide that number into the number of payments that had a PO number in the payment record. The measure to strive for is 100 percent of all payments from a PO (with the exception of purchasing cards).

Summary

This chapter has addressed a number of basic issues with procurement cost reduction—of which process analysis, supplier consolidation, and supplier relations are crucial components. In the next two chapters, we address two types of spend analysis, which is designed purely for the examination of a company's expenditures with the intent of reducing expenses. As a group, these three chapters reveal the tremendous extent of potential cost reduction in the procurement field.

CHAPTER 8

Spend Analysis

Introduction

Spend analysis is the process of organizing procurement information by suppliers and commodities and then using this information to achieve volume discounts and rebates with a reduced number of suppliers. While this process may sound simple, it most assuredly is not. A company must create and enhance a spend database as the source of its spend analysis and then gradually concentrate its ordering volume with a select group of suppliers; this is followed by continual efforts to monitor the company's compliance with the new system. This lengthy process can result in major cost reductions and is well worth the effort.

This chapter describes the steps required to create a spend database, the types of spend analysis that are used to create cost reductions, the reports that can assist in the process, the types of compliance actions needed for long-term control, and the types of spend management systems now available.

Spend Database

The spend database is at the core of spend analysis. This database is a highly organized cluster of files containing key information about *what* a company buys, *how much* it spends, and *whom* it buys from. A properly organized database makes successful spend analysis possible.

Interfaces

The spend database can be quite difficult to construct. It needs input feeds from the procurement systems of every company subsidiary, which should be updated on at least a quarterly basis. By aggregating all of this purchasing information, a company can see cost-saving opportunities at the corporate level that would not have been present at the subsidiary level.

Information Enhancement

The newly gathered information must be *cleansed* and *enriched*. *Cleansing* is improving on and correcting the information already contained within a database, while *enrichment* is adding new information to the database. As an example of cleansing, the same supplier may be recorded under a slightly different name in the feeds coming from different subsidiaries, such as International Business Machines, IBM, and I.B.M. When this happens, it is difficult to determine the amount of a company's total spend with a specific supplier. To fix the problem, the spend database should link all of the name variations for a single supplier to a single parent-level supplier name. For example, IBM could be used as the parent supplier name, and I.B.M. and International Business Machines are linked to it.

A considerable amount of cleansing may be required for item descriptions. An identical item listed in the item master records of five subsidiaries can easily have five wildly different descriptions, and it can be very difficult to match them. One way to correct the situation is to load supplier part numbers and part descriptions into the spend database, so that a part number arriving through a feed from a subsidiary will automatically pull in the correct part description. Doing this calls for a considerable amount of work and ongoing updating, but it is needed for aggregating the use of specific components.

Part of the database enrichment process includes adding commodity codes to each purchase. A commodity code is valuable because it assigns a general spend category to a supplier. The company can aggregate purchase dollars for each commodity code to see where it is spending the bulk of its money and use this information to negotiate volume purchase discounts with suppliers. Some subsidiaries may already record a commodity code in their purchasing records, but the codes may be incorrect or not detailed enough. Another problem is that subsidiaries may use different commodity code systems—either internal, home-grown varieties or an industry standard, such as the United Nations Standard Products and Services Code (UNSPSC) or the North American Industry Classification System (NAICS). If different subsidiaries use different commodity codes, then either the commodity codes arriving at the spend database must be mapped to a standard commodity code or the codes located in the originating procurement databases must be changed to match the company-standard code.

The commodity codes used may evolve over time to include entirely new commodities or subcodes to address differences among commodities.

If so, it is best to adopt a new version of an industry standard commodity code rather than an in-house code that will require continual updating, and to verify that the codes coming from subsidiaries are now mapping to the revised commodity codes.

It may also be useful to enrich the spend database with a supplier credit rating. This information is periodically updated through an input feed from a third-party credit rating agency, such as Dun & Bradstreet or Experian. The spend analysis system then issues reports containing just those suppliers whose credit ratings indicate that they are in financial difficulty, which the company uses to resource with different suppliers.

Another possible enrichment is to periodically update the spend database with the company's in-house supplier ratings. These supplier ratings are useful for steering more work toward those suppliers that consistently are rated highly on such issues as quality and on-time performance.

Given the massive size of a spend database, it would be cost prohibitive to cleanse and enhance information manually. Instead, the upgrades just noted should be accomplished to the greatest extent possible with automated systems. However, these systems will periodically insert the wrong commodity code or other information. Consequently, the spend analysis team should enlist the services of an experienced group of procurement staff who can suggest alterations to the information that appears to be incorrect. By continually improving database accuracy, the analysis team can classify information more correctly and thereby generate greater savings.

Report Writing

A fully loaded spend database is not usable unless it has an excellent report writing package, since the ability to drill down through the data is of paramount importance to spend management. Consequently, the database should be equipped with a report writer that can report on information at multiple levels, including by subsidiary, commodity code, and geographic region. It should also be able to report all of this information on a timeline, so that analysts can detect changes in spend. Sample reports are shown later in the "Spend Analysis Reports" section.

Summary

In summary, the spend database can be quite time consuming and expensive to construct. It calls for a considerable amount of database interface work and potentially endless amounts of cleansing and enrichment. However, the intent of spend analysis is to *save* money, so the project manager must exercise a considerable amount of judgment in determining how much effort to initially put into the database before initiating cost reduction activities. This concept is addressed further in the "Spend Analysis Rollout" section.

Spend Analysis

With the spend database in hand, a company can pursue a variety of strategies for concentrating its expenditures to take advantage of volume discounts and rebates. These cost reductions do not have to apply to just *direct spend*, which is the cost of goods sold. Cost reductions can also be applied to *indirect spend*, which encompasses all of the supporting materials and services needed by a company, such as utilities, supplies, advertising, travel, and insurance.

The primary spend analysis strategy is to consolidate purchases in order to increase buying volume with a smaller number of suppliers. It is also possible to use the information to standardize on a smaller number of components as well as to monitor compliance with supplier contracts. These topics and more are addressed within this section.

Supplier Fragmentation

Across a multisubsidiary company, there are bound to be too many suppliers. One subsidiary might use five suppliers to provide a specific commodity, while another supplier also uses five suppliers—but the two subsidiaries share only one supplier. This type of supplier fragmentation represents an excellent opportunity for consolidating business with a much smaller number of preferred suppliers and then extracting volume discounts or rebates from these suppliers in exchange for the extra business. Without the spend database, there would be no way to centralize sufficient information to determine the level of supplier fragmentation.

A good way to begin the supplier centralization process is to first determine the company's top five commodities by dollar value of spend and then determine the level of supplier fragmentation within these commodities. Supplier fragmentation can be determined by the volume of purchases from unapproved suppliers, by the volume of purchases not involving purchase orders, or simply by the total number of suppliers with which the company has done business over the past year. By concentrating on these fragmented areas, a company can focus its efforts on consolidating the largest-dollar opportunities first, which will likely yield the most savings from supplier consolidation.

A variation on supplier centralization is to base consolidation activities on the number of available suppliers and the dollar volume of goods

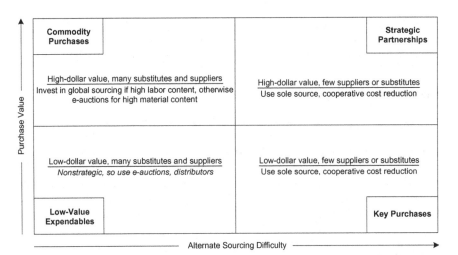

EXHIBIT 8.1 Cost Reduction Strategy Matrix

purchased. If there are few suppliers available, then single-sourcing in exchange for a cooperative approach to cost reduction may be the only cost reduction strategy. However, if there are many suppliers available and the dollar volume of purchased quantities is high, then a company can engage in a global search for the lowest-cost provider or reverse auctions to bid down prices. If there are many suppliers but dollar volumes are low, then global sourcing is probably not cost effective, but sourcing through a single distributor may yield the lowest overall cost. (See Exhibit 8.1.)

If a company elects to follow a global sourcing strategy, this will yield the greatest cost reductions if products have a very high labor content; international suppliers typically have access to labor rates far below those in the domestic market. Global sourcing does not work as well for raw materials, since international suppliers probably have no better access to low-cost raw materials than do domestic suppliers (and must incur higher freight costs to deliver to the company).

The result of a supplier consolidation process should be a small number of preferred suppliers to whom a company directs a large volume of its spend. These suppliers will have been selected for a combination of their financial status, delivery timeliness, product or service quality, and prices.

As a company gradually shifts its business toward its preferred suppliers, its spend analysis will focus on the remaining nonpreferred suppliers. This will be a substantial list, but one toward which an ever-shrinking proportion of the company's spend is directed. The most cost-effective approach is to continually review the highest-dollar commodities that have not yet been addressed, pick a preferred supplier within each one, and direct the bulk of the business in that commodity to that supplier.

Discount Tracking

The main point of concentrating purchases with a small number of suppliers is to earn volume discounts from them. However, the company should not rely on suppliers to calculate discounts and rebates, since they have no particular incentive for doing so. Instead, the company should closely monitor its spending levels by supplier so that it can determine specifically when spending levels have reached the trigger points where the company is entitled to lower prices or rebates.

Parts Duplication

Spend analysis also highlights problems with parts duplication. This issue arises when different subsidiaries use slightly different versions of the same parts; it can also arise within a single subsidiary. If the parts description fields in the spend database have been normalized so that descriptions are comparable, the spend analysis team can spot opportunities for standardizing on a smaller number of parts. If essentially the same part is coming from different suppliers, then immediate consolidation of parts with a single supplier is possible. However, this analysis may also call for a much longer-term solution, which is designing parts standardization into new versions of the company's products. In the latter case, cost savings may take years to realize.

Parts duplication analysis tends to be a distant second effort behind supplier consolidation, but it can provide significant savings. For example, if a smaller firm can standardize its parts, it can order the remaining parts in greater volumes; its cost per unit may therefore decline to the point where it can effectively compete on price against a much larger competitor that has not taken advantage of parts standardization. This effect comes from buying large quantities of a smaller number of items.

Other

Several lesser spend analyses can result in modest cost reductions. For example, the database can summarize the number of separate payments being made to each supplier from all of the company's various locations on a monthly basis. If a company were to centralize all of its supplier payments into a payment factory, it could make a single payment per month to each supplier, thereby eliminating the expense associated with all of the additional payments that would otherwise be made—either by electronic means or by check.

Another possibility is to use the spend database to locate those suppliers that are constantly issuing large numbers of credits to the company. This is a prime indicator of multiple supplier problems, such as low-quality or damaged deliveries, and can be used during the supplier consolidation process to determine which suppliers should be dropped.

Spend Analysis Compliance

The end result of spend analysis is a much greater concentration of a company's spend with a much smaller number of preferred suppliers. However, given the multitude of locations from which a large corporate can initiate purchases, and its ever-changing needs, it can be quite difficult to keep this small and select supplier base from rapidly expanding again, thereby diluting the effort of the original spend analysis. There are a number of ways to improve compliance with a completed spend analysis project, which are described in the next subsections.

Contracts Database The foundation for spend analysis compliance is to construct a database containing all contracts that the company has entered into with its approved suppliers. This database is used to match subsequent purchasing information against what should have been purchased through these key suppliers, and the terms at which items were purchased from them. Key fields to be included in the contracts database are:

Contract identification number	Contract name
Contract start date	Contract expiration date
Unit price	Contractual quantity at
	specified unit price
Discounts	Discount thresholds
Cumulative volume purchased	Rebates
to date	
Rebate thresholds	

As an example of how the contracts database can be used, Contractor ABC has agreed to issue Smith Company a 2 percent rebate once Smith purchases 30,000 widgets from ABC. The company matches its purchases against the contracts database and finds that Contractor ABC did not issued to Smith the rebate once the 30,000-unit threshold was surpassed. Smith contacts ABC and extracts not only the rebate but also interest income for the delayed payment.

Incumbent Rebates and Discounts The contracts database can be loaded immediately with any existing supplier contracts; by doing so, and matching it against the spend database, a company may realize an immediate benefit, which is that suppliers may not have issued rebates and discounts based on *existing* contracts and purchase volumes. Thus, there can be immediate cost savings without even engaging in any purchasing consolidation.

Centralized Purchasing If purchasing is being consolidated across multiple subsidiaries for a small group of suppliers, then it makes sense to consolidate purchasing in the consolidated commodities at the corporate level. This keeps local buyers from bringing in additional suppliers and watering down the impact of consolidated purchasing.

An alternative is to centralize only the official *designation* of preferred suppliers at the corporate level and allow local buyers to conduct purchasing using just that list of preferred suppliers. This pushes buying down to the local level, where the staff is likely to be more in touch with subsidiary-level needs, while still retaining the benefits of spend analysis.

Online Purchasing Catalogs The purchasing department can assemble frequently ordered items into an online purchasing catalog, from which employees can place orders. The purchasing staff either aggregates these orders and forwards them to suppliers, or the system does so automatically. The point of such a catalog is to funnel employees toward approved suppliers.

Mandatory Purchase Orders Larger-dollar purchases should be authorized only by a purchase order (PO). If something arrives at the receiving dock without an accompanying PO, then the receiving staff should reject it. This policy effectively routes all purchases through the purchasing department, which in turn can funnel all purchases toward preferred suppliers. This policy is extremely useful for limiting the activities of maverick spenders, who are discussed next.

Maverick Spenders There will always be people in a company who buy directly from any supplier they want. They do not route purchase requests through the purchasing department, and they do not purchase through the approved corporate online purchasing catalog. Their mind-set is either to buy their favorite brand or to use their favorite supplier. By doing so, they reduce a company's purchase volumes with preferred suppliers, which results in fewer rebates and discounts.

If there is a supporting purchase order for a supplier invoice, but the invoice date is earlier than the date of the PO, then the PO was created *after* the order placement and does not indicate that the subsidiary issuing the PO was really being compliant with the spend management program. Instead, it indicates that the purchasing staff has authorized a new supplier after the fact, probably at the behest of a department manager or some other senior-level manager, who is an aggressive maverick spender who is trying to avoid the spend management system.

There are several ways to deal with maverick spenders, including bringing their activities to the attention of senior management, incorporating maverick spending in their annual performance reviews, and charging their departments for lost savings. However, maverick spenders may very well be members of senior management themselves, which can make it difficult to deal with them.

Supplier Compliance   It is not just a company's own employees who do not comply with a spend analysis project. Suppliers may ignore the master purchase orders they have just signed with the company and keep billing at the same old prices. This is rarely intentional; they just do not have a good system for integrating new contracts into their billing systems.

To spot supplier noncompliance, have the internal audit staff compare master purchase agreements to the amounts billed by suppliers and bring variances to the attention of management. If a supplier has this problem once, its systems may be inadequate for correcting the problem again, so that supplier should be flagged for continuing audits.

Early Payment Analysis   An offshoot of spend analysis is to determine which suppliers are being paid earlier than is mandated in their contractual terms. Due date should be available in the contracts and spend databases, so the information can easily be linked into a standard report that will reveal specific early payments by individual supplier invoice. This is an especially useful analysis to conduct immediately after entering into a new contract where the payment terms have changed, to ensure that the accounts payable staff is aware of the change. The report can even show the monetary impact on the firm by listing the number of days of early payment and multiplying this amount for each invoice by the company's incremental cost of capital. An extract from such a report is shown in Exhibit 8.2.

Summary   To generate the highest level of compliance with a spend management system, it is best to implement *all* of the preceding improvements. Of the group, the most critical are the use of a contracts database and centralized purchasing. Over the long term, the most difficult issue will likely be maverick spenders, who will continually attempt to broaden the supplier base.

EXHIBIT 8.2 Early Payments Report

Corporate Cost of Capital = 8%

Supplier Name	Invoice No.	Invoice Total	Contractual Payment Days	Actual Days Payment Variance	Early Payment Financing Cost
Able Baker Co.	IN-5487	$1,009	30	−10	$2.24
Accurate Paper Corp.	8209	10,423	30	−12	27.79
Addie Supply	1031	742	45	−4	0.66
Affluent Grocers	54905	1,903	10	−5	2.11
Aggressive Attorneys	IN-00732	8,439	15	−14	26.25
			Total early payment cost		**$59.05**

Spend Analysis Reports

There is no better spend analysis report than one that clearly states exactly how much money a company can save if only it complies with directing orders to the lowest-cost supplier. The table shown in Exhibit 8.3 for a single part number illustrates the concept. The exhibit shows the lowest (and approved) price in the top row and then the various prices being paid to other suppliers (and even the same supplier by a different subsidiary; see the fourth row), along with the additional costs being incurred by continuing to use the other suppliers. This is a powerful argument for showing exactly how to reduce expenses for each subsidiary, supplier, and component.

Commodity codes are multilevel, and reporting only at the topmost level may not provide a sufficient level of detail regarding the volume of spend or the number of suppliers. If so, the report shown in Exhibit 8.4 drills down through multiple levels of commodity codes to provide this additional detail.

Another useful report is to show a quarterly trend of spend with the company's suppliers. Not only does it show the ongoing concentration of spend with top suppliers, but (of more importance) it can be used in ongoing negotiations to obtain further price reductions, discounts, and

EXHIBIT 8.3 Compliance Profit Impact

Widget, Part #123

Subsidiary	Supplier	Approved?	Unit Price	12-Month Purchase Volume (Units)	Variance from Approved Unit Price
Northridge	J.C. Hammonds	X	$1.00	25,000	—
Sonoma	Dithers & Sons		1.05	15,000	$750
Denver	Arbuthnot Corp.		1.08	18,000	1,440
Atlanta	J.C. Hammonds		1.10	42,000	4,200
Birmingham	Checkers Ltd.		1.15	15,000	2,250
			Total profit impact		**$8,640**

EXHIBIT 8.4 Multilevel Commodity Spend Report

Level 1 Commodity	Level 2 Commodity	Level 3 Commodity	Total Suppliers	Total Spend (000s)
Metal manufacturing	Steel product	Iron and steel pipe	8	$13,540
		Rolled steel	4	4,710
		Steel wire	3	3,900
	Steel product total		15	$22,150
	Aluminum product	Aluminum sheets	2	2,370
		Extruded aluminum	9	970
		Other aluminum	11	320
	Aluminum product total		22	$3,660
	Nonferrous metal	Extruded copper	14	1,900
		Copper wire	2	1,110
		Other nonferrous	5	880
	Nonferrous metal total		21	$3,890
Supplies total			50	$29,700

rebates as the company directs more business toward its top suppliers. The report also shows the remaining spend *not* with the top suppliers, which shows the company the extent of additional spend concentration that it can achieve. An example is shown in Exhibit 8.5.

EXHIBIT 8.5 Supplier Spend Trend Report

		Spend (000s)			
Ranking	Supplier Name	Quarter 1	Quarter 2	Quarter 3	Quarter 4
1	Columbus Framing	$17,980	$18,020	$18,400	$18,940
2	Masonic Metalcastings	9,730	10,030	10,170	10,500
3	Jacobean Fittings	7,090	7,260	7,605	7,865
4	Bricklin Supply	5,995	6,190	6,430	6,990
5	J.C. Hammonds Corp.	5,450	5,780	6,000	6,150
Subtotals		$46,245	$47,280	$48,605	$50,445
Remaining suppliers		90,410	89,045	86,830	84,060
Grand totals		$136,655	$136,325	$135,435	$134,505
Remaining suppliers percent of total		**66%**	**65%**	**64%**	**62%**

EXHIBIT 8.6 Preferred Supplier Concentration by Commodity

	20 × 1		20 × 2		20 × 3	
Commodity	Preferred Supplier Spend (000s)	Percent of Total Spend	Preferred Supplier Spend (000s)	Percent of Total Spend	Preferred Supplier Spend (000s)	Percent of Total Spend
Facilities	$1,400	14%	$1,623	18%	$2,044	29%
Fittings	170	3%	350	8%	482	11%
Fixed assets	13,079	32%	16,080	39%	15,750	37%
Materials	2,450	10%	5,030	20%	5,850	24%
Supplies	—	0%	80	4%	130	10%

It is also possible to aggregate information at a considerably higher level to see what proportion of total spend has been shifted to approved suppliers by commodity type. The purpose of this report is to measure progress toward gradually shifting spend into a small cluster of preferred suppliers. It does not measure cost savings, focusing instead on general levels of concentration. An example is shown in Exhibit 8.6.

An overall result of spend analysis is to reduce the number of suppliers. At a general level, it is useful to aggregate this information to see how much concentration is occurring. The intent is not to shift *all* spend into a small number of suppliers, since it is not cost effective to spend time

EXHIBIT 8.7 Spend Concentration Report

For the Year Ended December 31, 20 × 3

	Facilities	Fittings	Fixed Assets	Materials	Supplies
Total spend (000s)	$7,048	$4,382	$42,568	$24,375	$1,300
Total suppliers	108	240	42	289	98
Suppliers with 80% of spend	22	50	10	63	25
Suppliers with 90% of spend	51	82	18	90	31
Suppliers with 95% of spend	73	129	25	135	43

eliminating the smallest tier of suppliers. Instead, the focus of the report is to highlight the *proportion* of spend concentrated in the top tier of suppliers. An example is shown in Exhibit 8.7.

The spend concentration report reveals that the company has a considerable amount of supplier consolidation work to do; the suppliers with 80 percent of total spend in each commodity category comprise roughly 20 percent of the total number of suppliers, which does not depart appreciably from what a Pareto analysis would reveal. In other words, the supplier distribution does not depart significantly from what would be expected if the company had taken no action at all to concentrate its spend with preferred suppliers.

Spend Analysis Rollout

It can be quite expensive and time consuming to roll out a spend management project, particularly in regard to setting up and updating the spend database. A logical approach is to put sufficient effort into the project to yield information that can begin to generate savings and then put some of the savings back into the project, to further improve the database.

When initially looking for savings, a good method for locating the best targets is to first incorporate into the spend database those subsidiaries comprising 80 percent of the total company spend and then to pick the commodities making up 80 percent of the spend for this select group of subsidiaries. Only conduct data cleansing and enrichment activities within the selected commodity codes. This process avoids wasting time on interfaces to databases that will not yield much savings and concentrates attention on the largest-dollar categories of spend.

Thus, the key factor with a spend analysis rollout is not to try to set up a complete system right away. It takes a long time to do so, and there will be no offsetting cost reductions in the meantime, thereby leaving room for office politics to cancel the entire project. Instead, use a reduced number of data sources, reduced data enrichment activities, and only a few commodity codes to trigger initial gains. These early successes will build support for a more comprehensive rollout.

Spend Analysis for Acquisitions

When a company completes an acquisition, one of its first activities should be to interface the information from the acquiree's procurement systems into the corporate spend database. The spend analysis staff can then determine where the greatest savings can be found within the acquiree and develop a plan for realizing them. In addition, the analysis may reveal that the acquiree is buying some items at a lower cost than the company has been able to manage. If so, and the acquiree's supplier is acceptable, the company can shift all of its purchasing of that item to the new supplier. This can yield a significant company-wide savings that is completely out of proportion to the savings experienced by the acquiree. Thus, an acquisition is an excellent place in which to apply spend management, since cost reduction opportunities can be spotted and implemented quickly.

Third-Party Spend Management Systems

Spend management systems are available from a number of suppliers, including Ariba, Emptoris, and Ketera. By purchasing one of their systems, a company can significantly reduce implementation time. In addition, these systems can add contract management capabilities and even set up electronic supplier catalogs, so that users can conduct online ordering with a predefined set of suppliers. They also impose better controls over spending, since the systems require access passwords, approval cycles, contract compliance alerts, and supplier performance measurements.

Spend management systems are also available that are specifically designed to monitor a company's telecommunications spend. This is an extremely specialized area because the systems must build a database of supplier contracts, the company's telecommunications assets, and carrier tariffs and contracts, and then match this information to imported supplier invoices. The result is not only the identification of invoices that do not conform to contract terms, and billings for lines and phones that are not in use, but also recommendations to use different combinations of contracts that will reduce costs. An additional service offered by some telecommunications spend management companies is to assist a company with the renegotiation of supplier contracts. These systems cost anywhere from 1 percent to 2.5 percent of a company's telecommunications costs, with a minimum configuration starting at $150,000.

All third-party spend management systems are expensive. The next section describes an in-house system that is much less expensive but that still retains a considerable amount of functionality.

Low-Cost Spend Management Systems

Third-party spend management systems are extremely expensive to install and maintain, which puts them beyond the reach of most smaller businesses. So what can a smaller business do to emulate such a system? Here are some possibilities:

- *Add granularity to the chart of accounts.* To gain a better knowledge of costs, consider altering the chart of accounts to subdivide expenses by individual department, and then go a step further by adding subcodes that track costs at an additional level of detail. For example, if the existing account code is 5020 for the travel expense account, and the revised code is 5020-01 to track travel costs for just the engineering department, then consider adding a set of subcodes, such as 5020-01-XX, to track more detailed expenditures within the travel category, such as airfare (code 5020-01-01), hotels (code 5020-01-02), and rental cars (code 5020-01-03). Spending at the sublevels can then be added together across departments to reveal what is essentially spend by commodity code.

  This approach requires careful definition of spending categories and can result in data entry errors if there are too many subcategories of expenses. Also, it will not be of much use if reports cannot be created to properly interpret and present this extra level of expense information.

- *Identify unauthorized purchases with exception reports.* The reason for centralizing procurement contracts is to negotiate lower prices in exchange for higher purchasing volumes, so anyone purchasing from an unauthorized supplier is reducing a company's ability to reduce its costs. To identify these people, create a table of approved suppliers and match it against the vendor ledger for each period, yielding a report that lists how much was spent with various unauthorized suppliers. It is also useful to record in an empty purchasing or payables field the name of the requisitioning person, who can then be tracked down and admonished for incorrect purchasing practices.

- *Restrict procurement cards to specific suppliers.* If there is a procurement card system in place, it may be possible to restrict purchases to specific suppliers, thereby achieving centralized purchasing without any central oversight of the process. If there is no procurement card system, then consider obtaining a credit card from each designated supplier and restrict purchases to those cards.
- *Impose a penalty system.* People resist centralization, especially when it involves eliminating their favorite suppliers. Though penalties may be considered a coercive approach to solving the problem, the imposition of a graduated penalty scale will rapidly eliminate unauthorized spending. For example, a department may incur a $100 penalty for one unauthorized expenditure, $1,000 for the next, and $10,000 for the next.
- *Require officer-level approval of all contracts.* Department and division managers love to retain control over supplier relationships by negotiating their own deals with local suppliers. By enforcing a corporate-wide policy that all purchasing contracts be countersigned by a corporate officer, contract copies can be collected in one place for easier examination by a central purchasing staff.

These suggestions will not result in a seamless in-house spend management system. However, they will yield somewhat greater control over expenses and more visibility into the nature of a company's expenditures.

Metrics

The metrics discussed in this section show the general level of activity within a spend management program but do not drill down to a sufficient level of detail to reveal the reasons for the results. Consequently, these metrics serve only as the starting point for additional investigations in the spend database to determine underling causes. The spend analysis metrics are:

- *Percentage of spend under active management.* When a commodity is under active management, this means that it is being actively monitored for improvements. As a company gradually works through its various categories of spend, it should leave behind someone who monitors each one. Thus, a company with an active spend analysis program should experience a continually increasing percentage of spend under active management. The calculation is to divide the commodities that have already been improved and assigned to an analyst for permanent review by the company's total spend.

■ *Percentage of compliance with preferred contracts.* This is a critical metric, for it shows the organization's willingness to route purchases to preferred suppliers. It should also be available in a drill-down version, so that managers can see where compliance is the worst and where noncompliant purchases are originating. The calculation is to divide the dollars of total purchases within each commodity code into those purchases within each commodity code made with a preferred supplier.

■ *Percentage of receipts authorized by purchase orders.* A common control over spend compliance is to require that purchases over a certain minimum amount be preauthorized by a purchase order. By doing so, it is more difficult for maverick spenders to impose their own purchasing decisions on the company. The calculation is to divide the total receipt line items authorized by open POs by the total receipt line items for the measurement period.

Summary

Spend analysis is an extremely valuable tool that can generate significant cost reductions by consolidating the number of suppliers and parts that it uses. However, it requires a considerable amount of work to consolidate procurement information into a central database and then enrich the database information to the point where cost reduction opportunities can be discerned. Consequently, the management team must be willing to unswervingly commit to a significant up-front expenditure of time and funds in exchange for cost savings in the midterm.

This chapter did not encompass spend analysis for maintenance, repair, and operations, a specialized topic discussed separately in Chapter 9.

Maintenance, Repair, and Operations Analysis

Introduction

The spend analysis process described in the last chapter was designed to maximize earnings by focusing on the largest categories of spend, where the opportunities for cost reduction are the greatest. But what about the other end of the procurement spectrum, where there are massive numbers of parts being ordered from a multitude of suppliers? This is the province of maintenance, repair, and operations (MRO) procurement. MRO items include supplies used in the production process as well as a broad array of consumables, industrial equipment, plant upkeep supplies, and even furniture and fixtures. This is a more difficult environment in which to reduce costs, but there are certainly opportunities for doing so. In this chapter, we address the nature of MRO and how to analyze it in order to reduce costs.

Problems with MRO Cost Reduction

A number of problems with MRO items make them especially resistant to cost reduction activities. These issues are:

- *SKU volume.* Each MRO item that a company keeps in stock is known as a *stock-keeping unit* (SKU). A major problem is the sheer volume of these SKUs. There may be thousands of items, many bought in such small quantities that it initially does not appear cost effective to engage in any cost reduction analysis at all. For example, if a company only buys 10 units per year of an item that costs $20 each, then does it make sense for the procurement staff to research cost reduction opportunities where the entire annual spend is only $200?

- *Bidding disparities.* It is nearly impossible to competitively bid a large block of MRO items, because distributors do not carry the same brands and many of the items that a company may include in its request for bid are needed in such small quantities that it is not worth the distributor's time to prepare a bid response. Or, if a distributor does not carry a specific brand that is included in a request for bid, it may respond with a substitute that the company considers unacceptable. In essence, if a company insists that distributors bid on the same brands that the company already stocks, then its current distributor may be the only qualified bidder.
- *Item tracking.* MRO items are usually charged to expense upon receipt, which means that the accounting staff sees no reason to subsequently track them in an inventory database. This makes it difficult to determine how much of each item is in stock.
- *Identification.* Unlike materials used in the cost of goods sold, the recordation standards for MRO items are quite lax, if they exist at all, so that their descriptions can vary substantially between company locations. This makes it very difficult to determine if similar SKUs are used in different places.

Despite these problems, there are still a number of methods available for cost reduction within the MRO spend category. They are described in the next section.

MRO Cost Reduction Methodology

A number of techniques for reducing MRO are highlighted in this section. They are targeted primarily at the higher-volume MRO items, but some techniques have a sufficiently broad range that they can impact even items having an extremely small annual spend. The first three of the next items are preparatory steps that should be completed prior to any cost reduction activities.

MRO Spend Database

The MRO cost reduction process begins with the same step used in Chapter 8, which is the construction of a spend database that is specific to MRO purchases. As before, it requires a data feed of MRO purchasing information from each subsidiary, followed by data cleansing and enrichment. The database is then used to develop a variety of reports that can be used for further MRO analysis. Please refer to Chapter 8 for more information regarding this database and related reports.

MRO Inventory Record Keeping

It is impossible to reduce the cost of an MRO item if no one knows where it is stored or how many units of it are on hand. Thus, an initial step in MRO cost analysis is to create an inventory record-keeping system, much as would be used for the tracking of cost of goods sold inventory. The resulting inventory information is not used by the accounting department to charge MRO items to expense, since that is usually done upon receipt. Instead, the information is most crucial to the procurement staff, who can use the on-hand inventory quantities to determine reordering strategies.

Creating an MRO inventory record-keeping system differs in three ways from the same task for the cost of goods sold inventory.

1. The MRO inventories are likely to be dispersed throughout a company, so some effort must be made to consolidate them into a smaller number of locations. This simplifies counting activities, and also makes it easier to spot excessive inventory levels.
2. Create marked bins for each MRO item, and keep the same items in the same bins at all times. This makes it easier to conduct a visual check of inventory levels.
3. Place responsibility for each storage area on a specific person, who is responsible for organizing it and notifying the procurement team of any stock-out conditions.

These are the minimum requirements for creating a reasonably accurate MRO inventory system.

To attain a higher level of inventory record accuracy, a company can lock up MRO items, track them with bar codes, and conduct cycle counts. Also, inventory records can be stored in a central database, which is available to the procurement staff. However, these extra steps may not yield higher accuracy if there is not a sufficient level of control over each MRO storage location.

Pareto Analysis

The Pareto principle states that roughly 80 percent of the effects come from 20 percent of the causes in a population. In the case of MRO, this means that 80 percent of the total cost of MRO comes from just 20 percent of the MRO SKUs. Consequently, MRO cost reduction efforts should concentrate on that top 20 percent of the MRO population. Any additional cost reduction forays into the other 80 percent of the MRO population should first be reviewed from a cost-effectiveness standpoint to see if they really make sense to pursue.

Distributor Cooperation

Given the sheer volume of MRO items and the difficulty of putting them out for bid, it makes sense to enroll the services of a distributor in examining the company's MRO purchases. The distributor can recommend replacing SKUs with less expensive ones, or with ones that can be shipped at lower freight expense or have lower support costs. The distributor deals with these MRO items every day in much greater volumes than the company does, and so has greater knowledge of cost effectiveness. Distributors will perform this service if the company consolidates its MRO purchases with them.

This is the single most important MRO cost reduction initiative, because a company can essentially shift a large part of its investigative labor to a third party.

Distributor-Managed Inventory

If a company is willing to shift essentially all of its MRO purchases to a single distributor, it can take the additional step of inviting the distributor to own the entire MRO inventory at the company's locations on a consignment basis. Under this arrangement, the distributor is responsible for maintaining adequate on-site inventory stocks, which the company owns once it withdraws any items from stock. This approach shifts inventory ownership to the distributor, which eliminates a company's MRO investment in working capital.

If a distributor is not willing to engage in a consignment inventory arrangement, it may be willing to give the company assurance of 24-hour delivery. This reduces the company's safety stock requirements to a minimum, thereby reducing its working capital investment in inventory.

Example

AstroGraphics Corporation is considering having its MRO distributor, General Supply Inc., manage its entire MRO inventory of fittings and fasteners. It considers these costing changes that would occur:

The following table is part of the feature box.

Continued

Supplier monthly fee	$1,500 monthly fee × 12 months	=	+$18,000
Freight reduction	$25 delivery charge × 100 orders	=	−2,500
Process savings	1,000 hours of inventory tracking × $30/hour	=	−30,000
Inventory carrying cost	$150,000 inventory reduction × 10% carrying cost	=	−15,000
	Net cost reduction	=	−$29,500

The analysis shows that General Supply will charge a $1,500 monthly management fee, but this extra cost is comfortably offset by the elimination of inbound freight costs, inventory tracking labor, and the reduced cost of inventory ownership, resulting in a net cost reduction of $29,500.

Having a distributor-managed inventory is one technique for MRO cost reduction. If a company chooses to continue to maintain its own inventory, then the next cost reduction alternatives will apply.

SKU Consolidation

A company may need to keep hundreds or even thousands of MRO SKUs in stock. The sheer volume of SKUs introduces a number of expenses, including:

- *Inventory obsolescence.* If there are many types of approximately the same SKU in stock, it is very likely that some will be used a great deal and others will fall into disuse and eventually be discarded.
- *Inventory tracking labor.* MRO inventory is not normally tracked with a formal inventory tracking system, as would production materials. Instead, someone must manually check on-hand balances and manually reorder items, which is highly labor-intensive. This is especially difficult because MRO items may be stored in a multitude of locations throughout a company, each of which must be visited to obtain a complete count.
- *Holding cost.* Any MRO inventory is taking up space that could have been used for other purposes, or eliminated entirely. In addition, MRO storage usually requires an investment in shelving that could otherwise have been avoided.

- *Insurance cost.* The cost of MRO inventory should be included in a company's insurance coverage, the cost of which will increase as a result of the inclusion.

Given the high cost of storing a massive number of SKUs, an obvious cost reduction technique is to reduce their number. This represents one of the principal methods for MRO cost reduction, because typically a number of SKUs are very similar and can be consolidated into a much smaller total number of SKUs. For example, there may be mops with three different mop head sizes in stock, which can be consolidated down into a single size. By doing so, the number of SKUs in stock drops by two-thirds. Also, by having just one version of each SKU, there is a much lower risk of obsolescence, and the smaller number of SKUs also reduces the volume of storage space required. Further, with fewer SKUs to count, the cost of inventory tracking labor declines.

These are formidable arguments for consolidating MRO items, but there can be considerable resistance to consolidation at the local level. The primary problem is that the local staff has brand preferences. They like to buy a particular type of product and resist having a different version imposed on them.

MRO Specification Matching

Many MRO items are bought that are constructed for more advanced purposes, when a less expensive product would do just as well. By reviewing the use of the more expensive or high-volume MRO items, one can determine if a less expensive item would be sufficient for its actual use. This issue commonly arises when users are given a free hand in buying MRO items, since they tend to have favorite products and brands that are over-engineered for what they need.

OEM Parts

Parts sold by original equipment manufacturers (OEMs) are typically much more expensive than their generic counterparts. If so, then deliberately avoid the OEM parts in favor of third-party items. Also, it is entirely possible that the OEMs do not manufacture the parts themselves but are actually buying them from a third party. If so, ascertain the name of the third party and buy directly from it.

OEMs sometimes force their customers to buy parts from them by threatening to otherwise void warranties for the underlying product. If so, create a table showing the warranty expiration dates for all products, and start using third-party components as soon as the warranties expire.

Private Label Purchases

When buying commodity items, it makes little sense to buy a brand-name MRO item when the same item is available from a private label for substantially less. This can be an area of substantial savings if a company buys commodities in large volumes, so it makes sense to examine commodity purchase quantities at an early stage of MRO cost reduction work to see if this can generate an immediate cost savings.

MRO Order Sizes

Companies tend to order MRO items in small quantities, perhaps of as little as one unit at a time. However, an MRO item may normally sell in a standard package quantity that is considerably larger, and so the company is paying for a broken package quantity that is much more expensive. If so, the company must weigh the holding cost of buying in larger, standard package quantities against the reduced per-unit cost of those purchases. If the trade-off is cost effective, then it may be better to set aside more storage space for the larger quantities. If the items being used are liquid, this may involve buying large refill units and using them to periodically refill smaller-size containers for employee use.

Custom MRO Items

A company may ask its suppliers for custom-made items or standard items repackaged in unusual sizes or formulations. If so, see if they can be replaced with commodity products. There is usually a notable reduction in cost from a custom item to a commodity item. Also, since custom items require some preparation time by the supplier, they tend to require a longer backlog, which in turn requires a larger on-site safety stock to guard against stock-out conditions. By shifting to commodity purchases that have shorter lead times, there is less need for on-site safety stocks, which can accordingly be reduced.

However, there was originally a good reason why a custom MRO item was ordered, so some investigation must be made into what internal changes are needed to shift over to a commodity purchase. This may involve some type of expense or internal resistance that may make it difficult to justify the change.

Manufacturer Price Reductions

In some rare instances, a company may be able to generate such large purchase quantities for a specific SKU that it makes sense to go around the distributor, straight to the manufacturer, and negotiate a lower unit price. The manufacturer will probably not want to deal directly with the company on an ongoing basis, so the two parties can arrange for the lower price to flow through the company's usual MRO distributor, which in turn receives a small markup for handling deliveries to the company.

MRO Consumption

If the same MRO items are being used in different locations, then consider tracking consumption at an MRO unit level at each of the locations and then comparing their usage. It is quite possible that some locations have discovered how to prolong usage; this information can be shared with the other locations, thereby cutting purchase totals. Conversely, this practice may simply find that some locations are throwing out MRO items well before their rated usefulness periods have expired, which can also be stopped.

Another reason for tracking MRO usage at the local level is to pinpoint any evidence of theft. If there is extremely high usage in one area in comparison to another area that experiences similar activity levels, this is a good indicator of theft.

Theft Reduction

Given the dispersed and unsecured storage locations that are indicative of MRO items, it is extremely easy for employees to walk off with inventory. Many MRO items, especially tools, can be used at home or sold, and so are prime targets for theft. To curb these losses, there should be a centralized tool storage area, with a checkout system that assigns responsibility to the person checking out each tool. In addition, a company can etch tools with a company serial number, which may deter theft.

Locking up MRO items is another way to prevent theft, but employees need ready access to many such items, which makes this alternative highly inconvenient; it may be impossible during the second or third shifts, when there are fewer supervisors available to closely monitor MRO stores.

Tool Reuse

Tools are among the most expensive of all MRO items, and so are worth additional attention to either prolong their life span or obtain free replacements.

Many shop tools have a lifetime warranty, so there is no reason to ever throw them out. Instead, have employees toss all broken tools into a bin and then periodically return the bin to the manufacturer or distributor in exchange for a credit. This may seem minor, but the credits can add up in a tool-intensive environment.

Some tools can be salvaged simply by regrinding or resharpening them. If so, set up a tool maintenance bin, where older tools can be left, and have the maintenance staff periodically regrind or resharpen everything in the bin. Otherwise, employees might be tempted to buy new tools if there is not an easy refurbishment alternative available on-site.

MRO Recycling

Many MRO items can be recycled but instead are thrown directly into the trash. Metal scrap can yield a modest profit if it is segregated into a separate waste bin, although most other types of recycling do not yield much of a profit. However, shifting items out of the trash and into a recycling bin reduces a company's waste storage and disposal charges. Furthermore, recycling is correct environmental behavior and should be pursued even in the absence of a clear cost reduction.

A somewhat unusual approach to determining the potential for recycling is to periodically examine a batch of trash to see if any of its contents could have been recycled; the resulting information shows management where the largest amounts of potential recycling are located and can be the foundation for a new recycling program or at least an employee education campaign regarding recycling.

Returns for Credit

When a supplier ships MRO items to a company, the shipment may include items that the supplier would be willing to accept back in exchange for a credit. This can include the pallet on which the delivery was shipped, as well as the cores, spools, spindles, and other items that products may have been wrapped around or stored within. These items are reusable by suppliers, so it may be significantly less expensive for them to accept back in a slightly used condition than buying entirely new ones. The credit granted to the company on a per-unit basis will likely be small but can add up over time if the company's purchases are significant.

Distributor Invoicing

The number of a company's separate MRO orders to its distributors can be enormous, which results in a correspondingly large flow of invoices back to the company from the distributors. The administrative cost of processing this flood of invoices is substantial, so it makes sense to request that the distributors consolidate the invoices into a single weekly or monthly invoice. Better yet, distributors can reference the company's general ledger account numbers on the invoices for each purchase made and then submit the invoices in electronic format; the company can create an interface straight into its accounts payable module, which parses the various elements of the invoice and charges the correct departments and other expense codes with minimal human intervention.

Location Cooperation

Most of the cost reduction items noted in this section require a considerable amount of cooperation from local subsidiary personnel, who may not be too happy about using alternative MRO items that they are not accustomed to, as well as a variety of other new procedures. To gain their cooperation, be sure to credit all distributor price reductions, rebates, and discounts back to the subsidiary level, so that local managers see the positive results of the changes. Also, where possible, *do not* centralize MRO purchasing, only the negotiation of annual contracts with distributors. Instead, allow local buyers to make acquisitions under the master contract with the preferred distributor.

Summary

There are a number of tools available for MRO cost reduction. The key to success is knowing which ones to use on the massive number of MRO SKUs with which a typical company is burdened. Accordingly, Pareto analysis is critical: Do not waste time applying cost reduction techniques where the spend is very small, since the resulting savings will be equally small. Also, make extensive use of the expertise of the company's designated MRO distributors, which can point out easy cost reductions that the company's procurement staff might not have recognized.

Distributor's Viewpoint

The vast majority of all MRO items are sold by distributors, not the original equipment manufacturers. The reason is that most MRO items are bought in small quantities, which are easier for a distributor to fill as part of larger orders containing a number of other items. The typical distributor does not have an inordinate gross margin to work with and so cannot grant large discounts or rebates to a company that directs more business to it.

However, there is a fixed administrative cost associated with processing customer orders, and if a company concentrates its MRO purchasing with a single distributor, then that distributor will experience a lower administrative cost per order, simply because the size of each order increases. This presents an opportunity for the company, which can reasonably request a portion of that savings as a discount or rebate.

Also, if a company is aggressive in obtaining discounts directly from manufacturers, it can arrange to pass these discounts through its distributor, which handles the sales in exchange for a small markup. By doing so, the manufacturer can avoid direct interaction with the customer, the distributor increases its profits, and the company can continue to place all of its MRO orders with a single distributor, which benefits all three parties.

Finally, the successful distributor is quite willing to partner with its customers to advise on consolidating MRO SKUs and other issues that will save the customers money. By doing so, the distributor becomes closely linked with its customers, who will thereafter be extremely unlikely to go elsewhere to buy MRO items.

Metrics

The metrics already described in Chapter 8 are equally applicable to MRO analysis. However, the results may vary substantially from those found under non-MRO spend management situations. A company should centralize nearly all of its MRO spend with a small number of distributors, so the percentage of spend under active management will be extremely high. Conversely, the percentage of receipts authorized by purchase orders may be quite low for MRO purchases, if there is a supplier-managed inventory.

The key metric in an MRO environment is likely to be the percentage of compliance with preferred contracts. Given the vast array of MRO items and the extremely distributed MRO purchasing environment in many companies, the procurement staff will face a constant battle to ensure that purchases are made only with preferred suppliers.

Summary

Cost reductions associated with MRO items are not as large as those that can be achieved with the spend management program that was outlined in Chapter 8, and the reductions require more work to achieve. Nonetheless, a continuing program of consolidating and carefully reviewing MRO items will eventually achieve notable savings, and it is well worth creating a long-term cost reduction program. Keys to this success are partnering with a distributor that advises about potential cost reductions and avoiding cost reduction work on categories of spend that are too small to yield significant results.

PART III

Asset Reduction

CHAPTER 10

Inventory Analysis

Introduction

Inventory may be a company's largest asset, but it should not be regarded as an asset at all—it is really a liability, because much of it may become obsolete, not all of it is necessary to produce revenue, and its value is constantly declining. For these reasons, a considerable amount of analysis is needed to keep inventory levels as low as possible without damaging profitability.

The fundamental reasons for large inventory balances involve the policies used to run a business, such as how quickly customer orders are to be filled, and a variety of tactical considerations, such as the use of drop shipping and how close suppliers must be located. In this chapter, we group the discussion of these issues into the general categories of inventory purchasing, receiving, storage, the bill of materials, obsolete inventory, and miscellaneous topics.

Inventory Purchasing

The bulk of a company's inventory problems arise at the point of purchase, where the purchasing staff must use a potentially erroneous forecast to project purchasing needs and then decide how much to buy and from whom to buy it. The next points are useful ways to keep from making the wrong purchasing decisions.

Forecasting Accuracy

The purchasing department orders inventory based on its estimates of what customers are going to buy. No matter how sophisticated, these estimates are bound to be incorrect to some extent, resulting in the purchase of excess inventory or the rush ordering of other items. To reduce this forecasting error, a company should attempt to gain direct access to the inventory planning systems of key customers. This gives the purchasing staff perfect information about what it, in turn, needs to order from its suppliers, and thereby reduces excess inventory levels.

Supplier Distance

When the purchasing department orders inventory from suppliers, it asks them for the lead time they need to deliver orders and then creates a safety stock level to at least match the lead time. For example, if a supplier says that it needs two weeks to deliver goods, and the company uses $100,000 of its inventory per week, then the purchasing department creates a safety stock level of at least $200,000 to keep the company running while it waits for the next delivery. This lead time therefore requires $200,000 of funding. The purchasing staff should be aware that distant foreign sourcing will drastically lengthen lead times and therefore the amount of safety stock. Conversely, if a company can source its inventory needs from suppliers located very close to the company and work with them to reduce their lead times and increase the frequency of their deliveries, this results in lowered safety stock levels and therefore a reduced need for working capital.

Ordering Lead Times

Another contributor to long lead times is the manual processing of purchase orders to suppliers. If inventory needs are calculated by hand, then transferred to a purchase order, manually approved, and delivered by mail, a company must retain more safety stock to cover for this additional delay. Conversely, if a company can install a material requirements planning system that automatically calculates inventory needs, creates purchase orders, and transmits them to suppliers electronically, then the ordering cycle is significantly reduced, and corresponding lead times can be shortened.

Purchase Order Updates

Between the time when a company issues a purchase order to a supplier and the date when the ordered items arrive, three problems may arise that render the original purchase order inaccurate:

1. Customer orders to the company may change, resulting in a modified production schedule that no longer requires some materials.

2. Ongoing changes in the design of company products may render certain parts obsolete.
3. Adjustments to recorded inventory balances through the cycle counting process may result in a need for fewer or more parts than are currently on order.

For these reasons, by the date of their arrival, the amount of goods delivered by suppliers may vary significantly from a company's needs.

To alleviate this problem, design a report that compares the amount of outstanding balances on open purchase orders to the company's needs, as listed in the material requirements planning system. The purchasing staff can review this report every day and modify open purchase order amounts to more closely match current requirements.

Risk Pooling

Risk pooling is the concept that safety stock levels can be reduced for parts that are used in a large number of products, because fluctuations in the demand levels of parent products will offset each other, resulting in a lower safety stock level. For example, engineers are usually instructed to use common parts in more than one product, so that fewer total parts can be stocked. A useful side benefit of this technique is that the fluctuations in the demand levels of a single part by multiple parent products will offset each other. This results in a smaller standard deviation in usage levels for a part having multiple sources of demand, as opposed to the usage deviation for parts with fewer sources of demand.

In order to reduce safety stock levels for parts having multiple sources of demand, use a simple trial-and-error approach of determining the actual stock-out level of these items over a rolling three-month period and gradually reducing the in-stock balance until the mandated service level is reached. For these items, the safety stock level will likely be substantially below the average corporate safety stock level.

ABC Inventory Replenishment

The inventory reordering systems yielding the lowest inventory levels are just-in-time manufacturing and then material requirements planning. If a company does not use either system, it can set up inventory replenishment around a multilayered ordering designation system for inventory. Under an ABC layering approach, a company maintains significant inventory levels for any items that are constantly being used; these items are designated as A-level items. If items are used with only moderate frequency, they are designated as B-level items and only minimal inventory quantities are kept in stock. Finally, C-level items are not kept in stock at all until a customer places an order. This system presupposes a fair amount of customer tolerance, since C-level items may require quite some time to replenish.

Inventory Ownership

It may be possible to shift raw material ownership to suppliers, so that they own the inventory located on the company's premises. Suppliers may agree to this scenario if the company sole-sources purchases from them. Under this arrangement, the company pays suppliers when it removes inventory from its warehouse, either to sell it or to incorporate it into the manufacture of other goods. The resulting payment delay reduces the company's need for working capital.

Another alternative is to obtain a supplier guarantee of delivery within 24 hours. This approach works well for items that are not used frequently and whose use can be accurately forecasted a day or two in advance. If suppliers can deliver within such a short time period, then the company can shrink its safety stock to a minor amount or eliminate it entirely. However, this approach essentially means that suppliers must now store extra inventory at their locations, so there is a risk of being charged a fee to compensate them for their extra working capital investment or for a rush delivery charge. The latter item is less of a factor if the supplier is located near the company.

Volume Purchasing

All of the preceding changes in purchasing practices can reduce a company's investment in inventory. Conversely, a purchasing practice that contributes to startling increases in funding requirements is the bulk purchase of inventory. If the purchasing staff is offered quantity discounts in exchange for large orders, it will be tempted to proclaim large per-unit cost reductions, not realizing that this calls for much more up-front cash and a considerable storage cost and risk of obsolescence.

Phased Deliveries

When a company places an order, the supplier sometimes imposes a minimum order quantity that may exceed the company's immediate needs, resulting in an investment in excess inventory when the entire minimum quantity is delivered.

Though the supplier may impose a minimum *order* quantity, it may be possible to negotiate for a smaller *delivery* quantity, so that smaller quantities are delivered more frequently. This concept works best when the supplier delivers numerous items to the supplier and can still make the same number of delivery runs—just with smaller quantities of more items in each delivery.

Inventory Receiving

The receiving process is not a critical factor in managing the amount of a company's inventory investment, but two points are of use to ensure that only authorized items are accepted and that additional items are not inadvertently ordered.

Reject Unplanned Receipts

The receiving staff's procedures can have an impact on inventory-related funding. For example, a supplier may ship goods without an authorizing purchase order from the company. If the receiving staff accepts the delivery, then the company is obligated to pay for it. A better practice is to reject all inbound deliveries that do not have a purchase order authorization. Though this method sounds simple, it is quite difficult to implement. An item may be rejected that causes significant short-term problems in a variety of departments, so management must be firm in supporting this policy.

Immediate Data Entry

Another procedural issue is to require the immediate entry of all receiving information into a company's warehouse management system. If this is not done, the risk increases that the receipt will never be recorded, due to lost or misplaced paperwork. The purchasing staff will see that the inventory never arrived and may order additional goods to compensate—which requires more working capital. Similarly, a procedure should call for the immediate put-away of inventory items following their receipt, on the grounds that they can become lost in the staging area.

Inventory Storage

The concepts of drop shipping and cross-docking can substantially reduce a company's inventory investment, either by avoiding it entirely or by accelerating it through the warehouse. There are also a number of ways to compress inventory into the smallest possible warehouse space, which reduces a company's facility costs. Finally, there are very simple systems for ensuring that the oldest perishable goods are used first, thereby avoiding inventory obsolescence. These issues are addressed in the next subsections.

Drop Shipping

In a traditional distribution system, inventory arrives from suppliers, is stored in the company warehouse, and is shipped when ordered by customers. The company is funding the inventory for as long as it sits in the warehouse, waiting for a customer order. A better method is to avoid the warehouse entirely by using drop shipping. Under this system, a company receives an order from a customer and contacts its supplier with the shipping information, which in turn ships the product directly to the customer. This is a somewhat cumbersome process and may result in longer delivery times, but it completely eliminates the company's investment in inventory and therefore all associated working capital needs. This option is only available to inventory resellers.

Cross-Docking

Another option that severely reduces the amount of inventory retention time is cross-docking. Under cross-docking, when an item arrives at the receiving dock, it is immediately moved to a shipping dock for delivery to the customer in a different truck. There is no put-away or picking transaction and no long-term storage, which also reduces the risk of damage to the inventory. Cross-docking works only when there is excellent control over the timing of inbound deliveries, so the warehouse management system knows when items will arrive. It also requires multiple extra loading docks, since trailers may have to be kept on-site longer than normal while loads are accumulated from several inbound deliveries.

Use Temporary Storage for Peak Storage Requirements

Warehouse planning tends to focus on the maximum amount of storage needed, such as during those periods just prior to expected peaks in forecasted item demand, when materials planners stuff the warehouse in anticipation of orders. However, storage space is expensive, and if there is a large difference between maximum and average storage requirements, then a company may be investing in too much warehouse space.

An alternative is to offload some storage into less expensive overflow locations, such as rented trailers. By doing so, a company can shift inventory back into its primary warehouse facilities as soon as the peak period is over, thereby paying much less for storage space over the course of the year.

There are two cautions associated with temporary storage facilities:

1. It can be difficult to extract needed inventory from these locations, so be sure to only shift low-usage items into them.
2. Overflow storage has a habit of becoming permanent, resulting in complex materials handling problems and added storage costs.

Match Storage to Cubic Space

A great deal of space in a warehouse is unused because the cubic volumes in storage racks greatly exceed the volume of the items stored in them. The next points can be followed to fill this excess space, which may result in a substantial overall reduction in warehouse space requirements.

- *Case height adjustment.* The most efficient way to store inventory is to stack cases on a pallet and store the entire pallet-load in a multilevel rack. However, if the resulting pallet height does not match the cubic volume of the existing rack space, some reduced pallet configuration must be used, probably involving one less layer of cases on the pallet. This inevitably results in some cubic storage space not being used at all. A solution is to alter the height of the case so that the optimal pallet height can be achieved to fill all available rack space. Conversely, it may be less expensive to adjust the height of the existing storage racks rather than to modify the cases to match the racks.
- *Modular storage cabinets.* Some item quantities are very small and they have small cubic volumes, so they only occupy a tiny portion of their assigned storage space. For these items, it is better to use modular storage cabinets. These cabinets have multiple drawers with varying drawer heights, the contents of which can be reconfigured with dividers to achieve the optimal amount of storage space given the on-hand quantity. This approach yields excellent storage density.
- *Movable racking systems.* A warehouse may be completely filled, and the cost of acquiring additional space is high. In this instance, it may make sense to install movable racking systems, where racks are mounted on wheels and pushed together, thereby eliminating all but one aisle. When someone needs an item, he or she pushes the racks apart to create an aisle and then picks the part. However, movable racks are expensive, slow down picking times, and generally work better in smaller warehouse spaces.
- *Double-deep racking.* When there are excess pallet volumes of the same stock-keeping unit (SKU) on hand, consider setting up two rows of racks adjacent to each other, with only one rack exposed to an aisle.

This configuration allows storage of two pallets of the same item in a single storage location, one behind the other. The main benefit is the elimination of an aisle, so there is more storage per square foot. This form of storage requires the use of specially designed forklifts that can reach deep into a rack to remove a second-tier pallet.

- *Stacking lanes.* If there are many pallets containing the same SKU, consider using stacking lanes in an open warehouse area where multiple pallets are stacked on top of each other without any bracing system, many pallets deep. However, pallets can collapse under too much weight, so verify allowable weight limits on cases before stacking too high. This is a particular problem in high-humidity environments where the cardboard boxes used to contain items on some pallets can gradually lose integrity and collapse under the strain of extra stacks of pallets.

- *Narrow aisles.* The typical warehouse is laid out on the assumption that all aisles are of exactly the same width, which is usually sufficiently wide for a forklift to put away or extract items from racks. Though this makes for consistently wide aisles, there is a potential loss of storage space in those areas where the items stored are all so small that forklifts are not needed. The result is excessively wide aisles that could have been used for more storage. The solution is to plan for narrower aisles in the minority of situations where manual put-aways and picking are the norm. The main problem with narrow aisles is making sure that the aisles are still large enough for kitting carts to negotiate.

- *Extended racks.* If there is a significant amount of space between the highest racks and the ceiling, consider extending the racks. However, also consider the weight-bearing capabilities of the racks as well as the maximum reach of the company's forklifts.

FIFO Storage Systems

When inventory items have a short shelf life, the oldest items on the shelf must be used first. A good way to automatically position the oldest item in front of a picker is to install gravity-flow racking. This racking system requires put-away from the rear, where items slide down a slight angle in the rack, assisted by rollers, pushing any items in front to the front of the rack. As soon as a picker removes items from the front of the rack, the weight of items in the rear push the next oldest item to the front. Gravity-flow racks are somewhat more expensive than standard storage racks and are useful only up to a height of about seven feet, since they are used only for manual picking.

For larger case sizes, pallet-flow racking is available as a larger form of gravity-flow rack. A pallet-flow rack uses standard racks that are set at an even height, on which are built dynamic flow rails at a slight downward angle from the loading end to the unloading end. The flow rails incorporate rollers and a series of automatic brakes to slow the movement of pallets. A forklift operator places a pallet at the receiving end of the pallet-flow rack, and it slides along the rails, being slowed by the brakes, until it comes to a halt behind the next pallet in line. When someone removes a pallet from the other end of the rack, the whole line of pallets automatically slides forward to fill the void. Pallet-flow racks are less efficient for a small number of pallets, since a considerable amount of rack space will be wasted without large quantities of the same item on hand.

Centralize Storage for Selected Items

The normal distribution strategy is to store finished goods in a group of regional warehouses so that goods can be delivered to customers with minimal delay. However, this approach does not work well for the minority of products having uncertain demand levels. It is impossible for materials planners to forecast how much of these items to stock in each distribution warehouse, so they face the alternatives of frequent stock-outs or the expense of an excessive inventory investment.

A possible solution is to retain high-value items with uncertain demand levels in a central warehouse and use overnight delivery services to ship them to customers as needed. By doing so, one can consolidate a large number of small quantities into one larger one that is still lower than the combined inventory totals that would have been maintained in the regional warehouses. The cost of overnight delivery services is usually minor in comparison to the saved inventory investment. However, this technique is not so cost effective for bulkier items, which are more expensive to ship by overnight delivery service.

Bill of Materials

Bill of materials accuracy is key to the minimization of inventory, since errors can result in the accumulation of excess raw material quantities. It is also necessary to carefully monitor the timing of changes in the components of a bill of materials, to ensure that old parts are not left in stock when they are replaced by new ones. These issues are addressed in the next subsections.

Bill of Materials Audit

A bill of materials is the record of the materials used to construct a product. It is exceedingly worthwhile to examine the bills of material with the objective of reducing inventory. For example, a bill may contain an excess quantity of a part. If so, and the underlying purchase order system automatically places orders for parts, the bill will be used to order too many parts, thereby increasing inventory levels. A periodic audit of all bills, where the reviewer compares each bill to a disassembled product, will reveal such errors. For the same reason, the estimated scrap listed in all bills of material should be compared to actual scrap levels; if the estimated scrap level is too high, then the bill will call for too much inventory to be ordered for the next production run.

Parts Substitution

A significant bill of materials issue from the perspective of inventory reduction is the *substitution of parts*. This may occur when the engineering staff issues an engineering change order, specifying a reconfiguration of the parts that comprise a product. Ideally, the materials management staff should draw down all remaining inventory stocks under the old bill of materials before implementing the new change order. If this is not done, then the company will have a remainder stock of raw materials inventory for which there are no disposition plans.

Obsolete Inventory

A considerable proportion of a company's inventory may be obsolete. If so, there should be a system for selling it off for the best possible price, even if this results in a loss. Otherwise, the inventory will continue to lose value over time. Consequently, there should be a robust inventory dispositioning system in place, as described in the next subsections.

Inventory Disposition

Even if a company has built up a large proportion of obsolete inventory, continuing attention to an inventory disposition program can result in the recovery of a substantial amount of cash. The first step in this program is to create a materials review board, which is composed of members of the materials management, engineering, and accounting departments. This group is responsible for determining which inventory items can be used in-house and the most cost-effective type of disposition for those items that cannot be used.

The next step is to adopt a schedule of regular obsolete-inventory reviews. The foundation of these reviews is these periodic reports, which are used to locate potentially obsolete inventory:

- *Last usage date.* Many computer systems record the last date on which a specific part number was removed from the warehouse for production or sale. If so, it is an easy matter to use a report writer to extract and sort this information, resulting in a report listing all inventory, starting with those products with the oldest "last used" date.
- *No "where used" in the system.* If a computer system includes a bill of materials, there is a strong likelihood that it also generates a "where used" report, listing all the bills of material for which an inventory item is used. If there is no "where used" listed on the report, it is likely that a part is no longer needed. This report is most effective if bills of material are removed from the computer system as soon as products are withdrawn from the market; this more clearly reveals those inventory items that are no longer needed. This approach can also be used to determine which inventory *is going to be* obsolete, based on the anticipated withdrawal of existing products from the market.
- *Comparison to previous-year physical inventory tags.* Many companies still conduct a physical inventory at the end of their fiscal years. When this is done, a tag is usually taped to each inventory item. Later, someone can walk through the warehouse and mark down all inventory items with an inventory tag still attached to them. This is a simple visual approach for finding old inventory.
- *Acknowledged obsolete inventory still in the system.* Even the best inventory review committee will sometimes let obsolete inventory fall through the cracks and remain in both the warehouse and the inventory database. Someone should keep track of acknowledged obsolete inventory and continue to notify management of those items that have not yet been removed.

Any or all of these reports can be used to gain knowledge of likely candidates for obsolete inventory status. This information is the mandatory first step in the process of keeping the inventory up-to-date.

The materials review board then passes judgment on which items can be dispositioned and passes off responsibility for dispositioning to the purchasing staff. The purchasing staff's options are to send inventory back to suppliers (probably for a restocking charge), sell to salvage contractors, sell as repair parts through the service department, or even donate them to a nonprofit in exchange for a tax credit. Throwing out inventory is frequently better than keeping it, since retention requires the ongoing use of valuable warehouse space.

Reserve Obsolete Inventory with Service/Repair Designation

When inventory is designated obsolete, the entire on-hand balance is typically disposed of, usually at some loss to the company. However, it is possible that some parts should be kept on hand for a number of years, to be sold or given away as warranty replacements. This will reduce the amount of obsolescence expense and also keeps the company from having to procure or remanufacture parts at a later date in order to meet its service/repair obligations.

The amount of inventory to be held in this service/repair category can be roughly calculated based on the company's experience with similar products or with the current product if it has been sold for a sufficiently long period. Any additional inventory on hand exceeding the total amount of anticipated service/repair parts can then be disposed of.

Of particular interest is the time period over which management anticipates storing parts in the service/repair category. There should be some period over which the company has historically found that there is some requirement for parts, such as 5 or 10 years. Once this predetermined period has ended, a flag in the product master file should trigger a message indicating that the remaining parts can be disposed of. Prior to doing so, management should review recent transactional experience to see if the service/repair period should be extended or if it is now safe to eliminate the remaining stock.

Identify Inactive Inventory in the Product Master File

There are few things more frustrating than for someone to disposition obsolete inventory, only to find that more inventory is then ordered, requiring additional effort to disposition once again. This typically happens when a company's automatic reordering system notices that the inventory balance for this item has dropped to zero and sends a message to the purchasing department, asking for a new purchase to bring the inventory balance up to some predetermined minimum.

The solution is to reset the product's activity flag in the product master file to "obsolete," "inactive," or some similar code. This not only tells the system to stop buying more inventory but also makes it impossible for the purchasing staff to create a purchase order through the computer system. The main problem is getting the person responsible for rendering inventory obsolete to remember to reset the flag. This can be accomplished by noting the deactivation step in bold on the inventory deactivation procedure. However, if the person doing this work ignores the procedure, it may be necessary to include a pop-up reminder in the inventory software code that appears whenever an inventory balance is set to zero. Another alternative is to modify the software to automatically alter the product master file whenever an obsolescence code is used as part of a transaction to write down inventory.

Miscellaneous Topics

There are a number of other issues that do not slot into any of the preceding categories and yet have a significant impact on a company's inventory investment. These range from the decision to provide a high-end service policy to the component tolerance level designed into a company's products.

Customer Service

A company may feel that its primary method of competition is to provide excellent customer service, which requires it to never have a stock-out condition for any inventory item. This may require that an inordinate amount of finished goods inventory be kept on hand at all times. This policy should be reviewed regularly, with an analysis of the inventory cost required to maintain such a high level of order fulfillment. Part of the policy review should be a survey of users to determine how much of a fulfillment delay they are willing to accept.

Product Design

A number of design decisions have a considerable impact on the size of a company's investment in inventory. A key factor is the *number of product options* offered. If there are a multitude of options, then a company may find it necessary to stock every variation on the product, which calls for a substantial inventory investment. If, however, it is possible to limit the number of options, then inventory volumes can be substantially reduced. A similar issue is the *number of products* offered. If there is an enormous range of product offerings, it is quite likely that only a small proportion of the total generate a profit; the remainder requires large inventory holdings in return for minimal sales volume. Yet another design issue is *minimum tolerance levels.* If a product is designed with extremely tight tolerances, then it is quite likely that there will be higher scrap rates for manufactured parts or that suppliers will charge higher prices to meet the tolerance specifications. As an alternative, design products whose functions still meet customer expectations, but which do so with the lowest possible tolerances. This can yield lower scrap rates and lower purchase prices.

Price Protection

A company with a distribution network sometimes finds it necessary to engage in price protection, where it reimburses its distributors for any price reductions on products they still have in stock. By doing so, the distributor does not have to sell at a loss. This is a particular concern in the consumer electronics market, where product prices decline continually as a result of price wars.

There are two ways to minimize these price protection costs:

1. Deliberately ship in smaller quantities, with more frequent replenishment cycles, thereby preventing distributors from building up large inventory stockpiles on which price protection payments must be made. If distributors resist this approach, then offer them incentives to do so that cost less than the projected savings from the price protection costs. Also, do not offer customers discounts for ordering in large volumes, and restrict their ability to return goods.

2. Join with the distributors in using collaborative forecasting and replenishment. Ideally, this means that the company has direct access to each distributor's inventory database and can see sales trends and stocking levels in real time. This allows the company to precisely tailor the size and timing of shipments to avoid price protection costs.

NCNR Inventory

When a company decides that it cannot use some inventory, it attempts to send it back to suppliers, usually paying a restocking fee to do so. However, some types of inventory are categorized by suppliers as noncancellable and nonreturnable (NCNR), usually because the inventory is so customized that they cannot expect to resell it elsewhere. If declared obsolete, these items would normally be written off and disposed of at a loss.

A variety of up-front procedures can be used to ensure that less NCNR inventory is ordered or left unused by a company, thereby reducing the amount of future write-offs. Here are some options to consider:

- Designate a field in the inventory item master file as the NCNR flag, and use it to designate which inventory items are categorized as NCNR by suppliers.
- Using the NCNR flag, modify the corporate material requirements planning system to forward all automatically generated purchase orders for these items to the materials planning staff, who verifies that they are really needed.
- Use the NCNR flag to create reports showing any NCNR inventory that will no longer be usable when an engineering change order is activated, when a bill of materials is modified for some other reason, or when a customer cancels a sales order.

- Use the NCNR flag to report on any scheduled production requiring NCNR items that is based on a forecast rather than actual demand. When management realizes the extra risk associated with this type of inventory, they tend to reduce the size of their forecasts.
- The NCNR status of inventory will be altered by suppliers from time to time, so be sure to update the NCNR flags in the item master file at least once a year.

These steps are an excellent way to reduce the amount of inventory write-offs associated with NCNR inventory.

Focus Reduction Efforts on High-Usage Items

Inventory reduction is a daunting task, if only because there may be thousands of SKUs to review. The result is a pitiful effort on a per-unit basis, if the materials management staff allocates its time equally to each SKU.

A solution is to focus their attention only on the reduction of high-usage items. There are two reasons for doing so.

1. By definition, slow-moving items are not going anywhere soon, so the materials management staff would have to wait a long time before the natural ongoing usage of these items will bring about any sort of reduction. Conversely, the turnover speed of high-usage items will cause a rapid inventory reduction in short order.
2. High-usage items represent a small portion of total items in stock, so the staff can focus on reducing the quantity of far fewer items, resulting in more staff attention to fewer items.

Metrics

Inventory is an area demanding the use of metrics, so that managers can see the proportion of various types of inventory to overall activity levels. If they see the proportion of inventory rising, then they can take prompt action to disposition existing inventory and restrict the inflow of new inventory. It is also useful to know not only how much inventory is obsolete but how much of that obsolete inventory can be returned (which can then be actively managed). Finally, some inventory is needed to ensure that the bottleneck operation runs at all times, so a metric is available for monitoring this too. Descriptions of these metrics are presented next.

- *Raw material inventory turns.* This metric is useful for comparing the proportion of inventory to production activity; it is best viewed on a trend line to spot changes over time. The calculation is to divide the dollar volume of raw materials consumed during the measurement period by the total dollar value of inventory on hand at the end of the period, and multiply the result by 12.

- *Finished goods inventory turns.* This metric shows the proportion of finished goods to sales and is useful for spotting inventory increases that may be related to sales declines. The calculation is to divide the amount of finished goods dollars sold during the measurement period by the finished goods dollar amount on hand, and multiply the result by 12. In cases where there are highly seasonal sales, it is better to use an average annualized sales figure than the annualized sales figure for the month in which the measurement is made.

- *Obsolete inventory percentage.* The proportion of inventory that is obsolete informs management of the level of dispositioning work still to be done as well as the scale of inventory build issues that must be dealt with. The calculation is to add up the cost of all inventory items having no recent use, and divide by the total inventory valuation.

- *Percentage of returnable inventory.* If inventory is obsolete, management's first question will be about the proportion that can be returned to suppliers. The calculation is to add up all inventory items for which suppliers have indicated that they will accept a return in exchange for cash or credit, and divide by the book value of all inventory items designated as obsolete.

- *Ratio of throughput to inventory.* Inventory should support the amount of throughput that a company generates, so it is reasonable to link the two together in a ratio. This is used for incremental decisions to alter inventory levels. The calculation is to divide annual throughput (sales minus totally variable expenses) by the cost of on-hand inventory.

Summary

There are a multitude of methods available for reducing a company's investment in inventory without negatively impacting its ability to generate revenue. These methods involve the cooperation of many parties, such as senior management regarding the fulfillment policy, engineers for accurate bills of material and substitutions, customers for demand information, and materials managers for a variety of purchasing decisions. If these parties support the goal of inventory reduction, then the methods described here can lead to a considerable reduction in a company's working capital investment. For more information about inventory cost reduction, see the author's *Inventory Best Practices* book (Hoboken, NJ: John Wiley & Sons, 2004).

CHAPTER 11

Fixed Asset Analysis

Introduction

The standard approach for purchasing fixed assets is to create a net present value analysis of a project's future cash flows and fund whichever projects promise the greatest potential cash flow. This method can lead to serious funding misallocations, when investments should instead be focused on enhancing total corporate throughput (revenue minus totally variable expenses). There are also a variety of other cost reduction considerations, including outsourcing, lease versus buy, feature reduction, and asset commoditization, all of which are addressed in this chapter. We also cover fixed asset condition tracking, which is useful for determining the timing of asset replacements.

Fixed Asset Acquisition Analysis

The traditional capital budgeting approach involves having the management team review a series of unrelated requests from throughout the company, each one asking for funding for various projects. Management decides whether to fund each request based on the discounted cash flows projected for each one. If there are not sufficient funds available for all requests having positive discounted cash flows, then those with the largest cash flows or highest percentage returns are usually accepted first, until the funds run out.

There are three problems with this type of capital budgeting.

1. Most important, there is no consideration of how each requested project fits into the entire system of production; instead, most requests involve the local optimization of specific work centers that may not contribute to the total profitability of the company.

2. There is no consideration of the bottleneck operation, so managers cannot tell which funding requests will result in an improvement to the efficiency of that operation.

3. Managers tend to engage in a great deal of speculation regarding the forecasted cash flows itemized in their requests, resulting in inaccurate discounted cash flow projections. Since many requests involve unverifiable cash flow estimates, it is impossible to discern which projects are better than others. Thus, the entire system of cash flow–based investments results in a suboptimal return on investment.

The Bottleneck as the Investment Focus

Properly managing the bottleneck operation eliminates most of these problems. Funding priority should be placed squarely on any projects that can improve the capacity of the bottleneck operation, based on a comparison of the incremental additional throughput created to the incremental operating expenses and investment incurred.

Any investment requests *not* involving the bottleneck operation should be subject to an intensive critical review, likely resulting in their rejection. Since they do not impact the bottleneck operation, these projects cannot enhance the throughput of the entire company; their sole remaining justification must be the reduction of operating expenses or the mitigation of some kind of risk.

Timing of Bottleneck Investments

At what point should a company invest in its bottleneck operation? In many cases, the company has designated a specific resource to be its bottleneck, because it is so expensive to add additional capacity; thus, investing in it involves a great deal of money. The decision process is to review the impact on the incremental change in throughput caused by the added investment, less any changes in operating expenses. Because this type of investment represents a considerable step cost (where costs and/or the investment will jump considerably as a result of the decision), management must usually make its decision based on the perceived level of long-term throughput changes rather than smaller expected short-term throughput increases.

Capital Budgeting Form

The issues just noted have been addressed in the summary-level capital budgeting form shown in Exhibit 11.1. This form splits capital budgeting requests into three categories:

Capital Request Form

Project name: _____

Name of project sponsor: _____

Submission date: _____   Project number: _____

Bottleneck-Related Project	Approvals
Initial expenditure: $ _____	All
	_____
	Process Analyst
Additional annual expenditure: $ _____	
	$100,000
Impact on throughput: $ _____	_____
	Supervisor
Impact on operating expenses: $ _____	
	$100,001–
	$1,000,000 President
Impact on ROI: $ _____	
	$1,000,000+
(Attach calculations)	_____
	Board of Directors

Risk-Related Project	Approvals
Initial expenditure: $ _____	
	_____
	Corporate Attorney
Additional annual expenditure: $ _____	< $50,000
Description of legal requirement fulfilled or	Chief Risk Officer
risk issue mitigated (attach description as needed):	
	$50,001+
_____	_____
	President
_____	$1,000,000+
	_____
	Board of Directors

Non–Bottleneck-Related Project	Approvals
Initial expenditure: $ _____	All
	_____
	Process Analyst
Additional annual expenditure: $ _____	
	<$10,000
☐ Improves upstream capacity?	Supervisor
Attach justification of upstream capacity increase	
	$10,001–
	$100,000 President
☐ Other request	
Attach justification for other request type	$100,000+
	_____
	Board of Directors

EXHIBIT 11.1 Bottleneck-Oriented Capital Request Form

1. Bottleneck related
2. Risk related
3. Non-bottleneck-related

The risk-related category covers all capital purchases for which the company must meet a legal requirement or for which there is a perception that the company is subject to an undue amount of risk if it does *not* invest in an asset. All remaining requests that do not clearly fall into the bottleneck-related or risk-related categories drop into a catchall category at the bottom of the form. The intent of this format is to clearly differentiate between different types of approval requests, with each one requiring different types of analysis and management approval.

The approval levels vary significantly in this capital request form. Approvals for bottleneck-related investments include a process analyst (who verifies that the request will actually impact the bottleneck) as well as generally higher-dollar approval levels by lower-level managers—the intent is to make it easier to approve capital requests that will improve the bottleneck operation. Approvals for risk-related projects first require the joint approval of the corporate attorney and chief risk officer, with added approvals for large expenditures. Finally, the approvals for non-bottleneck-related purchases involve lower-dollar approval levels, so the approval process is intentionally made more difficult.

Once approved as part of the budgeting process, capital requests can be segregated in the budget into the three categories just noted. The basic format of this portion of the budget is shown in Exhibit 11.2.

Also, the example contains an additional section at the bottom, in which is listed the incremental additional capacity of the bottleneck operation resulting from the new investments. In this section, the new capacity is listed with a time delay, so that a capital expenditure is fully installed before the resulting capacity is assumed to be available. Though most of the budget contains nothing but financial information, this operational information may have an impact on the company's ability to increase its sales later in the budget period, and so is extremely useful reference information.

Upstream Workstation Investments

The bottleneck operation should always have an adequate inventory buffer directly in front of it, so that it can maximize its production rate, irrespective of any upstream manufacturing problems. If there are severe upstream problems, then the inventory buffer could be eliminated, leading to the shutdown of the bottleneck operation, which in turn directly reduces a company's profitability. Consequently, it is extremely important to have a

EXHIBIT 11.2 Bottleneck-Based Capital Budget

	1st Quarter	2nd Quarter	3rd Quarter	4th Quarter	Total
Bottleneck-related projects:					
Additional metal press	$500,000				$500,000
Refurbish old metal press			75,000		75,000
Conveyors into metal press		180,000			180,000
Subtotal	$500,000	$180,000	$75,000	$0	$755,000
Risk-related projects:					
Smokestack scrubber		850,000			850,000
Water filtration			175,000		175,000
Asbestos abatement				250,000	250,000
Subtotal	$0	$850,000	$175,000	$250,000	$1,275,000
Non-bottleneck-related projects:					
Automated stock carver			147,000		147,000
Paint booth replacement		263,000			263,000
Lamination department conveyors				82,000	82,000
Subtotal	$0	$263,000	$147,000	$82,000	$492,000
Grand Total	$500,000	$1,293,000	$397,000	$332,000	$2,522,000

Incremental Improvement in Bottleneck Minutes				
	1st Quarter	2nd Quarter	3rd Quarter	4th Quarter
Operational impacts:				
Additional metal press		299,520	299,520	299,520
Refurbish old metal press				42,500
Conveyors into metal press			2,860	2,860
Total	0	299,520	302,380	344,880

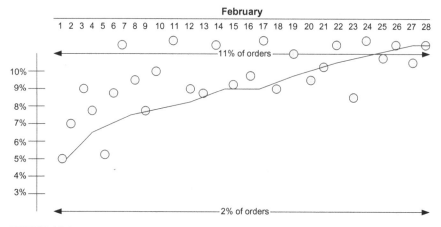

EXHIBIT 11.3 Inventory Buffer Trend Report

sufficient amount of upstream production capacity to refill the inventory buffer rapidly in the event of a manufacturing problem; this production capacity is called *sprint capacity*.

To guard against a drop in sprint capacity, the management team should regularly monitor the capacity usage levels of upstream workstations and make selective investments in those workstations whose sprint capacity has dropped sufficiently to present a risk of impacting the bottleneck operation's inventory buffer.

A good standard report is the inventory buffer trend report shown in Exhibit 11.3. The report shows an upper and lower boundary line, which represent tolerable boundaries for the percentage of all jobs where production problems caused the buffer to be eliminated. The small circles represent the daily percentage of jobs causing buffer elimination, while the line running approximately through the center of the boundary limits is a multiday moving average of the percentage of expedited orders experienced. The report reveals that the buffer is being eliminated with increasing regularity and that roughly one-third of all days now result in buffer elimination levels exceeding the tolerable limit.

In the situation shown in the exhibit, it would be reasonable to invest in those upstream workstations where capacity problems are causing the inventory buffer elimination in front of the bottleneck operation.

Downstream Workstation Investments

It is rarely necessary to invest in additional downstream capacity from the bottleneck operation, since doing so does nothing to increase a company's throughput. The only thing that a company achieves by making an investment in a downstream workstation is that it will improve the efficiency of an operation that will still be controlled by the speed of the bottleneck operation. In reality, the situation is even worse, for the investment in such an operation has no return on investment at all—so the company's total investment increases with no attendant improvement in its throughput.

Example

The industrial engineering manager of Circuit Board Corporation recommends that a $100,000 investment be made to improve the efficiency of the circuit board insertion machine, which is the next workstation in line after the bottleneck operation. This investment will double the speed of the machine. The projected results of this investment are shown in the next table, where total corporate throughput remains the same while the total investment increases and the return on investment declines from 20 percent to 19 percent.

	Annual Throughput	Total Corporate Investment	Return on Investment
Before investment	$400,000	$2,000,000	20.0%
After investment	$400,000	$2,100,000	19.0%

The problem with the investment was that it increased the efficiency of a machine that is still only going to receive the same amount of work-in-process input from the bottleneck operation. Since its input has not changed, neither can its output, despite a higher level of efficiency.

Fixed Asset Installation Reporting

Some fixed assets are acquired with a single purchase order and require minimal installation expense; the cost of these fixed assets is easily calculated. However, other fixed assets require multiple equipment orders and considerable installation activity over a prolonged period of time. A detailed appropriations and expenditures report should be used for these later assets, such as the one shown in Exhibit 11.4. Managers can use it to monitor installation progress and detect possible cost overruns.

EXHIBIT 11.4 Capital Appropriations and Expenditures Report

Capital Appropriation and Expenditure Status Report for the Period Ended April 30, 20xx (dollars in thousands)

Appropriation Number	Description	Work Order Number	Actual Completion Date	Outstanding Commitments	Actual Expenditures to Date	Estimated Cost to Complete	Indicated Total Cost	Original Estimate	Variance
42	*Northbridge Plant*								
	Site clearance	460	2/20/20xx	—	107	—	107	125	18
	Buildings	461	9/01/20xx	740	394	316	1,450	1,475	25
	Equipment	462	10/31/20xx	500	—	360	860	850	(10)
	Total, appropriation 42			1,240	501	676	2,417	2,450	33
46	*Delivery Fleet*								
	4 ton	495	6/30/20xx	300	40	10	350	360	10
	1 ton	496	6/30/20xx	75	30	60	165	180	15
	1/2-ton pickup	497	6/30/20xx	140	260	—	400	400	—
	Total, appropriation 46			515	330	70	915	940	25
50	*Miscellaneous*								
	Robot assemblers	525	5/20/20xx	100	214	20	334	350	16
	Fleet communications	534	7/01/20xx	30	50	5	85	75	(10)
	Lab pilot plant	542	11/30/20xx	40	160	55	255	290	35
	Forklift trucks	550	9/30/20xx	75	70	5	150	150	—
	Total, appropriation 50			245	494	85	824	865	41
	Grand total			2,000	1,325	831	4,156	4,255	99

In the exhibit, the key elements comprising each project are broken out, so that the spending variances associated with each one are clearly visible. For example, for the Northridge Plant project, the equipment purchases are running $10,000 higher than budgeted, while the site clearance and building expenses are $18,000 and $25,000 under budget, respectively.

This report is also useful from the perspective of investing on an incremental basis. If the costs associated with a fixed asset appear to be spiraling out of control, the report will reveal the problem before projection completion, which gives management the option of withholding further funding.

Postinstallation Audit

For larger fixed asset installations, consider conducting a postproject audit. The objective of this audit is to compare actual earnings or savings with the original proposal and to ascertain why any deviation occurred and what steps should be taken to improve capital investment planning in the future. These issues may be detected by a postinstallation audit:

- Weaknesses in strategic planning that led to a poor investment decision
- Weaknesses in policies and procedures that allowed a weak investment proposal to be approved
- Tendencies to have excessively optimistic revenue or cash flow projections
- Evidence of manufactured input data

Also, if employees know that their investment proposals will be subject to a postinstallation audit at some point in the future, they will be more cautious in making the projections contained within their proposals.

Outsourcing Alternative

It is possible to entirely avoid any fixed asset acquisitions through outsourcing. This means that a company signs a contract with a supplier, under which the supplier takes over an entire functional area. The supplier is now responsible for any asset acquisitions needed to maintain the appropriate level of service to the company and may even buy the company's fixed assets as part of the outsourcing deal. This situation is most common for information technology (IT) services and contract manufacturing.

Outsourcing can represent an excellent short-term cash savings for a company, which completely avoids investments for as long as the outsourcing deal continues. However, the supplier must also earn a profit, so the company will likely end up paying for the assets over the long term through its fee payments to the supplier. This situation will not arise if the supplier is so efficient that it can earn a profit while still charging less to its customers than they would pay to conduct the activity internally; This low-cost scenario arises when the supplier has such a high-volume operation that it can obtain very low costs per transaction, or when it has shifted its processing activities to a low-wage area. For example, an IT supplier has lower processing costs because it can run all of the program processing for many companies through one large data processing center that combines the overhead for all of those companies into one facility—this is a permanent cost advantage that a single company cannot match.

Shifting the responsibility for fixed assets to a supplier is certainly a worthwhile consideration but must also be balanced against three risks.

1. The supplier may go out of business, leaving the company hamstrung if a key outsourced function is suddenly completely inoperative.
2. The supplier may not fulfill its responsibility to update fixed assets on a regular basis, so that the company finds itself with aged equipment or software.
3. A company may so thoroughly shift a function to a supplier that it no longer has the capability to take back the function if problems develop in the relations with the supplier.

These are critical concerns and should be balanced against the benefit of shifting asset investments to a supplier.

In short, there are numerous situations where the outsourcing decision can save substantial amounts of cash in the short term but not necessarily over the long term. Against this short-term gain must be balanced the risks of supplier bankruptcy, inadequate supplier investments, and being excessively beholden to a supplier.

Lease versus Buy Decision

In a leasing situation, the company pays the lessor for the use of equipment that is owned by the lessor. Under the terms of this arrangement, the company pays a monthly fee; the lessor records the asset on its books and takes the associated depreciation expense while also undertaking to pay all property taxes and maintenance fees. The lessor typically takes back the asset at the end of the lease term, unless the company wishes to pay a fee at the end of the agreement period to buy the residual value of the asset and then record it on the company's books as an asset.

A leasing arrangement tends to be rather expensive for the lessee, since it is paying for the lessor's profit and for any differential between the interest rate charged by the lessor and the company's incremental cost of capital. However, leasing can still be a useful option, especially for those assets that tend to degrade quickly in value or usability, and that would therefore need to be replaced at the end of the leasing period anyway. It is also useful when the company cannot obtain financing by any other means or wishes to reserve its available lines of credit for other purposes.

The many factors used in calculating a lease payment (e.g., down payment, interest rate, asset residual value, and trade-in value) make it difficult to determine the cost of the underlying asset. Consequently, it is useful to use net present value analysis to independently verify the cost of a lease. An example is shown in Exhibit 11.5.

Based on the information in the exhibit, there is a net savings to be gained by buying the asset outright rather than leasing it. The net savings calculation is shown in the next table.

Present value of purchase	$1,000,000
Less: present value of related tax savings	272,230
Net purchase cost	$727,770
Net present value savings of purchase over lease:	
Present value of lease cost	$794,768
Net purchase cost (above)	727,770
Net savings	$66,998

By completing this analysis for each lease, one can determine the total cost difference between a lease and an outright asset purchase, which should be a part of management's approval process for acquiring an asset.

Feature Reduction Analysis

If the decision is made to acquire a specific asset, it does not mean the company has to acquire all of the features and functionality of the asset. For large-dollar assets in particular, it may make sense to review their features in considerable detail, especially in regard to the company's *specific* requirements. If a feature is not needed, then contact the supplier to see if it can be acquired without that feature. If the asset is expensive, the supplier may be willing to pare down a standard product in order to make the sale.

EXHIBIT 11.5 Net Present Value Calculation for Lease versus Buy Decision

Net Present Value Calculation

Lease versus Buy

A. Lease Basis

Year	Pretax Lease Payments	Income Tax Savings (35% Rate)	After-Tax Lease Cost	Discount Factor (9%)	Net Present Value
1	280,000	98,000	182,000	0.9170	166,894
2	280,000	98,000	182,000	0.8420	153,244
3	270,000	94,500	175,500	0.7720	135,486
4	270,000	94,500	175,500	0.7080	124,254
5	120,000	42,000	78,000	0.6500	50,700
6	120,000	42,000	78,000	0.5960	46,488
7	120,000	42,000	78,000	0.5470	42,666
8	120,000	42,000	78,000	0.5020	39,156
9	120,000	42,000	78,000	0.4600	35,880
	1,700,000	595,000	1,105,000		794,768

Net Present Value Calculation

Lease versus Buy

B. Buy Basis

Year	Accelerated Cost Recovery	Income Tax Savings (35% Rate)	Discount Factor (9%)	Net Present Value
1	200,000	70,000	0.9170	64,190
2	200,000	70,000	0.8420	58,940
3	200,000	70,000	0.7720	54,040
4	200,000	70,000	0.7080	49,560
5	200,000	70,000	0.6500	45,500
6	—	—		—
7	—	—		—
8	—	—		—
9	—	—		—
	1,000,000	350,000		272,230

This feature review can extend to the capacity level of the asset. If there is a specific capacity level for which the asset is needed, with no realistic expectation for any capacity spikes in the future, then only buy an asset with a rated capacity just above what the company needs.

If a company is buying the same type of asset in large quantities, then it may also be possible to purchase exactly the same configuration for every unit. By doing so, it can simplify its maintenance requirements and replacement parts storage. A good example of this is Southwest Airlines, which only buys the Boeing 737 in order to narrowly focus its maintenance facilities on that one airframe.

An interesting variation on feature reduction analysis is to alter the work environment in order to downgrade the features needed for an asset purchase. For example, two production cells are located sufficiently far apart that a forklift is needed to move work-in-process items between them. This would normally call for the purchase of a forklift. However, by shifting the two production cells closer together, it is now possible to downgrade the asset purchase requirement from a forklift to a few hand trucks and push carts—which are much less expensive.

Asset Commoditization

If there is a choice between acquiring a highly customized asset and a standard model that can be purchased off the shelf, then buy the standard model whenever possible. There are three reasons for doing so.

1. There is a larger resale market for standard equipment, which may translate into higher resale prices.
2. No third party will bother to create repair parts for a custom machine, whereas they may do so for a widely sold standard model; such parts are typically less expensive than parts produced by the original equipment manufacturer.
3. It is much more difficult to obtain repair parts for a custom machine, and they will be expensive.

Monument Analysis

A company's production facility may be poorly configured, because it has acquired a very large, high-capacity machine (a *monument*) that the rest of the facility is configured around. This can be a problem not only from a floor space usage standpoint but also because it is difficult to construct an efficient product flow and because the entire facility may grind to a halt if the monument stops functioning.

To avoid these issues, adopt a long-range plan of eliminating monuments in favor of a larger number of smaller assets that can be more easily moved, have less capacity on a per-unit basis, and have fewer features. The result will eventually be a production facility that has less downtime and that can be easily modified into a variety of different work cells, depending on the production mix.

Facility-Specific Considerations

When a company elects to expand its facilities, it is incurring a substantial long-term expense. Given the size of this liability, it is best to pursue additional analysis to see if the extra space is really needed, or if alternative arrangements can be made. Here are some considerations:

- *Eliminate storage space.* The typical office space contains a considerable amount of storage space. Consider shifting the stored items to less expensive warehouse space as well as throwing out any items that are no longer needed.
- *Compress space.* It may be possible to tear down offices and convert to more space-efficient cubicles as well as narrow open spaces and corridors (subject to fire code restrictions).
- *Hoteling.* If a significant number of employees housed in a facility are rarely on-site, then set up a hoteling situation where they can sit in any available open cubicles or offices.
- *Extra shifts.* If there is a possibility of moving work into the second or third shifts, assign the same work space to employees in multiple shifts. This is another form of hoteling.
- *Work from home.* A number of jobs can be handled from a home office. If so, shift staff home on a pilot project basis, and extend the concept, depending on employee acceptance and the impact on productivity.
- *Staggered shifts.* A company may be paying for a substantial number of extra parking spaces, because the cars owned by the last shift are still in the lot as well as the autos owned by the employees just starting the next shift. To avoid this temporary space shortage, stagger the start of employee shifts, so that employee arrivals and departures are spread over a longer period of time.
- *Delay the decision.* If there is a chance that employee headcount may spike and then decline during the short to medium term, it makes sense to endure some discomfort in the existing facilities until the situation is clarified. Otherwise, a company may find itself with a substantial amount of excess space.
- *Lease duration.* A landlord prefers to lock a tenant into a five-year lease, if not longer. It steers prospective tenants into these leases by requiring inordinately high lease rates on shorter-duration leases. However, existing tenants may be willing to sublease their space for

periods substantially shorter than five years, and at lower rates than those offered by the landlord.

The typical company will find that nearly all of the listed possibilities can be used to some extent; doing so not only keeps a company from having to obtain additional square footage but may even result in some facilities being closed down entirely.

Fixed Asset Retention Analysis

Fixed assets that are no longer being used tend to be shoved off into odd corners and clutter up a facility for years. This is not only a waste of valuable floor space but also represents the waste of their residual value; for every year that an asset sits unused, its resale value declines. To avoid this issue, the accounting staff should conduct a quarterly review of all fixed assets with the department managers, to see which assets should be sold. Further, in case some assets are no longer listed on the official company fixed assets register, the accounting staff should conduct an annual fixed asset audit; the resale value of any unlisted assets found should be determined and the assets targeted for sale. If an asset is considered to have such a low resale value that it is not worth selling, then it should still be disposed of, in order to make floor space available for other uses.

If fixed asset resale values are being driven down by excess industry capacity in the short term, it may make sense to mothball assets rather than sell them at a large discount. By doing so, the company retains the ability to use them again if demand increases in the future, or if there is a reasonable chance that resale values will increase in the near future.

However, if the industry appears to be mired in a long-term slump where asset values will remain correspondingly low for the foreseeable future and company sales are not likely to increase, then the much better option is to realize some cash by selling the assets now, which also reduces the company's floor space requirements.

Fixed Asset Maintenance Analysis

It may be tempting to replace old equipment once it completes its manufacturer-recommended life span. However, some additional analysis may be in order. If an asset is used for substantially less than a 24-hour period each day, then there is plenty of time available for ongoing preventive maintenance. If the maintenance staff has sufficient time available during

the equipment's nonoperative periods to complete the required maintenance, this helps to keep the equipment functional for a period that is
potentially much longer than its rated life.

This is a particularly fine solution if most of the maintenance is related
to labor (rather than parts replacements), so that the company only incurs
the cost of its maintenance staff, which would likely be working on-site
irrespective of the work required for the machine. Thus, this situation
involves minimal incremental cost, in exchange for keeping equipment
running past its expected life span.

Fixed Asset Location Tracking

Part of the effort of tracking fixed assets can be eliminated simply by reducing the number of items designated as fixed assets. A good option is to
increase the corporate capitalization limit; this excludes more purchases
from being designated as fixed assets, so that they are instead charged to
expense in the current period. In particular, try to set the capitalization
limit above the price of desktop and laptop computers, which are exceptionally difficult to track.

Smaller capital items may be moved around a facility with some regularity, making it extremely difficult to locate them when needed and can
result in their outright loss. To resolve this problem, use a radio frequency
identification (RFID) system. This requires the purchase of battery-powered
RFID tags that are affixed to each asset, and which have enough battery
life to send a signal every 30 seconds for about five years. The signals are
received by RFID readers, which pass along this information to a central
database for user viewing on a facility map and which determines asset
positioning based on the relative signal strength of the signals received by
the various RFID readers.

Using an RFID tracking system may reduce the need for extra assets
that might otherwise have been kept in reserve in case similar assets could
not be located. Thus, RFID could potentially reduce the total asset investment. Further, it eliminates the time spent searching for missing equipment,
allows for rapid asset counts, eliminates instances of equipment hoarding,
and tells the maintenance staff where to find equipment that is scheduled
for maintenance.

An additional benefit of an RFID tracking system is its ability to provide
hard evidence to an insurance company that an asset has actually been
stolen. To do so, have the RFID tracking system record an out-of-bounds
alert when an asset is moved off the company premises, and then use the
time and date stamp on this alert to access the appropriate video footage
from security cameras to document the theft.

This application is hardly necessary for truly "fixed" assets, since a transmitter tag is not needed to send a multitude of signals that the asset has not budged in the past five years. Consequently, affix RFID tags only to those fixed assets for which there is actually some likelihood of movement.

If an RFID system is too expensive, then formally assign each asset to a department manager, and send each manager a quarterly notification of what assets are under his or her control. Even better, persuade the human resources manager to include "asset control" as a line item in the formal performance review. These actions make it very clear to the management team that keeping adequate control over the company's assets is a key responsibility.

Fixed Asset Condition Tracking

Wireless sensors provide the information needed to determine when to replace a fixed asset. These devices can monitor changes in lighting, position, temperature, humidity, incline, vibration, and pitch/roll/yaw. When configured as wireless devices that transmit from difficult-to-reach locations, they are ideal for monitoring the condition of fixed assets, especially those on the factory floor. A typical setup is for the sensor to transmit a wireless signal to a local router when it senses a significant change, which passes the data along to a computer, which in turn matches the data against a predetermined out-of-specification condition. If the reported condition is considered to be outside the predetermined boundary, the computer sends a warning e-mail to the appropriate person.

The wireless sensor is extremely useful for determining the exact moment when a fixed asset is failing, since the asset's temperature or level of vibration may rise by a measurable amount shortly before it fails. By monitoring these key indicators, management can determine precisely when asset replacement is needed, rather than guessing and either replacing it much too soon or waiting until it fails, precipitating a replacement crisis.

Fixed Asset Metrics

In most cases, fixed asset analysis is on a case-by-case basis, and so is not affected by metrics that are normally calculated on a company-wide basis. Of the metrics shown in the next list, the key one that can be used for individual assets is bottleneck utilization. The other metrics provide only a general view of the condition of a company's assets.

- *Bottleneck utilization.* The bottleneck operation should be operated at a very high level of efficiency in order to maximize system throughput, which is most easily tracked with the bottleneck utilization metric. The calculation is to divide the actual production hours of the bottleneck operation by its hours available for production. This metric can be manipulated by running low-priority jobs through the bottleneck, just to keep the machine running. To detect such manipulation, consider also tracking which jobs are being run against the jobs listed in the production schedule. Also, the denominator can be artificially reduced in order to increase the apparent level of utilization. It is generally best to assume that there are 24 hours available per day at the bottleneck and not allow anyone to reduce this figure.
- *Repairs and maintenance expense to fixed assets ratio.* If this ratio follows an increasing trend line, then a company is probably in need of a considerable amount of asset replacement. Such a trend line may also be indicative of high asset-usage levels, which can prematurely require advanced levels of repair work. The calculation is to divide the total amount of repairs and maintenance expense by the total amount of fixed assets before depreciation.
- *Operating assets ratio.* This ratio is designed for use by managers to determine which assets can be safely eliminated from a company without impairing its operational capabilities. Its intent is to focus management on assets that are not generating a return on investment and that therefore can be eliminated. The calculation is to divide the dollar value of all assets used in the revenue creation process by the total amount of assets, with both the numerator and denominator values being prior to any depreciation deduction.
- *Return on operating assets.* This measure focuses on the return on only those assets that are needed to generate revenue. Its intent is to show managers a company's ideal return on assets, which they can attain by eliminating all unproductive fixed assets. The calculation is to divide net income by the gross valuation of all assets used to create revenue.
- *Sales to fixed assets ratio.* In some industries, a considerable fixed asset investment is needed in order to generate sales. If this metric reveals a low ratio of sales to fixed assets in relation to the same ratio results for competitors, then the company is probably investing too little. The reverse result can indicate overinvestment. The calculation is to divide the net sales for a full year by the total amount of fixed assets, net of depreciation.

Summary

This chapter has placed a strong focus on investing in fixed assets only if the result will be an increase in corporate throughput. Most other investments, other than those required by law or to reduce risk, can be avoided. By taking this approach to capital investments, it is possible to sidestep a considerable proportion of all new fixed asset proposals while still maximizing corporate profitability.

Also, a proposal to acquire an expensive asset should trigger a considerable amount of analysis to see if all of the proposed features, functions, and additional capacity are needed. The sheer size of some capital acquisitions will be so massive that the analysis may even be conducted by, or at least closely scrutinized by, the chief financial officer.

PART IV

Special Topics

CHAPTER 12

Throughput Analysis

Introduction

Cost reduction is not about slashing costs indiscriminately but rather about carefully analyzing a company's operations and selectively paring away those costs that will not impede its ability to generate a profit or its opportunities for future growth. Throughput analysis is especially concerned with how a company generates profits, so the cost reduction practitioner should be well grounded in the subject. This chapter addresses constraints (or bottlenecks) and how they can be properly managed to maximize profits. For a much more detailed discussion of the concept, please refer to the author's *Throughput Analysis* book (Hoboken, NJ: John Wiley & Sons, 2006).

Theory of Constraints

The theory of constraints is based on the concept that a company must determine its overriding goal and then create a system that clearly defines the main capacity constraint that will allow it to maximize that goal. The operational aspects of the theory of constraints requires some understanding of a new set of terms that are not used in traditional company operations. The terms are presented next.

- *Drum.* The drum is the resource in a company's operations that prevents the company from producing additional sales. This is the company's constrained capacity resource or bottleneck operation. It will most likely be a machine or person, or possibly also a short supply of materials. Because total company results are constrained by this resource, it beats the cadence for the entire operation—in essence, it is the corporate drum.

- *Buffer.* The drum operation must operate at maximum efficiency in order to maximize company sales. However, it is subject to the vagaries of upstream problems that impact its rate of production. For example, if the drum is located in the production department, then if the stream of work in process generated by an upstream work center is stopped, the inflow of parts to the drum operation will cease, thereby halting sales. To avoid this problem, it is necessary to build a buffer of inventory in front of the drum operation to ensure that it will continue operating even if there are variations in the level of production created by feeder operations. The size of this buffer will be quite large if the variability of upstream production is large and will be correspondingly smaller if the upstream production variability is reduced.
- *Rope.* The timed release of raw materials into the production process; this ensures that a job reaches the inventory buffer before the drum operation is scheduled to work on it. In essence, the rope is the synchronization mechanism driving the flow of materials to the drum operation. The length of the rope is the time required to keep the inventory buffer full, plus the processing time required by all operations upstream of the drum operation.

These three terms are frequently clustered together to describe the theory of constraints as the drum-buffer-rope (DBR) system. The next section discusses the mechanics of the DBR system.

Operational Aspects of the Theory of Constraints

Pareto analysis holds that 20 percent of events cause 80 percent of the results. For example, 20 percent of customers generate 80 percent of all profits, or 20 percent of all production issues cause 80 percent of the scrap. The theory of constraints, when reduced down to one guiding concept, states that 1 percent of all events cause 99 percent of the results. This conclusion is reached by viewing a company as one giant system designed to produce profits, with one bottleneck operation controlling the amount of those profits.

Under the theory of constraints, all management activities are centered on management of the bottleneck operation, or drum. By focusing on making the drum more efficient and ensuring that all other company resources are oriented toward supporting the drum, a company will maximize its profits. The concept is shown in Exhibit 12.1, where the total production capacity of four work centers is shown, both before and after a series of efficiency improvements are made. Of the four work centers, the capacity of center C is the lowest, at 80 units per hour. Despite sub-

Scenario One:

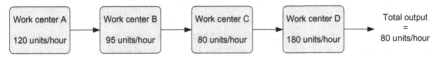

Scenario Two:

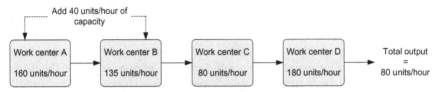

EXHIBIT 12.1 Impact of the Drum Operation on Total Output

sequent efficiency improvements to work centers A and B, the total output of the system remains at 80 units per hour, because of the restriction imposed by work center C.

This approach is substantially different from the traditional management technique of local optimization, where *all* company operations are to be made as efficient as possible, with machines and employees maximizing their work efforts at all times.

The key difference between the two methodologies is the view of efficiency: Should it be maximized everywhere, or just at the drum? The constraints-based approach holds that any local optimization of a nondrum resource will simply allow it to produce more than the drum operation can handle, which results in excess inventory. For example, a furniture company discovers that its drum operation is its paint shop. The company cannot produce more than 300 tables per day, because that maximizes the capacity of the paint shop. If the company adds a lathe to produce more table legs, this will only result in the accumulation of an excessive quantity of table legs rather than the production of a larger number of painted tables. Thus, the investment in efficiencies elsewhere than the drum operation will only increase costs without improving sales or profits.

The preceding example shows that not only should efficiency improvements *not* be made in areas other than the drum operation but that it is quite acceptable to not even be efficient in these other areas. It is better to stop work in a nondrum operation and idle its staff than to have it churn out more inventory than can be used by the drum operation.

Given the importance of focusing management attention on maximization of drum efficiencies, the use of buffers becomes extremely important. An inventory buffer should be positioned in front of the drum operation;

it is used to provide a sufficient amount of stock to the drum to keep it running at maximum efficiency, even when variations in upstream work centers create short-term reductions in the flow of incoming inventory. The need for a buffer brings up a major operational concept in the theory of constraints, which is that there will be inevitable production failures that will alter the flow of inventory through the facility. Buffers are used to absorb the shock of these production failures, though it is also possible to increase the level of sprint capacity to offset the need for large buffers.

Sprint capacity is excess capacity built into a production operation that allows the facility to create excess inventory in the short term, usually to make of up for sudden shortfalls in inventory levels. Sprint capacity is extremely useful for maintaining a sufficient flow of inventory into the drum operation, since the system can quickly recover from a production shortfall. If there is a great deal of sprint capacity in a production system, then there is less need for a buffer in front of the drum operation, since new inventory stocks can be generated quickly.

The concept of sprint capacity brings up an important point in the theory of constraints—that it is not only useful but necessary to have excess capacity levels available in a system. This controverts the traditional management approach of eliminating excess capacity in order to reduce the costs associated with maintaining that capacity. Instead, management should be aware of those work centers with high levels of sprint capacity, which require much lower levels of inventory buffer, and primarily focus its attention on areas with low sprint capacity, which require larger buffer stocks.

Thus far, we have seen that the theory of constraints places a premium on maximum utilization of the drum operation as well as the use of inventory buffers to support that utilization. One additional requirement is needed to ensure that the drum operates at maximum capacity at all times: the concept of the rope. The rope is the method used to release inventory into upstream production processes just in time to ensure that the drum operation and its buffer are fully supplied with the appropriate levels of work in process. If the rope releases inventory into the system too late, then the drum will be starved of input and will produce less than its maximum amount. Conversely, the release of inventory too early will result in a large backlog of unfinished parts in front of the drum, which both represents an excessive investment in inventory and may result in confusion regarding which jobs to process next through the drum operation.

Nature of the Constraint

The theory of constraints is based on the existence of a constraint, so it is useful to delve into the nature of this core concept. A constraint is a resource that limits a company's total output. For example, the constraint may be a machine that can produce only a specified amount of a key component in a given time period, thereby keeping overall sales from expanding beyond the maximum capacity of that machine. The key determining question to ask in locating this type of constraint is, if we had more of it, could we generate more sales? Physical constraints of this type tend to be easy to locate within a company, because there is usually a large amount of work in process piled up in front of it, waiting to be processed.

The most common system constraint cannot be seen or touched—it is the operational policy. A policy is a rule that dictates how a system is operated. Examples of policies are batch sizing rules and resource utilization guidelines. For instance, a policy may state that a workstation completely fill a pallet with work in process before sending it on the next workstation, since this makes it more efficient for the materials-handling staff to move inventory through the factory. The trouble is that the next workstation may be the constrained resource, which has to halt operations while waiting for the pallet to be filled. In this case, the policy should have allowed a more continuous flow of inventory to the constrained resource, which means that much smaller batch sizes would have improved the utilization of the constrained resource.

Policy constraints are usually difficult to find and eliminate. *Finding* them is difficult because policies are not physical entities that can be readily observed; instead, they must be deduced from the operational flow of the production system. *Eliminating* them can be even more difficult, since they may be strongly supported by employees, who require considerable convincing before agreeing to change a policy that they may have used for years. Though there may be considerable resistance to a policy change, the actual fix can be extremely inexpensive. Once eliminated, a policy constraint can result in a larger degree of system improvement than the elimination of any physical constraint.

A concept impacting the presence of policy constraints is the paradigm constraint. This is a belief that causes employees to follow a policy constraint. A classic paradigm constraint is the belief that every work center must be run at full tilt in order to increase its efficiency, which is something that traditional cost accounting theory teaches. However, this paradigm can result in a policy constraint to create a bonus plan that rewards factory managers for running all equipment at as close to 100 percent capacity as possible. The result is an excessive investment in inventory and the shift of resources away from the constrained resource. Thus, a paradigm constraint can be a powerful roadblock to the elimination of a policy constraint.

Another constraint may be a raw material, for which there is not enough to ensure that all orders can be filled. This less common problem tends to arise during bursts of peak industry-wide sales, when materials suppliers are caught with insufficient production capacity to meet all demand (which means that the constraint has now shifted to the supplier). This type of constraint will be immediately evident to the materials management staff, who cannot schedule jobs for release to the production area until sufficient materials are available.

Another possible constraint is the sales staff, when there are not enough people to bring in all possible customer orders. This constraint is made evident by a large number of sales prospects at the top of the sales funnel or a large potential market size but very few actual sales being generated.

A company may so improve its operations that its existing capacity can handle all orders currently placed by customers. If so, the constraint has now shifted into the marketplace. The company must now use its higher capacity to offer better pricing deals or service levels to the market in order to increase its share of the market.

A company can also intentionally position a constraint on a specific resource. This happens when the capacity of a particular resource would be extremely expensive to increase, so managers prefer to focus their attention on maximizing the efficiency of the work center without actually adding capacity to it. It is also useful to avoid positioning the constraint on a resource that requires a complex level of management, such as one where employee training or turnover levels are extremely high. Thus, the positioning of the constrained resource should be a management decision rather than an accident.

Definitions for the Financial Aspects of the Theory of Constraints

Explaining the financial aspects of the theory of constraints requires the use of several new terms (or old terms with new definitions), which are presented next.

- *Throughput.* The contribution margin that is left after a product's price is reduced by the amount of its totally variable costs (which is explained in the next bullet point). There is no attempt to allocate overhead costs to a product or to assign to it any semivariable costs. As a result, the amount of throughput for most products tends to be quite high.
- *Totally variable costs.* A cost that will be incurred only if a product is created. In many instances, this means that only direct materials are considered to be a totally variable cost, though subcontracting costs, commissions, customs duties, and transportation costs may also apply.

Direct labor is not totally variable unless employees are only paid if a product is produced. The same rule applies to all other costs, so no type of overhead cost will be found in the "totally variable cost" category.

- *Operating expenses.* The sum total of all company expenses, excluding totally variable expenses. Expenses usually categorized here are direct and indirect labor, depreciation, supplies, interest payments, and overhead. As a general rule, all expenses incurred as a result of the passage of time (rather than through the production process) are operating expenses. This group of expenses is considered to be the price a company pays to ensure that it maintains its current level of capacity. The theory of constraints does not care if a cost is semivariable, fixed, or allocated—all costs that are not totally variable are lumped together into the operating expenses category.
- *Investment.* This definition is the same would be found under standard accounting rules. However, there is a particular emphasis on a company's investment in working capital (especially inventory). The value of a company's investment in inventory does not include the value added by the system itself; so it does not include the value of direct labor or manufacturing overhead. The investment in inventory only includes amounts paid for components that are purchased from outside suppliers and used in the manufacture of inventory.
- *Net profit.* Throughput minus operating expenses.

These definitions are used to describe the financial aspects of the theory of constraints in the next two sections.

Financial Aspects of the Theory of Constraints

The earlier discussion of the operational aspects of the theory of constraints might not appear to have a great deal of application to cost reduction analysis, but its financial aspects are actually quite important. Cost reduction analysis is concerned with two aspects of the theory of constraints: investments in fixed assets and the impact of cost reductions on throughput. This section deals with both issues.

A key concept of throughput is the use of profitability analysis at the system level instead of gross margin analysis at the product level. In a traditional cost accounting system, costs from all parts of the production process are compiled and allocated by various means to specific products. When subtracted from product prices, this yields a gross margin that is used to determine whether a product is sufficiently profitable to be produced. Throughput almost entirely ignores gross margin analysis at the product level. Instead, it considers the production process to be a single system whose overall profitability must be maximized.

The key reason for this difference in perspective is that most production costs do not vary directly with the incremental production of a single unit of a product. Instead, most production costs are required to maintain a *system* of production, irrespective of the number of product units created by it. For example, a traditional cost accounting system will assign the depreciation cost of a production machine to an overhead account from which it is allocated by various means to each unit of a product manufactured. However, if one unit were not produced, would this result in a proportionate drop in the amount of overhead cost? Probably not. Instead, the same amount of overhead would now be assigned to the fewer remaining units produced, which raises their costs and lowers their gross profits.

To avoid this costing conundrum, throughput analysis uses an entirely different methodology, which is comprised of three elements: throughput, operating expenses, and investment. The key element of the three is throughput. To arrive at throughput, we subtract all *totally* variable costs from revenue. In reality, the only cost that varies totally with a product is the cost of its direct material. Even the cost of direct labor does not usually vary with the number of units produced. In how many companies can one find a situation where the staff immediately goes home when the last product is completed, or where employees are paid solely based on the number of units of production they create? Instead, the staff is employed on various projects during downtime periods to ensure that the same experienced staff is available for work the next day. The result of the throughput calculation is a very high level of throughput—much higher than a product's gross margin, which includes both labor and overhead costs.

The result of using throughput instead of gross margin is that hardly any products will *not* be produced due to a negative margin. This will occur in a throughput analysis environment only if a product's revenue is matched or exceeded by its raw material cost, which is rarely the case. Instead, products with a low throughput will still be included in the product mix, since they contribute to some degree to the total throughput of a company's production system.

The next element of throughput analysis is the concept of operating expenses. This is all other expenses besides the totally variable ones used to calculate throughput. Operating expenses are essentially all costs required to operate the production system. In throughput analysis, there is no distinction between totally fixed or partially fixed costs; instead, they are either totally variable costs or part of operating expenses. By avoiding the considerable level of analysis required to deduce the variable elements of most largely fixed costs, financial analysis is greatly simplified.

Throughput analysis also places considerable emphasis on investment, which is the amount of money added to a system to improve its capacity. When combined with throughput, totally variable costs, and operating expenses, throughput analysis uses the next formulas for a wide array of accounting decisions:

Revenue – totally variable expenses = throughput

Throughput – operating expenses = net profit

Net profit/investment = return on investment

When making a decision involving changes to revenue, expenses, or investments, these three formulas can be used to arrive at the correct decision, which must yield a positive answer to one of the next three questions:

1. Does it increase throughput?
2. Does it reduce operating expenses?
3. Does it improve the return on investment?

If a localized decision yields a positive answer to any one of these questions, then it will also improve the company-wide system, and so should be implemented.

When answering these three questions, it is best to favor decisions resulting in increased throughput, since there is potentially no upper limit to the amount of throughput that a company can generate. Decisions resulting in reduced operating expenses should be given the lowest action priority, since there is a limited amount of operating expense that can be reduced; also, a reduction of operating expenses may limit the production capacity of the system, which in turn may yield less throughput.

Opportunity Cost of Operations

A major concept of throughput analysis is to determine the true cost to a company of its capacity constraint. The capacity constraint is the drum operation, as described earlier in this chapter. If the use of the drum is not maximized, what is the opportunity cost to the company?

In a traditional cost accounting system, the cost would be the forgone gross margin on any products that could not be produced by the operation. For example, a work center experiences downtime of one hour, because the machine operator is on a scheduled break. During that one hour, the work center could have created 20 products having a gross margin of $4.00

each. Traditional cost accounting tells us that this represents a loss of $80. Given this information, a manager might very well not back-fill the machine operator and allow the machine to stay idle for the one-hour break period.

However, throughput analysis uses a different calculation of the cost of the capacity constraint. Since the performance of the constraint drives the total throughput of the entire system, the opportunity cost of not running that operation is actually the total operating expense of running the entire facility, divided by the number of hours during which the capacity constraint is being operated. This is because it is not possible to speed up the constrained operation, resulting in the permanent loss of any units that are not produced. For example, if the monthly operating expenses of a facility are $1.2 million and the constrained resource is run for every hour of that month, or 720 hours (30 days × 24 hours/day), then the cost per hour of the operation is $1,667 ($1,200,000 ÷ 720 hours). Given this much higher cost of not running the operation, a manager will be much more likely to find a replacement operator for break periods.

What about the cost of not running a *non*constrained resource operation? As long as its downtime does not impact the operation of the constrained resource, it has no opportunity cost at all. In fact, the situation is reversed, for it is actually better to run nonconstraint resources only at the pace of the drum operation, since any excess inventory produced will just increase the amount of inventory in the production system—and this represents an additional investment in the system for which there is no offsetting increase in throughput.

Thus, there are substantial differences in the opportunity cost of running various operations, which can be interpreted differently with different accounting systems. Throughput analysis focuses attention on the high cost of not running a constrained resource while showing that there is a negative opportunity cost associated with running a nonconstrained resource more than it is needed.

Locating the Constraint

Throughput analysis is centered on the total optimization of the constrained resource. However, in order to properly manage it, we must first locate this resource. It may not be immediately apparent, especially in a large production environment with many products, routings, and work centers. It is this noise in the system that prevents us from easily identifying constraints. Here are some questions to ask that will help locate it:

- *Where is there a work backlog?* If there is an area where work virtually never catches up with demand, where expeditors are constantly hovering, and where there are large quantities of inventory piled up, this is a likely constraint area.

- *Where do most problems originate?* Management usually finds itself hovering around only a small number of work centers whose problems never seem to go away. Continuing problems are common at constrained resources, because they are so heavily utilized that there is never enough time to perform a sufficient level of maintenance, resulting in recurring breakdowns. In addition, there tends to be a fight over work priorities when there is not sufficient capacity, which also means that managers will be regularly called on to determine these priorities among competing orders.
- *Where are the expediters?* An expediter physically steers a high-priority job through the production process. Because they frequently wait while their assigned jobs are being processed, their presence (especially several of them together) is a good indicator of a bottleneck where they must wait for available production time.
- *Which work centers have high utilization?* Many companies measure the utilization level of their work centers. If so, review the list to determine which ones have a continually high level of utilization over multiple months. If a work center attains high utilization only briefly, it could still be the constraint if the reason for the lower utilization is ongoing maintenance problems or employee absenteeism.
- *What happens to total throughput when the constraint capacity changes?* If we add to the capacity of the suspected constraint, is there a noticeable increase in throughput? Conversely, if we deliberately *reduce* the capacity of the targeted work center (not recommended as a testing technique), does overall throughput decline? If throughput does alter as a result of these changes, then we have probably located the constrained resource.

If, after this analysis, a company picks the wrong operation as its constrained resource, the real constraint will soon appear because of changes in the inventory buffers in front of the real and fake constraints. If the real constraint is upstream from the fake constraint, then the inventory buffer in front of the fake constraint will disappear. This happens because management will focus its attention on improving the efficiency of the fake resource, thereby wiping out its backlog of work. The real constraint will be readily apparent, because it still has an inventory backlog. Conversely, if the real constraint is downstream from the fake constraint, then a larger inventory backlog will build in front of it. This happens because the same improvement in efficiency at the fake resource will result in a flood of additional inventory heading downstream, where it will dam up at the real constraint.

If products are engineered to order, then consider the engineering department to be part of the production process. This is important from the perspective of locating the constraint, because the constraint may not be in the traditional production area at all but rather in the engineering department. Similarly, and for all types of product sales, the constraint may also reside in the sales department, where there may not be enough staff available to convert a large proportion of sales prospects into orders. This constraint is most evident when there are clearly many sales prospects at the top of the sales funnel, but there is a choke point somewhere in the sales conversion process, below which few orders are received. If this is the case, the solution is to enhance staffing for the sales positions specifically needed to improve handling of sales prospects at the choke point in the sales funnel.

Another constraint can also be raw materials. This problem arises during periods of excessive industry demand, resulting in materials allocations from suppliers. The location of this constraint will be immediately apparent to the materials management staff, which will have to reschedule production based on the shortage. However, this problem tends to be a short-term one, after which the constraint shifts back from the supplier and into the company.

It is also possible to *designate* a work center as the constrained resource. Taking this proactive approach is most useful when a work center requires a great deal of additional investment or highly skilled staffing to increase its capacity. By requiring that the constraint be focused on this area, management can profitably spend its time ensuring that the work center is fully utilized. It is also useful to avoid positioning the constraint on a resource that requires considerable management to operate properly, such as one where employee training or turnover levels are extremely high. Thus, positioning the constrained resource can be a management decision rather than an incidental occurrence.

Example

The Baroque Furniture Company specializes in the construction and gilding of carved furniture. Its production manager has just returned from a constraint management seminar, and wants to locate the constraint within Baroque's production process. Baroque uses these steps to create its signature line of gilded furniture:

1. Assemble furniture kits from subcontractor.
2. Hand carve designs on furniture.

3. Add a calcium carbonate and adhesive base layer to the furniture.
4. Apply pigment to adhesive base layer.
5. Apply gold leaf.
6. Burnish gold leaf.

Baroque's production policies have thus far emphasized high levels of efficiency for all production processes, so an examination of work center utilization levels only reveals that *all* parts of the production process are being heavily used.

Another way to locate the constraint is to determine which processes have the largest buildup of work-in-process inventory in front of them, which implies that they have insufficient capacity to handle the standard workload. The production manager obtains the backlog information shown in the next table, which itemizes the total minutes of processing time required to clear the backlog in front of each workstation:

Step	Process	Minutes to Process Backlog
1	Assemble furniture kits from subcontractor	895
2	Hand carve designs on furniture	3,050
3	Add adhesive base layer	290
4	Apply pigment to adhesive base layer	510
5	Apply gold leaf	1,400
6	Burnish gold leaf	3,425

The exhibit reveals that Baroque appears to have *two* constrained resources: the wood carving and burnishing departments. Both have large work backlogs of approximately the same size.

The production manager now has the opportunity to select which of the two processes will be the primary production constraint. Both departments require large quantities of manual labor to complete, so Baroque can hire additional staff or internally shift staff between workstations to reduce the backlog in both areas. However, the burnishing process requires minimal skill, whereas the wood carving process requires very expensive labor, which is also hard to attract and retain. Accordingly, the production manager shifts several employees from the furniture assembly area to the gold leaf burnishing department,

Continued

resulting in the modified work backlog shown in the next table, where 1,000 minutes of work backlog has been added to the furniture assembly area (because its staffing has been reduced) and 1,000 minutes of backlog have been cut from the burnishing area (because its staffing has been increased).

Step	Process	Minutes to Process Backlog
1	Assemble furniture kits from subcontractor	1,895
2	Hand carve designs on furniture	3,050
3	Add adhesive base layer	290
4	Apply pigment to adhesive base layer	510
5	Apply gold leaf	1,400
6	Burnish gold leaf	2,425

By shifting some low-skilled labor between work areas, the production manager has clearly identified the wood carving department as being Baroque's preferred choice for its constrained resource. Baroque can now focus on the management of this high labor-cost area, as is described in the next case study.

The pointers in this section are useful tools for locating a company's constrained resource. If not successfully located at once, a small number of iterations will soon cull out any "pretender" constraints, leaving the real constraint laid bare to a heightened level of management attention, as noted in the next section.

Management of the Constrained Resource

Once identified and isolated, management can use a number of ways to improve the throughput of the constrained resource. Several of the more common techniques are listed next.

- *Cover break time.* When employees stop a constrained resource to take a break from work, the company is suffering from the lost throughput that could have been generated during their break time. It is almost always cost effective to pay someone else to work at the constraint during the work break, thereby gaining back capacity that would otherwise be gone for good. It is also possible to schedule the maintenance staff to work on the constraint during a break period; this makes sense when the maintenance staff would have otherwise shut down the machine during some other time period; combining two types of scheduled shutdown into one is an effective way to increase throughput.

- *Avoid downtime during shift changes.* A common occurrence is for a machine or work center to be shut down during a shift change, since outgoing employees like to spend a few minutes cleaning up their work areas before leaving, while incoming employees may require some time to review work schedules or attend meetings before they begin work. To avoid this downtime, consider having overlapping shifts, so that the incoming shift is on-site before the outgoing shift is scheduled to leave. This arrangement is necessary only for the constrained resource, not for other work centers that have excess capacity.

- *Offload incidental work.* If a machine operator is required not only to process materials at his workstation but also to conduct maintenance and cleanup work, then there is a high likelihood that productive work will stop while the operator handles these additional tasks. This is a particular problem in companies where the maintenance department attempts to offload periodic minor maintenance onto the production staff; though this makes the job of the maintenance staff much easier, it can also reduce throughput. A better solution is to have an assistant handle all incidental work, thereby leaving the machine operator to ensure that the work center operates at maximum efficiency.

- *Replace equipment with staff.* In some cases, machines have replaced employees because of their higher processing speeds. However, employees may still be an alternative to the use of machines, since people can be more easily shifted in and out of constraint tasks. Thus, proper staff scheduling to handle work overloads at the constraint can result in a net increase in throughput.

- *Review for quality in front of the constraint.* The constrained resource has only a fixed amount of processing time available, so do not waste it by running materials through the constraint that already contain flaws that will lead to their rejection further in the manufacturing process. Instead, position a quality assurance person directly in front of the constraint; this person is responsible for culling out any low-quality materials before they are used by the constrained resource.

- *Avoid rework at the constraint.* If the processing work at the constrained resource is not done properly, then materials must be routed back through this work center, which uses up valuable throughput time. To avoid it, have the industrial engineering staff closely examine the reasons why rework problems arise here and reduce their causes to a minimal level.

- *Have backup staff available.* The operators of the constrained resource may not require the most extensive training (since this work center may not involve the most complex work in the facility), but it may still be a problem to locate replacements when the regular staff inevitably takes time off for a variety of reasons. To mitigate this issue, always have multiple, fully trained backup staff available. It may even be useful to give the backup employees regular training sessions, taught by the regular operators, just to ensure that they will operate at the highest possible level of efficiency when they are filling in for the regular staff. It is useful to pay a bonus to designated backup staff, just to ensure that there are enough volunteers available for this role.
- *Raise pay.* The best possible staffing should be used on the constrained resource. However, if the work is uninteresting, employees will be more likely to call in sick or transfer to other workstations. To ensure that the best possible staff is always manning the constraint, offer the highest pay rate in the facility to those operators willing to work there.
- *Offload work to in-house work centers.* If there are other work centers in the production facility that can create products that are normally processed at the constrained resource—no matter how inefficient they may be—it will likely be cost effective to shift some overflow work to these other work centers. By doing so, more throughput can be generated while excess (and free) capacity at the other work centers can be utilized.
- *Outsource work.* If there are no opportunities to use the preceding recommendations to improve the throughput of in-house operations, consider outsourcing some part of the production work to suppliers. As long as the throughput generated from this work exceeds its incremental outsourcing cost, outsourcing is a viable option. Also, the supplier must be willing to invest in enough capacity to meet maximum demand levels, consistently make deliveries in time for the company to meet its customers' delivery dates, and ideally have the potential to grow beyond current production quantities as demand levels increase over time.

Example

In the preceding example, the Baroque Furniture Company has chosen its wood carving process to be its constrained resource. This is an excellent choice of constraint, because of the high cost of the skilled labor needed for the wood carving process. Baroque's production manager, Ms. Stark, finds that this work area currently has a backlog of 3,050 minutes of work. At an average throughput per minute of $8.00 or $480.00 per hour, this represents $24,400 of throughput that Baroque is unable to recognize.

Due to the highly individual nature of the work, Ms. Stark finds that it is impossible to cover employee break time or lost time that occurs at shift changes; it is simply impossible to have more than one person carve a single piece of furniture. However, further analysis reveals that the wood carvers divide their work into two stages: the tracing of their proposed design on the furniture, followed by carving in multiple stages to attain the proper level of relief. Ms. Stark finds that by hiring lower-cost artisans who first trace designs onto the wood surfaces of the furniture, the carvers can concentrate their attention strictly on the carving work, resulting in a higher level of capacity.

Ms. Stark now divides the wood carving department into two departments, the first for design tracing and the second for wood carving. By more narrowly defining the scope of the constrained resource, the same group of wood carvers now has extra time to devote to carving, which results in a drop in the number of backlog minutes.

Ms. Stark also discovers that an occasional piece of furniture develops cracks that are only discovered during the gilding stage, when the gold lamination tends to highlight irregularities in the underlying material. This problem applies to only 1 percent of all furniture pieces used, but this means that it wastes 1 percent of the throughput of the wood carving operation, since the results of its efforts must now be scrapped. Ms. Stark finds that it is possible to discover these flaws with a high degree of accuracy simply by scanning the wood with a small magnifying lens, called a hand loupe. Since the new design tracing team positioned immediately in front of the carving department has excess time available, she arranges to have them conduct the quality assurance review with hand loupes. By doing so, Baroque incurs no additional labor expenditure and only a tiny investment in hand loupes, and effectively increases the throughput of the carving operation by 1 percent.

Ms. Stark also finds that an excessive degree of burnishing in the last production step can heat the underlying wood surface to such an extent that the gold surface becomes discolored. When this happens, all gilding must be removed, the wood surface sanded down by the wood carving department, and the gilding reapplied. In the most recent month, this rework required 550 minutes of work by the wood carvers. At $8 per minute of throughput time, this represented the loss of $4,400 of throughput. However, by positioning thermal sensors near the wood surfaces during the burnishing stage, employees could be warned of

Continued

temperature increases likely to cause discoloration and stop burnishing until temperature levels drop. Buy purchasing 10 of these thermal sensors for $250 each, Ms. Stark can invest $2,500 and earn back her investment in saved throughput in just a few weeks.

By shifting some tasks away from the constrained resource, moving the quality assurance function immediately in front of the constraint, and reducing rework, Baroque has increased the amount of throughput generated by its furniture wood carving department without adding any expensive staff to this operation.

There are two other ways to manage the constrained resource, which are the use of proper inventory buffering and production scheduling (which are the "buffer-rope" elements of the "drum-buffer-rope" system). After a short diversion to address policy constraints, we will describe the proper management of buffers and production scheduling.

Types of Policy Constraints

A policy constraint is an extremely common problem that can reduce throughput levels. A policy is a rule that dictates how a system is operated, such as a *batch sizing rule* that a crate must be filled with work in process before being moved to the next downstream workstation. The trouble is that such a policy may keep materials from arriving at the downstream workstation in a timely manner, which is starved of materials until the appropriate delivery crate is filled and is then flooded with work when the crate arrives. Spotting the policy constraint in this example is relatively simple, because it results in downstream operations being alternatively flooded with materials or starved. This boom-famine cycle occurs because inventory builds up at an upstream workstation until a sufficient quantity has been completed to meet the policy guideline, triggering delivery of a large quantity to the downstream workstation.

Conversely, if an operation is continually starved of materials (but never flooded), then the constraint is likely to be caused by an upstream work center with inadequate capacity rather than a policy.

There are a number of other common policy constraints. For example, a negotiated *break rule* that allows all machine operators a half-hour break period is a constraint when this means that no one is operating the constrained resource during that half-hour period. In this case, the problem caused by the policy is obvious, but the solution may require painful labor negotiations to achieve. This problem arises for all types of *work rules*, which are frequently imposed by union agreements.

Another policy causing a constraint is the requirement to always have *production runs that do not drop below a set minimum level.* An excessively long production run creates too much inventory and also uses up valuable time at the constrained resource; thus, shorter production runs that only match immediate customer requirements are to be encouraged. This policy is usually engendered by a cost accounting analysis that points out that the cost of an expensive equipment setup can be reduced if spread over the cost of a great many units of production. However, since most work centers have excess capacity, the time required to make extra equipment setups for shorter production runs is actually free. This type of policy is discovered by investigating whether the scheduled amount of a production run matches demand, or if an excessive quantity has been scheduled by the production planner. Another form of evidence is the presence of economic lot sizing rules where the computer recommends a lot size rather than using the amount of actual customer orders. A secondary investigative approach is to review recent additions of finished goods to the warehouse and determine if they were added because of excess production.

Another policy constraint is *overtime avoidance.* Plant managers are frequently judged on their ability to keep employee overtime levels to a minimum in order to reduce labor expenses. However, when the incurrence of overtime can keep the constrained resource operational, the resulting increased throughput should easily outweigh any overtime costs. This constraint can be spotted by investigating the reasons for downtime at the constrained resource.

A policy that causes considerable trouble for the constrained resource is the concept of attaining *production line balance.* Under this concept, the best production process is one where there is just barely a sufficient level of production capacity in all work centers to complete the work listed in the production schedule. This approach assumes that costs can be stripped out of the production process by deliberately limiting capacity levels in all areas. The problem with it is that any production shortfall in any work center will almost certainly limit the production of the constrained resource and so will reduce throughput. This policy is readily apparent in most cases, because it takes a great deal of deliberate effort to achieve product line balance. A form of indirect evidence of line balancing is when constraints appear to crop up in many places and seem to move around the production floor even during a single day.

Perhaps the worst policy constraint is the general belief that a company *must run all of its resources at their maximum levels* in order to gain the highest level of efficiency and therefore (supposedly) the highest level of profit. This is not precisely a policy constraint, since it is not always formally enunciated, but is more of a *paradigm constraint,* where everyone's underlying view of the production process is that all resources are to be run flat out. In reality, only the constrained resource must be run at the highest level of efficiency; many other resources should operate only when needed. This constraint is most easily spotted by checking for work center efficiency reports for areas that are not constrained resources.

Most of the policy constraints noted in this section share one bond: They are based on the concept of *local optimization*. Each one is designed to optimize a specific performance measurement rather than the throughput of the entire system. For example, banning overtime will reduce labor costs, not paying delivery charges will cut freight costs, and long production runs will cut the average setup cost. However, in all cases, they also reduce the total amount of throughput generated. Because of this common underlying problem, it is useful to analyze every production policy and determine if it is based on local optimization. If so, it is probably having a negative impact on throughput, or has the potential for doing so.

Given the number of examples shown in this section, it is evident that a production process may be rife with policy constraints. Accordingly, one should devote a considerable amount of time to the investigation of all policies that could impact throughput.

Having covered numerous aspects of the constrained resource, including its location, management, and mitigation, we will now move on to the use of buffers, which are key tools for enhancing the productive efficiency of the constraint.

Constraint Buffer

The buffer of inventory placed immediately in front of the constrained resource is critical to the throughput maximization of the constraint, because the buffer protects the constraint from a work shutdown caused by a shortage of processed materials coming from upstream workstations. An inadequate buffer will result in periods when there are no materials to feed the constraint, yielding a throughput decline just as severe as if the constraint itself were mismanaged. These shortages can be caused by a wide array of production problems that are bound to occur to some degree, despite a company's best efforts to root out their causes. Though it may be possible to reduce the size of these production variations, there will *always* be variations—and the buffer is used to protect the constraint from them. If the level of production variation is high, then the protective buffer will be commensurately large, while smaller variations will call for the use of a much smaller buffer.

If a company has minimal excess capacity in its nonconstraint areas, it will have an extremely difficult time recovering from a production shortfall, since it is only barely able to keep up with the demands of the constrained resource. This will likely result in a very long time to rebuild the inventory buffer if the buffer has been reduced to cover a production shortfall. Consequently, if there is a minimum amount of excess production capacity upstream from the constraint, management must choose between maintaining a large buffer or investing in more excess capacity. Since it is difficult to establish a large buffer in the first place (because there is so little excess capacity), the only real choice left is to invest in extra capacity or tolerate stock-out conditions at the constraint.

This does not mean that a company should invest in inordinate amounts of excess capacity throughout its facility—far from it. Instead, managers can measure the amount of capacity that would have been needed to rebuild inventory buffers within a reasonable time period and then invest only in that incremental amount of capacity. If the capacity problem relates to a work center that uses labor, rather than machine time, then the appropriate response is to engage in enough employee cross-training to ensure that staffing levels can be rapidly increased if a significant amount of extra inventory is needed.

An alternative to increasing the size of the inventory buffer is to intentionally replace it with so much upstream sprint capacity that the system can very rapidly replenish inventory shortages in front of the constrained resource. However, this is not normally a cost-effective solution, since capacity increases are usually much more expensive than incremental increases in inventory at the buffer. It can be a useful technique if used solely to address recovery from very large upstream variances that would otherwise call for the use of an inordinately large buffer.

Example

In the preceding two examples, the Baroque Furniture Company has chosen its wood carving department to be its constrained resource and has taken a number of steps to improve the throughput of that operation. Another problem faced by Baroque is its furniture source, which is located in Italy. For highly precise wood carving, the best wood choice is Italian walnut, which Baroque purchases from the Lombardy region of north-central Italy. The supplier processes the wood into precut furniture kits, which Baroque's assembly operation drills and glues together before passing them along to the wood carving department. Because of the distant location of its furniture source, Baroque has historically taken advantage of large shipping container sizes and ordered in bulk, thereby reducing its shipping costs. However, this also

Continued

means that replenishment deliveries only arrive at long intervals, which increases the risk that a materials shortage may occur that shuts down the wood carving department.

The production manager, Ms. Stark, faces the alternatives of doing nothing, placing smaller furniture orders that are delivered more frequently, or creating an inventory buffer to protect the wood carving department from materials shortages. An evaluation of each alternative reveals:

1. *Do nothing.* A review of stock-out conditions at the wood carving department reveals that the department averages 500 minutes of downtime per month that is caused by materials shortages. At an average throughput rate of $8.00 per minute, this equates to $4,000 per month of lost throughput (500 minutes of downtime × $8.00/ minute average throughput). Thus, Baroque loses $4,000 per month by taking no action.

2. *Place smaller orders.* If Baroque places orders of half the usual size and does so twice as frequently, then the duration of the average stock-out period should be cut in half, which reduces the minutes of downtime per month by half, to 250. This equates to a reduction of lost throughput of $2,000 (250 minutes downtime saved × $8.00/minute average throughput). However, because furniture is now shipped in smaller quantities, freight charges increase by $1,750 per month, resulting in a net profit improvement of only $250 per month.

3. *Create inventory buffer.* Ms. Stark calculates that if Baroque invests in an inventory buffer costing $10,000, this will be of a size sufficient to prevent 300 minutes of downtime per month that would otherwise be caused by material shortages. To eliminate the entire 500 minutes of downtime caused by material shortages will require a much larger inventory buffer of $40,000. In the first case, increased throughput of $2,400 per month (300 minutes × $8.00/ minute average throughput) equates to a payback period of the $10,000 investment of about 4 months. In the second case, increased throughput of $4,000 per month (500 minutes × $8.00/minute average throughput) equates to a payback period of the $40,000 investment of about 10 months.

Of the scenarios presented, Ms. Stark would be well advised to build a $40,000 inventory buffer in front of the wood carving department, thereby earning a significant return on this working capital investment within one year.

In some cases where proper buffer management can have a large impact on throughput, there may even be a "buffer manager" whose sole responsibility is the monitoring and replenishment of the buffer. The buffer manager will note the reason for delays causing buffer penetrations and work with the production manager to mitigate these delays in the future. The buffer manager may also engage in *dynamic buffering*. This is the careful management of buffers and upstream capacity levels to achieve the smallest possible investment in inventory and sprint capacity to ensure that throughput levels are maximized at a cost-effective level.

A hole in the buffer occurs when a planned upstream work center does not complete work by the scheduled date and time, resulting in the late arrival of materials in the buffer. Usually, only a small number of upstream work centers cause these buffer holes. These work centers can be easily spotted by using a buffer penetration chart such as the one shown in Exhibit 12.2. The report shows when buffer penetrations occur and identifies the originating workstation. The buffer manager uses this report to target problem areas requiring immediate resolution.

In summary, proper management of the buffer placed in front of the constrained resource is crucial to the attainment of high throughput levels.

Production Scheduling

The final key element of constraint management in the factory is the rope, which is the timed release of raw materials into the production process to ensure that a job reaches the constrained resource when it is needed. The person driving this work is the production scheduler, who must ensure that all nonconstraint resources are working on the right jobs and in the right sequence and batch quantities to meet the constrained resource's

EXHIBIT 12.2 Buffer Management Report

Date	Arrival Time Required	Actual Arrival Time	Originating Workstation	Cause of Delay
Sept. 11	9/11, 2 p.m.	9/12, 3 p.m.	Paint shop	Paint nozzles clogged
Sept. 14	9/14, 9 a.m.	9/16, 4 p.m.	Electrolysis	Power outage
Sept. 19	9/19, 10 a.m.	9/19, 4 p.m.	Electrolysis	Electrodes corroded
Sept. 19	9/19, 4 p.m.	9/25, 10 a.m.	Paint shop	Paint nozzles clogged
Sept. 23	9/23, 1 p.m.	9/24, 9 a.m.	Paint shop	Ran out of paint

schedule. This section shows how constraint management is used to clarify and simplify the role of the production scheduler and, in so doing, describes the rope mechanism.

The first issue a scheduler must deal with is the order of priority for jobs. The overriding corporate goal is to maximize total throughput, but the scheduler must ensure that *all* orders accepted by the company are delivered to customers in a timely manner. Thus, the maximization of throughput is a fine goal but is handled at a strategic level by top management. The production scheduler has been given a specific set of orders to fulfill, and must find a way to do so—irrespective of the throughput associated with each one. Consequently, the amount of throughput associated with a job is not a valid criterion for its order of production priority.

Instead, the production scheduler must work with other scheduling criteria. First in importance is any job that would otherwise be delivered late to the customer. Any company cannot stay in business for long if it persistently delivers late, since customers will find more reliable suppliers in the future. Next in importance is inventory that can be reworked. There are two reasons for this enhanced level of priority.

1. Rework usually sits in the production area until fixed, and so interferes with the flow of production.
2. It is frequently associated with specific customer jobs, and so must be completed in order to meet required ship dates.

The third level of scheduling priority is all other jobs on a first-in, first-out (FIFO) basis. This third priority covers most production scheduling jobs, and merely states that a customer order will be handled in the order in which it was received. However, if a job is currently located directly in front of the constraint, the constraint can process it at once, and other higher-priority jobs are delayed, then that job should be handled in front of other FIFO-scheduled jobs in order to maximize resource usage. There will also be cases where special customers will receive priority treatment, but this modified FIFO rule works well in most situations. The fourth level of priority is any in-house inventory replenishment. Thus, production is scheduled in this order:

1. Orders in danger of being delivered late
2. Rework
3. All other customer orders sequenced as of their receipt dates, subject to their physical location near the constrained resource
4. Inventory replenishment

By requiring that all other orders follow the listed priorities, a company will experience a relatively smooth flow of orders through its production area.

Production priorities are impossible to assign if the scheduler is basing her scheduling calculations on an unreasonable amount of available constraint time. For example, the absolute maximum number of minutes available at the constraint per week is 10,080 minutes (7 days × 24 hours × 60 minutes). However, this assumes that the resource is actually operational for that period of time, which is virtually never the case. There will be downtime for both preventive and unscheduled maintenance as well as stoppages caused by raw material or work-in-process shortages, or staffing problems. There may be a number of other Murphy's Law issues that will further reduce the amount of available capacity, so the actual available amount of time is substantially lower than 10,080 minutes per week. Consequently, the production scheduler should formulate a schedule based only on the average number of constraint minutes available, based on a rolling average over the past few weeks or months.

A similar limiting factor in the determination of available constraint time is the consideration of how many batches will be run by the constrained resource, and in what size. An excessive number of small jobs and related setups will adversely impact the number of minutes available at the constraint. This issue is covered in the next section.

Another factor in the production scheduling task, besides the amount of available constraint time, is the amount of available labor. Labor costs are theoretically more fixed than variable, and so are irrelevant to the scheduling decision, on the assumption that there will be sufficient labor capacity to meet all reasonable production scheduling requirements. However, there are some types of processing that require specific types of skilled labor that may not be so readily available. If so, the production scheduler must also make use of a labor capacity planning model that multiplies the prospective production schedule by the types of labor required, as noted in the labor routing files, in order to compare the amount of required labor to available resources. This may result in rescheduling to match available labor resources.

Another scheduling issue is the timing of the release of raw materials into the production process. The production scheduler should never release materials too early or in excessive quantities, because this merely clutters the work area with a large amount of inventory that is not yet needed and that can confuse the production staff regarding which waiting work-in-process items should be processed next. Instead, raw materials should be released at the pace of the constraint, so that the materials arrive at the constraint buffer shortly before they are needed, and only in the amounts needed. The timing of materials release can be calculated as the time required to keep the constraint buffer full, plus the processing time required by all operations upstream of the constrained resource.

Example

As noted in the preceding three case studies, the Baroque Furniture Company constructs furniture from kits delivered from its Italian supplier, carves ornate patterns in the furniture, and applies gilding to the results before shipping them to customers. Baroque's production manager, Ms. Stark, is having problems determining the precise point in time when furniture kits should be released from the warehouse into the furniture assembly department, which in turn feeds the constrained resource, which is the wood carving department. There is some pressure from the sales staff to tell Baroque's demanding customers that their orders are "in production," which means that orders are released into the manufacturing area before they can be processed. By doing so, the furniture assembly department becomes flooded with work in process, making it difficult to determine which jobs are to be completed next.

During a seminar on constraint management, Ms. Stark learns that materials should be released based on the processing time required by all operations upstream of the constrained resource while still ensuring that the inventory buffer in front of the constraint remains full. Since there is only one department upstream of the wood carving department (i.e., the furniture assembly department), the release of materials into the production area is calculated based on the time required to assemble each furniture model. There is no batching policy requiring several items of furniture to be completed before being transported to the inventory buffer; instead, each completed item is transported to the buffer at once. The furniture department assembles four types of furniture, which are identified in the next table along with their assembly times.

Furniture Type	Assembly Type
Chair, Louis XIV style	9 hours
Console table, duke style	7 hours
Cupboard, imperial style	20 hours
Mini chaise, viscount style	12 hours

Multiple furniture kits of each model are being assembled at any given time. To create a controlled release of materials, Ms. Stark prepositions a one-day supply of kits in front of the assembly area and then releases then into that department using a kanban system, whereby the completion of one item of furniture triggers the release of a corresponding kit into the assembly area. For example, there are always five imperial style cupboards being assembled; given a total assembly time of 20 hours each, one cupboard should be completed every 4 hours. Accordingly, the warehouse staff positions two cupboard kits in front of the assembly area (comprising one day of demand), and moves one into the assembly area every 4 hours, as soon as a completed unit is sent to the inventory buffer in front of the wood carving department.

The result is a considerable reduction in work in process, with more inventory being retained in the warehouse rather than cluttering the production area.

There is also a strong production scheduling tendency to impose a large number of concurrent jobs on the production staff. When this happens, work centers keep shifting between multiple projects, with the result that their focus becomes diluted, and all jobs are delivered later than scheduled. A better approach is to reduce the number of jobs allowed into production to an optimum amount that can be discerned through trial and error. This reduced number sharpens the focus of the production staff, resulting in faster job completion.

This job release approach runs contrary to many scheduling systems, where customers want to hear that their orders are "in production," even if this only means that their order is languishing somewhere on the shop floor until such time as the manufacturing staff can get to it.

Finally, when work-in-process inventory *leaves* the constraint, there should be a sufficient amount of downstream production capacity to use standard labor routings to estimate the amount of effort required to predict the final ship date. It is then possible to use this calculated ship date to work backward and accurately determine the material release dates for other items that do not need to pass through the constraint operation. By doing so, all items required for final assembly, no matter what course they may follow through the production process, will arrive at the final assembly area with sufficient time to meet the shipment date.

In summary, the production scheduler must use a combination of scheduling priorities, realistic constraint capacity estimates, labor constraint planning, minimal nonconstraint production, and restrictive material releases to ensure that throughput will be optimized. These are the basic tenets of the "rope" element of the drum-buffer-rope constraint management system.

In the next section, we expand on the use of batch sizing to maximize the number of available constraint minutes.

Batch Sizes

Batch sizing is a key aspect of constraint management, because it impacts the rate at which inventory reaches the constrained resource and therefore the amount of throughput to be realized. This section covers the impact of smaller batch sizes on overall throughput.

The inventory buffer situated in front of the constrained resource must be maintained at an adequate size, or else there is a heightened chance that the constraint will run out of materials, thereby reducing throughput. Though it is always possible to invest in a larger inventory buffer (if upstream capacity will allow it), an alternative scenario is apparent in Exhibit 12.3. In the exhibit, Case A reveals a buffer requiring a maximum stocking level of 100 units in order to ensure that buffer holes never reach the expedite zone. This stocking level is mandated by the use of large batch sizes, whereby the buffer is drawn down to low levels while large

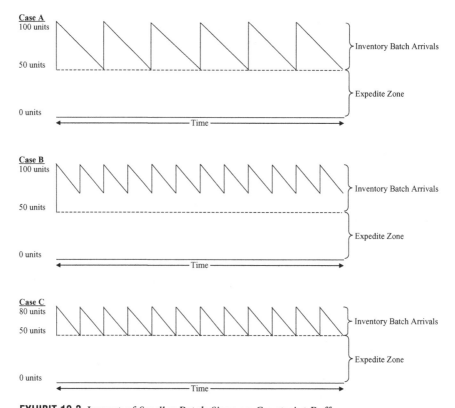

EXHIBIT 12.3 Impact of Smaller Batch Sizes on Constraint Buffer

inventory batches are being produced upstream. Case B shows the impact of half-size batches, where smaller inventory amounts arrive more frequently. Because of the more rapid replenishment, inventory levels drop less drastically, allowing for a smaller (and less expensive) inventory buffer as shown in Case C.

Though smaller batch sizes clearly have a favorable impact on the size of the inventory buffer, it would seem reasonable that the much larger number of setups would make this concept prohibitively expensive. However, we are talking about increasing the number of batches *upstream* from the constrained resource, not *at* the constraint. Because these upstream work centers have excess capacity, there is no cost associated with the extra setups—they are free. Consequently, the production scheduler could theoretically continue to schedule ever-smaller jobs in front of the constraint until such time as the extra setup burden requires the incremental addition of operating expenses. If a company has a large amount of excess capacity in these areas, it could afford to schedule exceedingly small job sizes.

An entirely different scenario arises when batch sizing is applied to the constrained resource. In this case, the production scheduler must be much more careful in allocating the limited number of available production minutes toward job setups, since many setups for small jobs results in fewer minutes of available production time and therefore a reduced level of throughput. Because of this issue, the scheduler has a tendency to plan for larger production runs at the constraint than in other work centers. The decision to authorize a longer production run than needed is based on the belief that any excess inventory will be rapidly sold off, so the scheduler must balance the savings from reduced setup time against the estimated time that extra production will be held in inventory prior to being sold.

One way to handle batch sizing at the constraint is to use bulk rate pricing management. For example, one could offer bulk-rate discounts to customers, thereby convincing them to place a smaller number of large orders. This pricing decision makes sense to the company, because it offsets the reduced throughput on the lower price point with its added capacity from avoiding an excessive number of setups.

In summary, small batch sizing is a no-cost option when jobs are passing through nonconstraint work centers but will be the subject of intense analysis when it involves the constrained resource.

Capacity Reduction Analysis

A particularly knotty problem is when the analyst identifies an excessive level of capacity in a nonconstraint area and proposes that the company save money by eliminating some portion of the excess capacity. What the analyst misses is how important that excess capacity may be. The total capacity at each work center should be divided into three parts. The first is *productive capacity*, which is that portion of the total work center capacity needed to process currently scheduled production. The second part is *protective capacity*, which is that additional portion of capacity that must be held in reserve to ensure that a sufficient quantity of parts can be manufactured to adequately feed the bottleneck operation. Any remaining capacity is called *idle capacity*. Only idle capacity can be eliminated from a work center.

If the capacity to be eliminated is protective capacity and not idle capacity, then the constrained resource will not have any inventory on which to work and must shut down until its inventory inflow can be replenished. Thus, the reduction in capacity in order to cut costs may seem like a reasonable decision in the short term, until such time as a sufficiently large manufacturing problem results in a throughput drop precisely because of the missing capacity.

Work Center Utilization

A traditional cost accounting system requires the analyst to spend a great deal of time calculating the gross margin of each product, which includes a large proportion of allocated costs. Throughput analysis has no interest in the fully burdened cost of a product, focusing instead on enhancing the performance of the entire system.

A major result of this change in philosophy is the utilization level of work centers from which production is not currently needed. A traditional costing system would hold that it should continue to operate as much as possible with long production runs, on the grounds that the average cost per unit must be kept low by spreading the cost of the work center over the largest possible number of units. Throughput analysis would require the work center's operations to be stopped, on the grounds that any additional output would simply result in a greater investment in inventory that the company does not need, as well as additional operating expenses to store the excess inventory.

Metrics

A traditional set of performance metrics and reports cause managers to focus their attention in a multitude of areas rather than on the constrained resource, and so should be largely avoided. The proper use of a constraint-based management system requires the use of an entirely different set of supporting performance measurements. The key concept behind this new system is to use a measurement or report that focuses only on the performance of the corporate production system as a whole, with the measurement of localized performance optimization targeted only at the constrained resource. Suggested metrics are:

- *Ratio of throughput to constraint time consumption.* If a product has a low throughput in proportion to the amount of constraint time used, the company should consider giving it a price increase in order to increase its net profits. Conversely, there should be an aggressive sales effort behind any product with a high throughput to constraint time consumption ratio, since this will lead to the highest possible profits.

- *Ratio of maintenance downtime to operating time on constrained resource.* The maintenance staff should be measured based on its ability to keep the constrained resource running for long periods of time. This means that the effectiveness of its maintenance is more important than its efficiency in conducting a repair. In other words, the maintenance staff should be considered less successful if they spend just a few minutes correcting a problem that keeps the constrained resource running for only a short period of time; conversely, it is better to spend more time on a maintenance operation if this will result in a substantially longer operating period before the next machine stoppage for additional maintenance. The calculation is to compare the total time required for maintenance to the total machine downtime for the constrained resource.

- *Throughput of postconstraint scrap.* An excellent way to increase the total amount of system throughput is to avoid scrap that occurs after the constraint. These items have already been processed by the constrained resource, and so have used up constraint capacity that cannot be recovered. Consequently, one of the best throughput-related measurements relates to scrap occurring after the constrained resource. The measurement is to compile the constraint hours spent to produce all scrap occurring after the constraint, and then multiply this by the average throughput per hour generated by the constraint.

- *Constraint utilization.* The constrained resource should be operated at a very high level of efficiency in order to maximize system throughput. A good measure for this core operation is constraint utilization, which is the actual hours of constraint run time divided by the number of constraint hours available for use.

Summary

This chapter gave a general overview of the operational and financial underpinnings of the theory of constraints and throughput analysis. The key points are that a company's results are largely driven by its management of a single constrained resource and that one should focus on the total throughput of a system rather than on optimizing local operations.

The examples in this chapter have focused on the manufacturing process, but throughput analysis can also be directed toward any part of a company, ranging from engineering to sales. In all areas, throughput analysis should be considered when conducting cost reduction analysis, in order to avoid making a mistake in cutting an expense that might have contributed to the generation of valuable throughput.

CHAPTER 13

Cost Reduction in Mergers and Acquisitions

Introduction

A special area of cost reduction is the acquisition. The most surefire way to make the cost of an acquisition succeed is to locate duplicate costs within the buyer and acquiree and successfully reduce them, which requires the careful and detailed integration of many functional areas. If the buyer does so effectively, it can realize substantial synergies that more than offset the cost of the purchase. If not, then the buyer will soon realize that it has spent an inordinate amount of money and time on a "boat anchor" acquisition. Thus, the effectiveness of the acquisition integration process is absolutely crucial. In this chapter, we address numerous integration topics, including the integration team, the planning process, and how to integrate an acquiree's employees, processes, and specific functions. These issues are critical to the full realization of an acquisition's full cost reduction potential.

The discussion in this chapter is not just about locating specific cost reductions; the focus is also on the *process* of implementing the integration changes that yield cost reductions, which is especially difficult to accomplish with a newly acquired entity.

Integration Timing

The integration of an acquiree into the buying entity can be slow and painful or fast and painful. There is simply no way to avoid a significant amount of dislocation within the acquiree, especially if the buyer wants to achieve major synergies. Consequently, the best thing a company can do is to move as rapidly as possible to complete all integration tasks, thereby reducing the period of dislocation through which the acquiree will undoubtedly suffer.

A good target period over which to complete the bulk of all integration activities is one year, even for a very large acquiree. Due to their complexity, some efforts will linger on for multiple years after the purchase, but at least 80 percent of the integration activities should be completed within one year. This is in opposition to many acquisitions, where large-scale integration projects are still in process as much as five years later.

It is even possible to begin integration work before a purchase transaction has closed, though this is mostly limited to preparatory work. To do so, any of the buyer's employees who are involved in the integration effort must work under the assumption that the deal could still collapse. This means that the buyer's team must track the receipt and disposition of all documents received from the potential acquiree and catalog them for destruction or return, if the companies do not combine. Further, the buyer should not dictate business decisions to the potential acquiree at this time.

The key point with integration timing is to not delay—there are few activities in a corporation where haste is of more importance. However, the speed of integration must go hand in hand with a detailed project plan.

Integration Planning

The integration of an acquiree's operations into the buyer requires a considerable amount of planning. The planning process should begin with an implementation charter that sets forth the statement of overall objectives, synergy targets, and the resources available to the team. The team then uses this information to create an integration plan that itemizes the tasks to be completed in achieving the objectives noted in the charter as well as measurement systems to ensure that targets have been achieved.

Portions of the integration plan can be written during the due diligence process, to include any issues arising at that time. The due diligence teams will be too busy with their own work to volunteer this information to the integration manager, so the manager should meet frequently with the teams to elicit this information. At a minimum, a first draft of the plan should be completed as soon after the purchase transaction as possible.

The plan should identify all key personnel resources and the time period during which they are available. Examples of this group are the integration manager and all function-specific experts, such as process analysts and outside consultants. Since the integration requires the active participation of a key group of experts, this part of the plan is crucial.

The basic timing of the plan is that most of the key decisions should be finalized within the first 100 days. This should certainly include all staff and organizational structure decisions (which, if possible, should be completed within the first week). All key customers should have been contacted multiple times during this period to increase the odds of their retention, as noted later in the "Sales Integration" section. Also, the most obvious quick-hit synergies should have been identified and addressed. The team should also have a good idea of how the processes of both organizations compare to each other and what steps should be taken to integrate them. In addition, the plan should have been fleshed out with a full set of budgets, timelines, and allocation of responsibilities. In short, 100 days is sufficient time to uncover the easier synergies, restructure human resources, and give the team a detailed view of what tasks must still be completed.

The integration plan must also go through an approval process, since many of the proposed synergies may be difficult or expensive to achieve, require special resources, or have risky side effects. This calls for a review by an expert, typically the line managers who are responsible for taking over various sections of the acquiree. Since these people have a long-term incentive to ensure that the integration goes well, they will be most inclined to critique the plan heavily.

The plan should also be reviewed by the analysis team that originally proposed the purchase price for the acquiree. This group will have made certain assumptions about the types of synergies to be obtained in order to justify the purchase price, and so will have an interest in the amount of savings that the integration team feels it can achieve.

Once the integration process begins, the integration plan will be tweaked constantly, as the integration team goes on-site and finds that conditions do not match its initial expectations. Thus, a staff person should constantly assess progress against the plan and recommend adjustment steps to the integration manager. By the time an integration has been completed, the integration plan will look substantially different from the first version that was initially compiled.

The internal audit department is scheduled last in the integration planning process. After all other integration work is completed, the internal auditors review the various synergies and process integrations that have been completed. They compare these results to the initial plan, as well as the buyer's expectations at the time of the acquisition, and issue a report that evaluates the impact of the acquisition on the buyer. Beyond the usual cost/benefit analysis, this report itemizes what the buyer did well and those areas in which it could do a better job when it integrates other acquisitions.

Synergy Realization

The most important part of the integration plan centers around the realization of synergies, since this is where the buyer justifies the price paid for the acquiree. A financial buyer may be content simply to wait for appreciation in the value of the acquiree. However, a strategic buyer has usually paid a higher price, because it feels it can achieve cash flow improvements through a variety of synergies where the combined entities can be more profitable than if they operated separately. Cost reduction synergies fall into the general categories of cost savings, capital spending, financial engineering, and tax benefits.

Cost Synergies

Of the various types of synergies, the most reliable ones to achieve are cost savings, since they are entirely within the control of the buyer. The areas most commonly targeted for cost reductions are:

- *Administrative expenses.* There are strong possibilities for cost reduction by centralizing a variety of administrative positions. Several accounting areas may be integrated, with the most common being accounts payable, payroll, and treasury, while billing and collections tend to be more localized.
- *Duplicate management.* One of the most common cost-saving areas is in the elimination of duplicate management teams. Since the acquired company's management may have just sold its shares or been paid significant severance packages, this can involve a downright cheerful set of employee departures.
- *Duplicate research and development.* In industries where product development is a key determinant of success, there is a possibility for staff reductions, especially when the research and development (R&D) staffs of both companies are working on the same product. However, this area is also fraught with political maneuvering because senior managers may support their pet projects while outside analysts may question why there are R&D cuts going on that may negatively impact future sales. The usual result is a modest cutback in expenses that is less than initial expectations.
- *Duplicate sales staff.* If the intent is for the sales staff to sell the products of the combined companies, then there is a strong likelihood of overlapping or overstaffed sales territories. While this may involve the departure of a number of salespeople, it more commonly is preceded by a significant shuffling of sales territories, so that the best salespeople

(a precious commodity) can be retained while the worst performers are pushed out.

■ *Field service consolidation.* If both companies operate similar field service staffs, it may be possible eventually to integrate them, thereby reducing the combined headcount to some extent. However, it takes time to achieve this synergy, since the surviving staff must be cross-trained in the servicing of new products. Also, since servicing volumes are likely to remain consistent from before the acquisition, the same staff totals probably will still be needed. If there are aggressive plans to boost sales, the entire existing field service staff still may be needed to service the increased sales base.

■ *Marketing consolidation.* The two companies may have been conducting similar advertising campaigns, attending the same trade shows, and so on. These duplicate costs can be consolidated, though the savings will be significant only if the two entities operate in the same market and sell very similar products. Even if marketing activities cannot be consolidated, there is a possibility that greater purchasing volumes can result in somewhat reduced costs.

■ *Pension plans.* If the acquiree has a defined benefit plan, the buyer can shut it down and shift employees over to a defined contribution plan, which is much less expensive. While this conversion is certainly hazardous to employee relations, the cost savings can be substantial. If the acquiree has a union, its collective bargaining agreement may require continuation of the defined benefit plan, leaving no possibility of a cost reduction in this area.

There are a multitude of issues involved with merging any kind of pension plan. One way to avoid them is to require the selling entity to terminate its plan prior to the acquisition date. Once the acquisition takes place, the acquiree's employees can then roll over their plan benefits into the buyer's plan, with much less risk of any further problems arising.

If the buyer has a defined benefit plan and intends to shift the acquiree's employees into it, then a significant cost issue is whether to credit their years of service prior to the acquisition. This issue should be settled as part of the purchase negotiations, since it can greatly increase the overall cost to the buyer.

■ *Process improvements.* Either the buyer or the acquiree may have unusually efficient processes that are the result of a gradual buildup of best practices over time. If so, an enlightened integration effort will not just impose the buyer's processes on the acquiree but instead will compare all systems and select the best from either side. While this can result in significant long-term cost reductions, the mutual enhancement of processes is a lengthy endeavor.

- *Product overlap.* If the companies support similar products, the buyer may elect to phase some out. This is not a simple decision, since there may be long-term warranties or field service operations that require ongoing support for a number of years. Thus, cost reductions in this area tend to be of a more long-term nature.
- *Purchasing power.* When companies combine, there is always a prospect for greater purchasing power, due to greater buying volume. (See Chapter 8, "Spend Analysis.") This can result in a gain of several percent in net profits. However, it also requires a great deal of coordination in purchasing activities and may not be possible at all if the acquiree is outside of the area occupied by the buyer's supplier distribution regions.

Cost savings can be especially great when the buyer acquires a company within the same industry and in the same geographical region in which it already operates. By doing so, there is a high probability of function duplication, which can be eliminated. Likely targets for cost reduction will be duplicate sales forces, production facilities, and administrative staff.

Though the simplest way to immediately achieve gains is through cost reductions, one must also consider the costs associated with achieving them. For example, if the buyer plans for massive layoffs, it must factor in the cost of severance and plant closures, which may also be impacted by firing restrictions in some foreign countries. In addition, if it plans to retain some employees for knowledge transfer purposes and then let them go, there is the cost of retention bonuses to consider. Consequently, when modeling potential synergies, these new costs must be offset against the planned cost reductions. Depending on the circumstances, the net effect of cost reductions and new costs may not yield any significant cost reductions until more than a year has passed.

Capital Expenditure Synergies

An area in which few companies consider the possibility of synergies is in the avoidance of capital expenditures. If either party to an acquisition has already made a significant expenditure, then it is entirely possible that the other party can avoid a similar payment by using the excess capacity generated by the preceding investment. Consequently, part of the integration process should be a comparison of planned capital expenditures by both companies to see if any can be combined.

Financial Engineering Synergies

There may be savings to be gleaned in the area of financial engineering. Combined entities can pool their foreign currency positions for receivables and payables, resulting in fewer foreign exchange transactions. Also, the buyer may be able to refinance the acquiree's debt at a more favorable borrowing rate, if the buyer has a significantly higher credit rating. Further, the buyer can sweep the acquiree's cash balances into a centralized bank account, where it can take advantage of overnight investments, and also handle the acquiree's short-term borrowing needs from its own cash pool. These improvements are not overwhelmingly large by themselves but can add a noticeable amount to the total synergies achieved.

Tax Synergies

It is also possible to develop tax synergies. This can be achieved by acquiring an entity within a low-tax region and then transferring brands and other intellectual property to it. Alternatively, if the buyer acquires a company in a high-tax region, it can push debt down into that subsidiary in order to create interest expenses and reduce its reported level of income. However, it is unwise to base acquisition synergies entirely on their tax ramifications, since tax rates are under the control of governments and they may change rates at any time. Instead, acquire for other synergies and then take advantage of tax synergies if they happen to exist.

Synergy Reporting

When itemizing synergies, it is useful to record the information on a chart that shows the value to the buyer of each item. A sample is shown in Exhibit 13.1.

This table is then used by the integration manager to determine which synergies will yield the most benefit and justify the largest amount of attention.

EXHIBIT 13.1 Synergy Valuation Chart

Synergy Description	One-Time Profit	Recurring Profit	No Profit Change
Capital expenditure merge	—		$400,000
Centralize bank accounts	—	$5,000	—
Merge company names	—	—	—
Merge facilities and sublease	—	130,000	—
Payroll centralization	—	70,000	—
Product rebranding	—	150,000	—
Shift to defined contribution plan	—	62,000	—
Total synergies	$0	$417,000	$400,000

Integration Manager

The integration of a newly acquired company into the buyer is an extremely complex affair and so requires the services of a single talented manager to achieve. This integration manager serves in the role only until the main integration targets have been met, and then moves on to other projects. The integration manager is responsible for these tasks:

- Supervise integration planning
- Monitor integration progress
- Identify synergies
- Facilitate team reviews
- Interpret and mitigate cultural issues
- Mobilize project teams

While these bullet points appear to indicate a rigid job description, it usually begins as an extremely sketchy one and gradually fills out over time as the integration manager learns more about the tasks to be completed and the types of problems to be overcome. By keeping the job description relatively fluid, the integration manager can shift efforts into a variety of areas, as needed.

The integration manager is always an employee of the buyer. This is because this manager must have direct links to the more powerful people within the buyer's organization who can support the integration effort. In addition, this manager must have an in-depth knowledge of the buyer's key processes and who controls each one. This allows the integration manager to directly access those individuals within the buyer's organization who can most readily assist with and support the manager in achieving integration goals. If the integration manager were to come from the acquiree, there would be no such support network, and this manager would also have no knowledge of the buyer's organization.

Because the integration manager has such strong ties into the buyer organization, he or she can also assist acquiree employees in locating their counterparts. This manager can also educate them about how a variety of buyer processes function, such as annual personnel reviews, pay change procedures, and the budgeting cycle. Further, if reports are available that might be of assistance to the acquiree, this manager can arrange to have them fitted to the acquiree's specific needs and sent to them on a predefined distribution schedule.

The integration manager's role between the organizations also works in the other direction. This person can educate the buyer's management team about the acquiree's culture and any idiosyncrasies that may impact relations between the two companies. Also, whenever this manager feels there is a need for closer links between the entities, he or she can arrange for social events to bring together specific groups of people.

Though this person comes from the buyer, he or she cannot have a bull-in-a-china-shop mentality and forcibly impose buyer practices on the acquiree. Instead, this manager must have a singular ability to appreciate and work with the acquiree's culture. Doing this requires extraordinary listening skills as well as the ability to determine how integration goals can be achieved within the confines of cultural issues.

The integration manager is extremely independent and must be able to operate with almost no supervision. By working in this manner, he or she can make snap decisions on-site, without having to run them up through the buyer's management structure for approval.

Being an integration manager involves that person's physical presence at the acquiree location. The designated person cannot manage the integration process long distance, from an office at corporate headquarters. Given the extraordinary amount of time needed in face-to-face meetings with acquiree employees, the integration manager must spend nearly all of his or her time on-site. This requires a commitment to live near the acquiree for the duration of the integration process. Further, because some issues will require the participation of the buyer's management team, the integration manager should be prepared to make numerous trips back to corporate headquarters to consult with senior management.

In brief, the integration manager occupies the central role in an acquisition. The individual must have sufficient heft within the buyer's organization (as defined by experience, skill, and leadership ability) to coordinate all aspects of the integration effort. This is an extremely involving role, requiring more than a normal working day, dealing with a broad range of conflicts, and necessitating living away from home for long periods of time. Consequently, a high-grade integration manager should be treated as a prized asset.

Integration Team

The integration manager is only one member of a large integration team. This group is responsible for completing dozens or even hundreds of integration activities. The team's skill sets will be extremely broad, covering every functional area of the acquiree. There may even be subteams of specialists who are responsible for very specific activities (such as merging pension plans). Among the more common subteams will be ones responsible for human resources, manufacturing, legal, environmental, research and development, purchasing, finance, information technology, sales and marketing, and culture. For buyers that do not make a regular practice of acquiring companies, there may also be a consultant who dispenses advice as well as assistance with management of the integration effort and ongoing maintenance of the project plan.

Specialization within the integration team is an excellent idea, because it focuses efforts on tightly defined projects that yield fast results. Where possible, try to include acquiree employees in the subteams, since they can be of great assistance in bridging cultural gaps between the companies. This approach is most useful when a high level of acquiree cooperation is needed to achieve a goal, and less so when the project involves a technical issue (such as consolidating legal entities).

A key member of the integration team is the assistant to the implementation manager. This person should come from the acquiree. His or her role is to represent the acquiree on the team at a senior level. This means the assistant should collect feedback from employees regarding a number of implementation initiatives and advise the implementation manager regarding how targets can be achieved while disturbing the acquiree to the minimum extent possible. This person should have considerable seniority with the acquiree and be well known and trusted within that organization.

The integration team should have a strong incentive not only to meet its management-imposed integration targets but to exceed them. Since team members are already deeply involved in the operations of both companies, they are in the best position to spot additional synergies that might have been missed during the initial creation of the integration plan. Thus, the integration manager should be given control over several types of bonuses, such as spot bonuses to be paid out for minor improvements and major bonuses for exceeding the initial cost reduction target.

While the integration team is extremely useful, especially for larger integration projects, it is not intended to be a permanent fixture. Instead, the integration plan should include a milestone (typically one year) after which the team is disbanded. At that point, any remaining integration activities become the responsibility of the business unit managers who are now running the integrated businesses.

Integration Communications—Internal

Once the integration process is under way, an integration team of any size will find that it loses touch with the progress of other team members. This is a particular problem when they are operating in multiple locations. Given the extremely tight timelines normally associated with an integration effort, usually it is not possible to bring the team together for periodic status meetings. The usual result is a weekly conference call involving all subteam managers, which uses an agenda, structured reporting, and a follow-up report that itemizes who is responsible for the issues discussed during the call.

In addition to a conference call, consider introducing a more personal touch by authorizing a periodic team newsletter. This can be used to document integration "wins" as well as progress scorecards and recognition of those teams completing major milestone projects.

The integration team must also maintain an issues log. This is an itemization of unresolved problems that are interfering with the completion of various tasks in the implementation plan. The log is intended to be a summary of remaining issues, who is responsible for each item's resolution, and the date by which it should be completed. A sample issues log is presented next.

Issues Log Issue	Responsibility	Action	Due Date
Select sales personnel for layoff	M. Sarnoff	Facilitate selection meeting with sales managers	Jan. 15
Legal entity not shut down	A. Weatherby	Rewrite landlord contract for new entity	Jan. 21
ABC facility not subleased	T. Arnold	Meet with leasing agent to determine market rate for sublease	Jan. 27

The communication systems outlined here are especially important for large teams, where it would otherwise be impossible for participants to remain knowledgeable about overall activities.

Integration Communications—External

Communicating with the acquiree's employees is a large part of the integration staff's job. Employees will be ultra sensitive about any changes to the content of their jobs, their compensation, and their reporting relationships and will interpret every contact, question, and request for information with suspicion. Integration team members can fully expect that their most inconsequential comment will be magnified far out of proportion and misinterpreted, sometimes to an extraordinary degree.

Due to the sensitivity of the acquiree's staff, there should be a system for regular communication. This system can involve a combination of methods, such as a Web site, newsletter, voice mails, video conferences, and so on. Whatever methods are used, the integration team must be careful to present a consistent message about the acquisition, what the team intends to do, and when it plans to complete its work. These messages cannot prevaricate in any way, since acquiree employees are poring over them in detail to see if the buyer is doing what it says. Further, communications should not react to events but rather be issued as soon as the integration team becomes aware of anything that may impact employees. That being said, some communications will be reactive, since events will arise that were not planned.

Communication frequency is also important. There should be at least weekly updates on progress. If information is not released at these intervals, then employees will make up their own news about the integration, which may vary wildly (and inaccurately) from the real situation. There should be some communication, even if there are no concrete accomplishments to report. Merely stating that there is some progress toward a milestone is better than a period of prolonged silence.

One person should be responsible for all information dissemination. This individual ensures that the same message is consistently stated across all forms of communication and that communications are made as soon as new information becomes available to the integration team. Do not consider this position to be secondary—the cooperation of acquiree employees is essential, so they must be treated as partners by keeping them informed through a first-class communications system.

Some buyers may think that they are already handling the communications process, because the top-level managers from each entity are actively engaged in conversations with each other, every day. However, these people forget to inform those lower-level managers working for them, who in turn have no information to pass along to the nonmanagement staff. Further, even if the top-level managers were diligent in imparting information, they would be doing so individually—which abrogates the principle of having a consistent message across all forms of communication. Thus, it is not sufficient to assign responsibility for communications to a group of people; only a single communications manager will do.

Employee Integration—Qualification Assessment

Once the legal aspects of a purchase transaction have been completed, the most pressing issue for the buyer is to assess the qualifications of the acquiree's employees. Those functions that are handled strictly by the acquiree are normally left in the hands of the existing employees, using their in-place reporting structure. However, the integration team must

EXHIBIT 13.2 Employee Evaluation Scoring Grid

	Change Management	Communi- cations	Leadership	Problem Solving	Task Planning	Technical Skills
Reviewer 1	3	2	1	4	4	5
Reviewer 2	4	1	1	5	3	4
Reviewer 3	3	3	3	4	4	5
Reviewer 4	5	2	2	4	5	4
Averages	3.8	2.0	1.8	4.3	4.0	4.5

Note: Scores are 1 to 5, with 5 being the best.

determine whether functions *to be combined* shall be run by the personnel of the acquiree or the buyer. This calls for a rigidly defined and time-compressed evaluation process.

The integration team must use a standard evaluation form when reviewing acquiree employees, so that each person is evaluated using the same criteria. While a very compressed process may call for a single interview of each person, it is better to obtain a more rounded view by conducting multiple interviews, preferably by interviewers having different skill sets. Their numerical scores for each person can then be summarized in a grid and averaged to arrive at scores across various skill categories. While the scoring grid shown in Exhibit 13.2 can be used, it is designed to evaluate lower-level managers and should be altered to match the requirements of each job position. The integration team should also compile all ancillary comments into a single comment sheet that accompanies the scoring grid. By using this rigid approach, it is much simpler to arrive at a quantitative score as well as qualitative opinions and comments.

The sample scoring matrix shows results for an individual who obviously has considerable technical skills but poor people skills. The scores relating to each of these attributes would be more difficult to discern if the scores for all columns were summarized into a single overall score. Thus, it is best not to arrive at a single numerical score but rather to present a set of scores addressing a broad range of categories, thereby giving decision makers a better view of an employee's entire set of attributes.

When using the scoring system to decide who will be given certain jobs, it is extremely helpful to conduct a transparent and unbiased review that results in the retention of the most qualified candidates. By demonstrating that the system is fair, the acquiree's personnel will be more inclined to stay with the company. The best way to immediately show how the system works is to deliberately review several highly qualified people at the start of the evaluation process, so that they can be placed in high-profile positions at once.

Employee Integration—Job Positioning

During a normal eight-hour working day, studies have shown that employees are effective for about six hours. However, this number drops to just one hour when there is a change in control and will continue at that level until such time as all control issues are resolved. For example, if a 100-person company were to experience just one hour of reduced productivity per day, this would extrapolate into roughly 26,000 hours of wasted time per year. Thus, consider the enormous cost of lost productivity if employees are not properly integrated into the buying company. This is a sterling incentive for the integration team to move rapidly to establish employee roles and reporting relationships.

Many employees will fear for their jobs and will likely be conducting job searches, if only to keep their employment options open. While it is inevitable that some will leave, losses can be reduced by emphasizing rapid integration of employee roles. By doing so, there is a shortened period of uncertainty, which should effectively stop a number of informal job searches.

The integration team assists in determining who reports to whom. Team members are not responsible for making these decisions but can facilitate the process of doing so. By rapidly clarifying reporting relationships, the responsibility for job positioning now passes to the line managers who are taking over groups of employees. By swiftly settling this issue, employees will shift their focus away from internal matters and back to the customer-centric focus that builds profitability. This also eliminates wasted time among the respective management teams, whose members would otherwise jockey for position to take over the combined operations.

The reporting relationship decision is so important that the integration manager should essentially put the responsible decision makers in one room and not let them out until all decisions have been made. Further, they should establish secondary choices for each key position, since some acquiree employees can be expected to leave despite any incentives to the contrary. Once all decisions are made, the integration manager immediately notifies all affected staff. If a decision involves a change to a new location, then give people additional time to decide if they will accept. (See the next section, "Employee Integration—Relocations.")

Any employees who do leave the acquiree represent a unique opportunity for the buyer. There should be an exit interview with key departing employees, to determine what specific actions by the buyer caused the departure. The implementation manager can use this information to alter the integration process to reduce any further employee losses. Also, the company should continue to recruit any employees who leave, because bringing them back can be trumpeted as an indicator that the acquiree is still a good place to work. Returning employees can be a powerful motivator for other staff members who are contemplating a job switch.

Employee Integration—Relocations

A major fear for employees is being required to move to a different company location. This impacts their perceived quality of life, since they are being uprooted from neighborhoods and school systems to which they may have strong ties. While the retention rate for employees being moved is normally low, there are three techniques for increasing the odds of success.

1. Involve employee families in the decision. This means flying entire families (or at least spouses) to the new location for visits to local communities.
2. Remove all economic issues from the decision by paying for 100 percent of the moving costs, altering people's compensation if they are moving to a higher-cost area, and even offering to buy out their homes if they cannot sell them.
3. Do everything possible to welcome them into the new location by assigning a manager to introduce them to employees and sponsor informal off-site gatherings.

All of these techniques will improve the odds of success, but many employees simply will not move, no matter what inducements are offered.

Conversely, some employees will be *very* interested in a relocation. They may feel that, because their company is now a subsidiary, the best job opportunities have shifted to corporate headquarters. They then perceive a reduced level of job growth, reduced autonomy, and perhaps even a worsening work environment—all of which contribute to more employee turnover. In these cases, the company should actively advocate relocating employees, if this is the best option for retaining them.

Employee Integration—Key Employees

In any acquisition, the acquiree will have a key cluster of employees who are subject matter experts or rainmakers responsible for the bulk of all sales. These employees are likely at the core of the acquiree's central value proposition and so are extremely valuable. In addition, they may be the key drivers behind the acquiree's overall level of productivity and quality of work. The problem for the integration manager is that these people, because of their skills, are most likely to have held shares in the acquired entity and may now have sufficient wealth to walk away from the company. If they leave, there may be a devastating decline in organizational knowledge and morale, along with a very high replacement cost.

To retain this core group, the first task is to create a retention matrix, showing the impact of losing each key employee, what issues might cause them to leave, what tactics shall be used to retain them, and who is responsible for implementation. The integration manager uses this matrix to select the most appropriate retention tactics and to assign responsibility for follow-up with the targeted employees.

Retention tactics can cover a considerable range of options and can be narrowed down to the most effective alternatives only by talking to each key employee individually to determine their concerns. Here are some options:

- *Altered benefits.* An employee may have a special need, such as short-term disability coverage, that is not addressed by the standard company benefits package. In many cases, these additional requirements are not overly expensive and can have a profound impact on their decision to stay with the company.
- *Autonomy.* This is one of the most cherished prerogatives of an independent-minded manager, but only allow it if the employee is still linked to highly quantitative goals.
- *Change reporting relationship.* An employee may have conflicts with an oppressive manager, so switching to a different manager may not only improve retention but also increase the effectiveness of the employee.
- *Culture.* Employees may identify strongly with their company's culture and will leave if it changes. Culture issues may include a relaxed dress code, working from home, periodic beer bashes, and so on. The integration team should be very careful about altering any cultural issues that might alienate key employees.
- *Importance.* Some employees are used to being crucial to an enterprise's success, because of some unique skill. If so, retention may simply require the buyer to periodically reassure individuals that they are needed and important to the company—and then prove it through whatever methods are needed to provide assurances to the targeted persons.
- *Increased pay.* An increase in pay will certainly gain the attention of an employee, but keep in mind that pay changes can be matched by a competing firm and may also shift an employee into a pay level that is well outside of the normal range for the position.

- *Job content.* Simply making a job more interesting can retain employ ees. This may require a process change, so that more tasks within a process are concentrated on one person.
- *Learning opportunities.* An employee may want to obtain a technical skill or an entire college degree, so offer to either pay the entire cost or to share it with the employee. However, this situation sometimes results in the prompt departure of individuals once they have obtained the extra education, so require a payback agreement if they leave the company within a certain period of time following completion of the training.
- *New location.* Moving employees against their wishes to a new company location is a prime method for losing then to a competitor. If there is another company facility where they might *prefer* to work, however, then allow the change and pay for a housing move too—but only if the employees can be effective in the new location.
- *New title.* While a new title is the ultimate in inexpensive perks, it is also easily matched by a competing company and so does not help much to retain an employee.
- *Promotion.* Promoting an employee to a higher-grade position with more responsibility is a strong inducement to remain, though there is a risk of promptly losing anyone who becomes uncomfortable in the new role.
- *Work from home.* With the pervasive use of mobile communications, working from home, at least to a limited extent, is an excellent option, especially for those employees with long commutes or medical care issues.

Key employee desires may require some items entirely outside of the preceding list, so be open to other options that they may bring up.

Another solution is to give them enough additional shares to gain their attention, but only if there is a sufficiently long vesting period associated with the shares to retain them for a number of years. The most common approach is proportional vesting (e.g., 20 percent vesting in each of five years), but as key employees gradually gain vested shares, they have less inclination to stay with the company. As a result, some firms prefer to vest a larger proportion of stock near the end of a vesting period, as an incentive to keep key personnel for as long as possible. Also, there is a risk that employees will wait out their retention periods without adding any value to the company. To avoid this problem, consider tying any retention payments to a specific performance metric or deliverable.

Dealing with key employees is similar to the political stratagems used by a candidate for political office—one must determine what promises are needed to create a majority of backers. However, and as is the case with a politician, it is not necessary, nor always desirable, to issue a vast number of assurances to obtain the support of *all* key employees. Some employees will be so disaffected or demanding that it is not economical or prudent to accede to their demands. Instead, the integration manager seeks to work with as many key personnel as possible and to mitigate the negative opinions of a select minority.

There will be cases where the opinions of key personnel cannot be swayed in favor of the buyer. This is most common in hostile takeovers, where vigorous defenses are raised against an acquisition attempt, and public statements may extend to smear campaigns against opposing managers. In these cases, the buyer may have no other choice than to replace a large proportion of the acquiree's staff with new employees who do not hold prior allegiances within the organization or who have been brought in from other buyer locations.

Layoffs

Part of the integration plan may include the layoffs of some acquiree employees. The integration team should pay special attention to the mechanics of the layoff process, because it can have a major impact on the attitudes of the remaining staff. For example, if layoffs are made abruptly, with minimal severance pay, and with little respect for the people being let go, then this sends a strong message to the remaining employees regarding the type of company that they are now working for. Conversely, if departing employees are given reasonable severance packages, job search support, and the use of company facilities, then employees will realize that they may now have an excellent employer.

The integration team must also pay particular attention to the very real possibility of litigation by those employees being let go. Many states have right-to-work laws that allow for layoffs without a significant amount of proof by the employer. Nonetheless, employees can claim that they were discriminated against as minorities. There are so many groups of minorities, such as veterans, women, or those over 40 years old or with disabilities, that employers may sometimes wonder which staff are *not* minorities. In fact, about 10 percent of all litigation involving companies is for wrongful termination, with minority status being the core reason for the lawsuits. Thus, it is wisest to establish a logical and defensible layoff ranking system, such as by seniority, but to also review this list for minority concentrations. When in doubt, employ a labor attorney to review prospective layoffs and ascertain where there may be some risk of litigation.

Also, disseminate a clear statement of termination benefits to all employees being laid off, so there is no confusion about payments to be made. Where possible, pay termination benefits at once; doing so tends to reduce resentment.

If acquiree employees are part of a union, then the layoff process is more involved. Their union contract may state that they must be given a certain amount of notice prior to either a layoff or a plant closing. Not only does this create a significant and potentially costly delay, but it also gives the union more time in which to devise various legal barriers to throw in the way of the layoff or to bargain over the effects of the change. The integration team should use the services of a labor attorney to determine the likelihood of union-related problems and what mitigation steps can be taken.

If a company has at least 100 employees, then it must be in compliance with the Worker Adjustment and Retraining Notification Act (WARN). In essence, the act requires that a company provide 60 days' written notice to workers of impending plant closings and mass layoffs. This applies only if there will be a plant closing resulting in employment loss for 50 or more workers within a 30-day period or a mass layoff that does not result from a plant closing, but which will yield an employment loss for 500 or more employees, or for 50 to 499 employees if they make up at least one-third of the active workforce.

Compensation Integration

Unless subsidiaries are to be kept totally separate, the buyer must at some point address the problem of pay disparities between the employees of the buyer and the acquiree. While it is certainly possible to use pay cuts to achieve postacquisition equality, there are few actions more likely to bring about a significant number of employee departures. Instead, the buyer should consider enacting a small number of pay raises among key employees to achieve pay equality, without making significant pay rate increases elsewhere. By doing so, key staff members are less likely to leave, while the company as a whole does not incur a significant increase in payroll expenses.

However, companies may have pay plans so radically different that there is no way to achieve a reasonable degree of payroll integration. For example, a mature business is more likely to pay employees within rigid pay ranges and pay smaller bonuses. Conversely, a company in a high-growth field may have a compensation system structured to pay out much larger bonuses, possibly in stock, though with reduced base pay. Any attempt to integrate these plans will be more likely to cause serious disruption among the staff. If so, the only reasonable alternative may be to leave the compensation systems entirely separate in the short term. Over the long term, the operating environments of the companies will gradually change, which eventually makes it possible to incrementally alter the pay systems to bring them into greater alignment.

Even if pay systems cannot be integrated, there are still excellent opportunities for integrating benefit plans. If the buyer acquires companies on a regular basis, it can be quite expensive to maintain and administer a multitude of benefit plans. Instead, there are significant opportunities for cost savings by combining all benefits into a single, centrally administered plan. While this will likely call for some changes to the benefit plans of every acquired company, the scale of change is not normally so significant as to cause undue employee dissatisfaction.

The bonus plans of both companies may also be substantially different. If so, a common practice is to allow employees to complete the current fiscal year under their existing plans. This is especially common if a number of employees are close to completing their targeted goals and only need a few more months to meet targets. If the buyer were to eliminate these plans just prior to award dates, disaffection among the acquiree's employees could be high. However, if the fiscal year has just begun, it is not especially difficult to replace existing bonus plans with those of the buyer. Another alternative is to buy out existing bonus plans, based on the proportion of the year that has been completed under the plan and the degree of success thus far achieved in completing goals. This last option allows the buyer to immediately alter bonus targets so that they support integration goals.

Sales Integration

The success of any company begins with its customers, and this is precisely where an acquiree tends to suffer directly after an acquisition. Some customers will be concerned about changes in service, product, or pricing and will take their business elsewhere. In addition, competitors will view an acquisition as an opportunity to poach customers and will actively solicit them as soon as the deal is announced.

To avoid these problems, it is essential that the sales departments of the two companies meet immediately after the purchase transaction for a comprehensive briefing on the acquiree's key customers as well as its products, pricing, and sales strategy. The key result of this meeting should be a plan for how to deal with all key customers. In addition, the meeting should yield a general direction for the treatment of products and pricing, so that the sales force can give a general idea of the situation to those customers who inquire about what will happen next.

To keep from losing customers, senior managers should travel to the major customers several times to hear their concerns and to discuss issues related to the integration. For smaller customers, the acquirer can use other forms of communication, such as memos, e-mails, newsletters, or even the services of a public relations firm. The mind-set at this point should not be to pressure customers for more sales but simply to ensure that they do not take their business elsewhere.

As the combined companies gradually determine how they will integrate their products together and establish pricing, they should communicate this information back to the customers, preferably through personal visits. By transmitting this information face-to-face, managers can immediately ascertain customer reactions and adjust their plans if those reactions are excessively negative.

Another way to avoid a short-term decline in sales is to counteract it with a short-term sales incentive plan. This can include bonuses for the acquiree sales team for simply matching or slightly exceeding their normal sales volumes. The marketing department can also run additional repetitions of its normal advertising campaigns. The intent is to avoid the initial drop in sales that might otherwise trigger a continuing decline in sales.

A common practice is to have the sales staffs of both companies represent each other's products and services before the combined customer base. The theory is that combining sales forces will increase the total dollar value of each sales call. However, if the products being sold are not similar, it will take more time for the sales staffs to learn about the products and will also require longer sales calls. Thus, even though the total dollar value of each sales call may indeed increase, there may be fewer sales calls made, with offsetting results.

Also, it is difficult to combine sales forces if the underlying products have substantially different sales strategies. For example, if a product has a very high price point, then it likely involves different buyers and permission levels and therefore a much longer sales cycle. In this case, a sales team with a long-term compensation arrangement will probably be more successful than an individual salesperson whose compensation is based on short-term sales. Thus, the type of sale may mandate entirely different sales forces, even if the buyer and acquiree share exactly the same customers.

In brief, the integration team initially should be less concerned with ramping up sales and more involved with the retention of existing customers. In many cases, hoped-for sales gains through merging the sales forces will be structurally difficult to achieve. Thus, sales integration carries with it a significant risk of loss rather than the gains to which many buyers aspire.

Process Integration

Few areas cause more resentment than when a buyer unilaterally imposes its own processes on the acquiree, especially if the acquiree feels that it has the better process.

The most critical point is not to immediately impose the buyer's processes on the acquiree without some initial discussion. Ideally, this should include a side-by-side analysis of the processes used by each entity, with acquiree representatives participating in the analysis. A likely offshoot of this review will be comparative matrices showing the strengths and weaknesses of each process, and which ones require more or fewer steps. This review may result in a blended process that incorporates the best features of both systems.

A company that engages in frequent acquisitions does not have time to engage in the aforementioned comparative process analysis. Instead, it has already adopted a core system and must impose it on every acquiree in order to maintain its pace of acquisitions. When this scenario arises, the implementation team should make the acquiree's staff thoroughly aware of why the process changeover must be made, without any changes to accommodate their local needs or preferences.

An alternative that stands midway between the preceding alternatives is to compare the process metrics of the acquiree and buyer; if the buyer's metrics are clearly better, then the integration team immediately imposes the buyer's process on the acquiree with minimal further investigation. However, if the acquiree can quantitatively prove that it has a better process, then the integration team can take a deeper look at the acquiree's process.

A significant amount of history has probably built up around each process, including periodic process training, improvement rewards, and the simple inertia of many people growing accustomed to a fixed methodology over time. The integration team can knock some supporting struts from beneath these process edifices by eliminating anything that perpetuates them. This includes the elimination of training classes and any rewards geared to the ongoing use of the process. Also, most processes are strongly supported by long-term employees who have used them for many years, and who may have originated them. If so, it may be necessary to reassign these people, possibly into another facility entirely, so that they will be unable to interfere with any process integration activities.

Because of their significant impact on day-to-day work, process revisions can be exceedingly disruptive, so be sure to use a considerable amount of change management while doing so.

Technology Integration

Among the most difficult integration chores is that of consolidating disparate information technology platforms. It is exceedingly common for the two parties to an acquisition to use heavily modified legacy software solutions, which makes it extremely difficult to achieve a reasonable degree of integration. However, without integration, the combined company must maintain separate support staffs as well as diverging hardware and software maintenance agreements and upgrade paths.

The best solution for the acquirer is to first purge all of its own legacy systems in favor of the most reliable and scalable commercial solutions on the market. By doing so, the acquirer will have a much easier time shifting acquiree systems over to its own systems. Despite this level of preparation, the buyer will likely find that several years will be needed to fully integrate the systems of both companies.

It is also possible that the buyer has bought the acquiree *only* for its technology. If so, the integration process may involve the complete elimination of all other parts of the acquiree, with the integration team spending nearly all of its time creating a comfortable environment for the development and support staff surrounding the acquiree's technology.

Metrics

The success of an acquisition is ultimately measured by the increase in value of the combined firms over their values just prior to the purchase transaction. For a publicly held firm that acquires another public company, this result can be measured approximately by determining their average market capitalizations over a few weeks just prior to the announcement of the transaction. For private companies or mixed public–private transactions, the best approach is to measure discounted cash flows before and after the transaction, including the payout to the selling company's shareholders.

In order to achieve these before-and-after valuation metrics, the integration team must use a multitude of additional metrics. Many are based on the simple achievement of milestones, such as the variety of intermediate steps needed to eventually arrive at a single payroll system for the entire company or the combination of multiple company locations into one. In these cases, individual steps will not increase profitability by themselves but are still necessary for proving the ultimate value of the transaction. Thus, the integration team may deal with dozens of transient metrics which all roll together into the planned level of cash flow needed to justify the acquisition.

Metrics can span an extraordinary range of activities. For example, from a cultural integration perspective, an appropriate metric might be the weekly dissemination of a newsletter to the acquiree's employees. If treasury activities are to be combined, then another metric could be the number of acquiree bank accounts still open. If a computer system is to be replaced with one used by the buyer, then metrics would include a series of milestones, such as converting acquiree databases, completing system training for new users, and shutting down software licenses for the system being discontinued. Thus, the metrics used will vary based on the exact types of integration contemplated.

Metrics should also track signs that an acquisition is *not* working. If an acquiree's staff is not happy, this may appear through a higher total number of customer service calls or the loss of key customers or employees. These examples are quantitative and can be tracked easily. Other indicators of failure are more qualitative, such as the persistence of a them-versus-us mentality or difficulty in transferring the buyer's core values to the acquiree's management team. In these latter cases, a periodic survey can uncover the extent of attitudinal problems. Of course, the overriding indicator of a problematic integration effort is when the integration team remains on-site past the planned date and is not available to work on other acquisitions.

Integration Pacing

The buyer may have a strong interest in conducting a rapid series of acquisitions. This desire may be triggered by opportunities in an industry that is suffering an economic downturn or because the buyer wants to roll up a significant portion of an industry. While a rapid pace of acquisitions may be exciting for the chief executive officer, it is a logistical nightmare for the integration team.

Smaller companies do not have enough employees to appropriately staff a multitude of integration teams, and even larger companies may feel the strain if there are several large integrations going on at once. This results in an integration bottleneck, where some acquirees may not see an integration team for months, or integrations are only perfunctory, and do not attempt to achieve any synergies. Thus, companies that go on buying sprees without proper integration planning will find themselves at high risk of not meeting their performance goals.

The best solution to this quandary is to use a proper level of acquisition pacing. By spreading out acquisitions, the integration team will have sufficient time to address all issues at the last acquiree before moving on to the next one. While acquisitions are by their nature "lumpy" (i.e., acquisition dates cannot be predicted with precision), a company can adopt a policy of restricting itself to a certain amount of acquired sales volume per year, which generally will allow integration efforts to be completed at a reasonable pace.

If the buyer has multiple divisions, then it can achieve a faster pace by shifting acquisitions around the various divisions in rotation. This spreads out the integration efforts among different line-management people in the divisions, without placing an undue burden on any single group.

Summary

If the buyer treats an acquisition as a financial transaction where the acquiree is a stand-alone operation, there is a good chance that only the most minimal integration activities will be needed. However, if the buyer treats it as a strategic transaction, where it plans for full integration with the rest of the company in order to maximize cost reductions, then it must deal with a complex series of activities that will be difficult to coordinate and that will be at considerable risk of failure.

The key factors in the integration of a strategic acquisition are to have a dedicated integration team and to act at once. When a decisive manager announces all major changes within a few days of a purchase transaction, it keeps the acquiree's personnel from squandering time worrying about their circumstances. Conversely, a creeping integration that spans several years causes ongoing uncertainty and drains value from the combined companies.

Index

Printed in the United States
By Bookmasters